Understanding Health Literacy

Implications for Medicine and Public Health

EDITORS

Joanne G. Schwart
Jonathan B. VanGeest, PhD
Claire C. Wang, MD

SECTION EDITORS

Julie A. Gazmararian, MPH, PhD

Ruth M. Parker, MD   Rima E. Rudd, MSPH, ScD

Debra L. Roter, DrPH   Dean Schillinger, MD, MPH

Understanding Health Literacy:
Implications for Medicine and Public Health

Internet address: www.amapress.org

Additional copies of this book may be ordered by calling 800 621-8335.
Secure on-line orders can be taken at www.amapress.com
Mention product number OP323404

ISBN: 1 57947-630-9

Library of Congress Cataloging-in-Publication Data

Understanding health literacy: implications for medicine and public health/
    editors, Joanne Schwartzberg, Jonathan VanGeest, Claire Wang; section editors,
    Julie A. Gazmararian . . . [et al.].
      p.; cm.
    Includes bibliographical references and index.
    ISBN 1-57947-630-9
    1. Health education—United States. 2. Patient education—United States.
    3. Literacy—United States.
  I. Schwartzberg, Joanne G. II. VanGeest, Jonathan. III. Wang, Claire.

[DNLM: 1. Health Education—United States. 2. Communication Barriers—United States.
3. Educational Status—United States. 4. Health Knowledge, Attitudes, Practice—
United States. WA 590 U44 2005]

RA440.5.U485 2005
613'.0973—dc22   2004016090

BP07:04-P-059: 12/04

CONTENTS

iii

FOREWORD

Our concept of health literacy continues to evolve in a very meaningful way. Our health system is becoming increasingly complex, in great part, due to the amount of technology involved. This technology influences the availability of information about health, disease processes, and treatments. Our research continues to contribute new technology to aid the prevention, diagnosis, and treatment of diseases. It is difficult even for physicians to keep up with this technology. So it is understandable that patients find it difficult to keep up as well.

But health literacy can no longer be viewed as just a characteristic of the patient influencing how health and illness are experienced and dealt with. Health literacy is also crucial to the doctor–patient interaction and the environment in which that interaction takes place. All of these combine to influence the outcome of a patient's visit to a physician. Health literacy is reflected in the answer to questions such as: Was the service timely? Was there understanding on the part of the patient and the doctor? During the visit was the patient empowered to enhance his or her health, prevent and control disease? Was there motivation to act?

Health literacy is clearly influenced by the level of the patient's education. It is also influenced by the culture and the perspective that culture brings to an experience with illness. Culture influences how patients communicate about their illness with their physician. However, culture also influences what the physician hears and how a physician responds. In addition, culture and communication underlie many of our findings on health disparities.

As a nation, we have made a commitment to the reduction and ultimate elimination of disparities in health among different racial and ethnic groups. Areas of major disparities among those racial and ethnic groups include cardiovascular disease, cancer, diabetes, infant mortality, and the epidemic of HIV/AIDS. Great disparities have been also noted in diagnosis and treatment of mental health, as outlined in our report ***Mental Health: Culture, Race, and Ethnicity*** (US Department of Health and Human Services, 1999). Health literacy is a major factor in our understanding of these disparities, and in our quest to ultimately eliminate them. Many of the disparities and health outcomes are closely related to disparities in education and other socioeconomic measures and, therefore, must be dealt with as an integral part of the solution. However, we also know that even when we control for differences in socioeconomic status, some disparities still remain. By the same token, health literacy issues remain, even after we control for differences in education and socioeconomic status.

It is clear that barriers to and issues about health literacy must be dealt with as a part of our strategy for reaching the national goal of elimination of health disparities. It is time to bring the same level of concern, sophistication, and technology to the issue of health literacy that we have brought to other health issues. The role of computerized messaging, the internet, and electronic medical records will all be important in this endeavor.

This book, **Understanding Health Literacy: Implications for Medicine and Public Health**, is a very important contribution to this very critical issue of health literacy. The issue is placed in its proper context of patients, patient/provider interaction, and the environments (including culture) that influences them. The book describes challenges, experiences, and opportunities to improve levels of health literacy. This volume raises questions that will lead to more communication and investigation around the issue of health literacy in the context of the individual, the community, and patient–physician interaction.

David Satcher, MD, PhD
Sixteenth Surgeon General of the United States and Director of the National Center for Primary Care, Morehouse School of Medicine, Atlanta, Georgia

PREFACE

The fields of medicine and public health are moving forward with advances in disease prevention, diagnosis, and treatment, but are they leaving the patient and public behind?

The health sector's initial interest in literacy arose following the 1992 National Adult Literacy Survey (NALS), which unexpectedly identified nearly half of the United States adult population as being ill-equipped to meet the literacy needs of the 21st century. These findings raised concern over an individual's ability to function in health contexts, which often involve unfamiliar and complex materials and literacy tasks. The term "health literacy" subsequently came to refer to an individual's ability to read, comprehend, and act on medical information—with the health care system, health care professionals and the community partnering with the individual to achieve health literacy.

More than 10 years later, health literacy remains a pervasive, yet under-recognized, challenge in health care. Health care becomes ever more complex, while reliance on patient self-management continues to increase. Neither the American public's literacy skills nor the medical community's efforts to improve communication have kept pace. When an individual's ability to understand and utilize health information is unequal to the complexity of the information, and the communication efforts to bridge the gap are inadequate, this leads to failure in the delivery of health care.

The ineffective delivery of care due to health literacy barriers constitutes nothing short of a crisis for medicine and public health, with low health literacy linked to lower quality health care, poor health outcomes, and billions of dollars in avoidable health care costs. This crisis, in turn, has generated considerable activity in addressing health literacy—including the American Medical Association's *Health Literacy: Help Your Patients Understand* awareness program for health care professionals, recent reports from the Agency for Health Research and Quality and the Institute of Medicine entitled *Literacy and Health Outcomes* and *Health Literacy: A Prescription to End Confusion*, respectively; and now this textbook.

In preparing this textbook, our goal was to present a comprehensive resource of health literacy findings for researchers and educators in medicine, public health, nursing, pharmacy, and related fields, as well as for public health professionals and policymakers. We strove to examine the evidence from multiple perspectives, and we brought together expertise from a breadth of fields—including medicine, public health, adult learning, communication, and sociology.

This textbook is organized into four sections. Section 1 introduces the factors that determine whether health literacy is achieved—namely, the individual's literacy attributes, the content of specific health messages, and how these health messages are communicated—and presents a descriptive epidemiology of low health literacy in the United States. Section 2 focuses on the patient's literacy skills with relation to literacy demands encountered in health care, while Section 3 describes the effect of health literacy on patient-provider communication (and vice versa). We conclude with Section 4, which presents a framework for understanding how low health literacy might influence health outcomes, the research that supports this framework, and the literacy assessments that are instrumental to this research.

Readers will note that this textbook lacks an emphasis on interventions and recommendations for improving health literacy. We strongly feel that more research is needed before we can advocate certain approaches as being most appropriate and effective. It is our hope that readers will use this textbook both to enhance their understanding of health literacy and to stimulate much-needed progress toward eliminating health literacy barriers in the delivery of health care.

EDITORS AND CHAPTER AUTHORS

Editors

Joanne G. Schwartzberg, MD
Director, Aging and Community Health
American Medical Association
Chicago, Illinois

Jonathan B. VanGeest, PhD
Associate Professor
College of Health and Human Services
Kennesaw State University
Kennesaw, Georgia

Claire C. Wang, MD
Scientist
Medicine and Public Health
American Medical Association
Chicago, Illinois

Section Editors

Julie A. Gazmararian, MPH, PhD
Associate Professor
Emory Center for Health Outcomes and Quality
Department of Public Health and Management
Rollins School of Public Health
Emory University
Atlanta, Georgia

Ruth M. Parker, MD
Professor of Medicine
Emory University School of Medicine
Emory University
Atlanta, Georgia

Debra L. Roter, DrPH
Professor
Johns Hopkins Bloomberg School of Public Health
Department of Health Policy and Management
Baltimore, Maryland

Rima E. Rudd, MSPH, ScD
Senior Lecturer on Society, Human Development and Health
Harvard School of Public Health
Harvard University
Boston, Massachusetts

Dean Schillinger, MD, MPH
Associate Professor of Clinical Medicine
Division of General Internal Medicine
University of California, San Francisco
Primary Care Research Center and General Medicine Clinic
San Francisco General Hospital
San Francisco, California

Chapter Authors

Cynthia E. Baur, PhD
Health Communication and e-Health Advisor
Office of Disease Prevention and Health Promotion
US Department of Health and Human Services
Washington, District of Columbia

Mary Catherine Beach, MD, MPH
Assistant Professor of Medicine and
Health Policy and & Management
Johns Hopkins University
Baltimore, Maryland

Jay M. Bernhardt, PhD, MPH
Center for Public Health Communication
Department of Behavioral Sciences and Health Education
Rollins School of Public Health
Emory University
Atlanta, Georgia

Erica D. Brownfield, MD
Assistant Professor of Medicine
Department of Medicine
Co-Director, Medicine Clerkship
Emory University School of Medicine
Emory University
Atlanta, Georgia

Sarah L. Clever, MD, MS
Assistant Professor
Department of Medicine
Johns Hopkins University School of Medicine
Baltimore, Maryland

John P. Comings, EdD
Graduate School of Education
Harvard University
Cambridge, Massachusetts

Lisa A. Cooper, MD, MPH
Johns Hopkins University School of Medicine
Baltimore, Maryland

Lawren Daltroy, DrPH[†]
Harvard Medical School
Harvard School of Public Health
Brigham & Women's Hospital
Boston, Massachusetts

Rosalind Davidson, EdD
Graduate School of Education
Harvard University
Cambridge, Massachusetts

Terry Davis, PhD
Professor of Medicine and Pediatrics
Louisiana State University Health Sciences Center
Shreveport, Louisiana

Darren A. DeWalt, MD, MPH
Clinical Instructor
Divisions of General Internal Medicine and Community Pediatrics
University of North Carolina at Chapel Hill
Chapel Hill, North Carolina

Julie A. Gazmararian, MPH, PhD
Associate Professor
Emory Center for Health Outcomes and Quality
Department of Public Health and Management
Rollins School of Public Health
Emory University
Atlanta, Georgia

Estela M. Kennen, MA
Health Education Consultant
Lafayette, Colorado

Irwin S. Kirsch, PhD
Senior Research Director
Educational Testing Service
Princeton, New Jersey

---

† Dr Daltroy died in September 2003.

Michael K. Paasche-Orlow, MD, MA, MPH
Assistant Professor of Medicine
Section of General Internal Medicine
Boston University School of Medicine
Boston, Massachusetts

Ruth M. Parker, MD
Professor of Medicine
Emory University School of Medicine
Atlanta, Georgia

Anne Pereira, MD, MPH
Hennepin County Medical Center
Office of Medical Education
Department of Medicine,
University of Minnesota
Minneapolis, Minnesota

Michael Pignone, MD, MPH
Assistant Professor of Medicine
Associate Chief
Division of General Internal Medicine
University of North Carolina at Chapel Hill
Chapel Hill, North Carolina

Diane Renzulli, ScM
Communications Director
Philadelphia Health Management Corporation
Philadelphia, Pennsylvania

Debra L. Roter, DrPH
Professor
Johns Hopkins Bloomberg School of Public Health
Department of Health Policy and Management
Baltimore, Maryland

Rima E. Rudd, MSPH, ScD
Senior Lecturer on Society, Human Development and Health
Harvard School of Public Health
Boston, Massachusetts

Dean Schillinger, MD, MPH
Associate Professor of Clinical Medicine
Division of General Internal Medicine
University of California, San Francisco
Primary Care Research Center and
General Medicine Clinic
San Francisco General Hospital
San Francisco, California

John Strucker, EdD
Research Associate and Lecturer in Education
National Center for the Study of Adult Learning and Literacy
Graduate School of Education
Harvard University
Cambridge, Massachusetts

Barry D. Weiss, MD
Editor, Family Medicine
Professor, Department of Family and Community Medicine
University of Arizona College of Medicine
Tucson, Arizona

Mark V. Williams, MD, FACP
Professor of Medicine
Director, Hospital Medicine Unit
Emory University School of Medicine
Executive Medical Director, EHCA
Atlanta, Georgia

Reviewers

Cecelia C. Doak, BS, MPH
Director of Education
Patient Learning Associates, Inc.
Palm Springs, California

Leonard G. Doak, BS, PE
President
Patient Learning Associates, Inc.
Palm Springs, California

Fred A. Kobylarz, MD, MPH
Florida State University College of Medicine
Department of Geriatrics
Tallahassee, Florida

Sunil Kripalani, MD, MSc
Assistant Professor, Department of Internal Medicine
Assistant Director for Research
Grady Hospitalist Program
Emory University School of Medicine
Atlanta, Georgia

Scott C. Ratzan, MD, MPA
Vice President Government Affairs, Europe
Johnson & Johnson
Brussels, Belgium

Audrey C. Riffenburgh, MA
President, Riffenburgh & Associates
Specialists in Health Literacy and Plain Language
Albuquerque, New Mexico

Susan C. Scrimshaw, PhD
University of Illinois at Chicago
Chicago, Illinois

Michael S. Wolf, PhD, MPH
Assistant Professor of Medicine
Center for Healthcare Studies
Division of General Internal Medicine
Feinberg School of Medicine
Northwestern University
Chicago, Illinois

ACKNOWLEDGMENTS

We wish to thank the American Medical Association (AMA) Press for the opportunity to create this textbook. Special thanks and appreciation go to the section editors, chapter authors, and reviewers for contributing their expertise, energy, and enthusiasm to this project. Last, but not least, we wish to thank Patricia Dragisic and Pat Lee of the AMA Press for their guidance and editorial support.

Joanne G. Schwartzberg, MD

Jonathan B. VanGeest, PhD

Claire C. Wang, MD

Overview of Health Literacy in Health Care

Editors: Julie A. Gazmararian, MPH, PhD, and Ruth M. Parker, MD

INTRODUCTION

What is health literacy? Health literacy begins and ends with the patient; however, a growing body of literature defines health literacy as a shared function between patients and those with whom they interact to obtain and understand health information. Health literacy requires more than reading ability; it represents a constellation of skills necessary for understanding and communicating health information. A clear comprehension of the meaning of health literacy is needed in order to appreciate what is known about its epidemiology and associations.

In Chapter 1, Bernhardt and associates define health literacy, explaining it as an individual-level construct composed of attributes that can explain and predict one's ability to access, understand, and apply health information. The authors explore health literacy attributes that include the individual's prose literacy, document literacy, and quantitative literacy skills; two-way communication ability; motivation to receive and process information; and the presence and extent of external assistance. However, individuals do not learn in a vacuum; rather, it is the intersection of their attributes, the content of specific health messages, and how these health messages are communicated that determines whether functional health literacy is achieved. To demonstrate these intersections, the *health literacy and communication matrix* is introduced.

Chapter 2 explores why health literacy is gaining prominence as a factor in health research. In this chapter, Weiss characterizes the epidemiology of low health literacy, exploring the scope of the problem and the demographics of low health literacy in the United States.

1

Consequences of inadequate health literacy are introduced here (and described in greater detail in Section 4), as well as system, provider, and patient factors contributing to our nation's health literacy problem. Chapter 2 concludes with a discussion of barriers to improved health literacy.

Understanding Health Literacy

Jay M. Bernhardt, PhD, MPH; Erica D. Brownfield, MD, and Ruth M. Parker, MD

The challenges of health literacy are somewhat akin to those a driver faces when lost in an unfamiliar area. To reach his or her destination, the driver must find a source of accurate directions, correctly understand the language and meaning of necessary information, and then follow the directions properly from beginning to end. Written information such as street signs and printed information maps can be helpful but may be hard to find and difficult to read and understand. Calling someone for help is an option, if the traveler has access to a phone and can reach a person who actually knows the way and can communicate the directions accurately and effectively. Interactive feedback from an onboard navigational system would certainly help, but access to such systems is extremely limited and may not provide the most direct route. Moreover, many people are uncomfortable with this newer, less familiar technologic tool. Stopping to ask for directions may be a good option for some, but others may feel embarrassed or shamed in admitting they are lost, and the person giving directions must use language and landmarks that the driver can understand.

With two noteworthy differences, the skills and abilities needed to navigate successfully through unfamiliar territory are similar in many respects to those needed to navigate successfully through today's complex health care system and its nonstop barrage of health messages and information. These skills and abilities are collectively known as *health literacy*. Like a driver trying to reach a destination, a patient must learn how to navigate his or her way to health. He or she must be able to correctly understand appointment slips and directions within a hospital in order to see the doctor and receive necessary tests. He or she must be able to communicate health information with nurses and physicians in order to reach the correct diagnosis. He or she must be able to apply for health insurance and understand informed consent forms. And he or she must be able to follow instructions given by the doctor to stay healthy. Although navigation challenges exist for both drivers and patients, the consequences of being lost due to health literacy can be far more dire for individuals and far more costly to society.

This chapter provides an overview of health literacy. We begin with a basic definition of health literacy and the individual-level attributes that contribute to health literacy. We then explore these attributes to help distinguish between literacy, health literacy, and functional health literacy. Finally, we examine the relationship between functional health literacy and the communication of health information via the health literacy and communication matrix.

HEALTH LITERACY DEFINED

The term health literacy was first used in a 1974 monograph by Simonds that described how health information impacts the educational system, health care system, and mass communication.[1] Although health literacy is currently viewed as a policy issue at the intersection of health and education, the magnitude of the problem stems from much more than the history of our educational system.[2] Health literacy skills are required to function in health care systems that are increasingly characterized by technologic sophistication and complexity.[3] At the same time, individuals are being asked to assume more responsibility for the self-management of their wellness and illness and to make many more informed choices about their health.

Health literacy has been defined by the American Medical Association (AMA) as "a constellation of skills, including the ability to perform basic reading and numerical tasks required to function in the health care environment."[4] *Healthy People 2010*[5] defines health literacy as "the degree to which individuals have the capacity to obtain, process, and understand basic health information and services needed to make appropriate health decisions." Taken together, these two definitions demonstrate that health literacy is an individual-level construct composed of a combination of attributes that can explain and predict one's ability to access, understand, and apply health information in a manner necessary to successfully function in daily life and within the health care system.

People who possess the skills and ability to successfully function are considered to have "functional health literacy," which includes the ability to successfully complete tasks such as reading and comprehending prescription bottles and appointment slips and completing forms on financial eligibility.[1,6] Functional health literacy also involves accessing, understanding, and applying health information received from other nonclinical sources and settings, such as reading and understanding newspaper and magazine articles about emerging infectious disease threats; searching for online health information and assessing its accuracy and credibility; using problem-solving skills to compare the nutrition information of foods in the grocery store; reading and comprehending labels on the thousands of perceived "harmless" over-the-counter drugs; and critically considering the messages within televised advertisements for health care products and services.

It is important to note that many studies and publications that have explored the relationships between literacy and health have used the terms *literacy* and *health literacy* somewhat interchangeably. To help distinguish these terms, it may help to consider that literacy skills are content and setting specific and that people who have the requisite literacy skills to access, understand, and apply information on some topics may nonetheless lack the health literacy ability to access, understand, and apply information about their health.[7] To avoid confusion and promote clarity, the term *health literacy* may be preferable for describing situations and settings in which individuals or groups receive health-related information and messages.

HEALTH LITERACY ATTRIBUTES

Functional health literacy encompasses more than a single skill or ability. To function in the complex and multidimensional health care environment, one must possess a combination of individual-level attributes including abilities in prose, document, and quantitative literacy; ability to engage in two-way communication; skills in media literacy and computer literacy; motivation to receive health information; and freedom from impairments and/or communicative assistance from others (eg, a surrogate reader). However, at its core, functional health literacy also requires the skills and abilities traditionally known simply as literacy.

Historically defined as the ability to read and write, the concept of literacy recently has advanced to include higher level skills such as comprehension, problem solving, and reasoning. In 1991, the National Literacy Act defined literacy as "an individual's ability to read, write, and speak in English, and compute and solve problems at levels of proficiency necessary to function on the job and in society, to achieve one's goals, and develop one's knowledge and potential."[8] In 1992, the National Adult Literacy Survey (NALS) was conducted to assess the functional literacy skills of the adult population and provide vital information to policymakers, business and labor leaders, educators, researchers, and citizens on the condition of literacy in the United States.[9] The NALS measured literacy along three dimensions: prose literacy, document literacy, and quantitative literacy.

Prose literacy is the ability to locate requested information within written text documents (eg, editorials, news stories, poems, and fiction), to integrate disparate information presented in the texts, and to write new information based on the texts.[10] *Document literacy* is the ability to locate selected information on a short form or graphical display of everyday information (eg, job applications, transportation schedules, and maps), to apply selected information presented in documents, and to use writing to complete documents and survey forms that require filling in information.[11] Finally, *quantitative literacy* (or numeracy) is the ability to locate numbers within graphs, charts, prose texts, and documents; to integrate quantitative information from texts; and to perform appropriate arithmetic operations on text-based quantitative data.[12] Examples of this ability could include using a bank's automated teller machine, understanding a bar graph, or completing an income tax return.

Although proficiency in prose, document, and quantitative abilities are necessary for functional health literacy, especially for processing quantitative and text-based written health information, these literacy abilities alone are not sufficient for overall functional health literacy. Processing health information received through communication channels such as video, interactive multimedia, or interpersonal communication also requires skills such as speaking and listening. These additional skills are essential for functional health literacy and were included in the International Adult Literacy Survey, which assessed five domains necessary for functional literacy: reading, writing, numeracy, speaking, and listening.[13]

The ability to engage in conversations by speaking and listening, known as two-way communication ability, is essential for accessing, understanding, and applying health information received from a physician or other interpersonal source. This ability involves being able to clearly and accurately express physical, mental, and emotional states to health care providers; to hear, process, and understand spoken information expressed by another person; and to confidently interrupt and ask questions despite the power differential between patient and provider or patient and insurance administrator. Differences between the two communicators' spoken language, cultural heritage, perceived power, education level, and other factors can make the positive exchange of health information in interpersonal interactions difficult or impossible.

Several new abilities and skills are now required for overall functional health literacy because health information comes from so many different communication channels. One such ability is called *media literacy*.[14] Media literacy has been defined as the ability to "develop an informal and critical understanding of the nature of mass media, the techniques used by them, and the impact of these techniques."[15] People with media literacy are able to assess the degree of truth within media-based health information.[16] In contrast, people who lack media literacy may be less likely to resist inaccurate or irrelevant health information and media messages, which, in turn, could lead them to believe inaccurate health information and to adopt risky health behaviors.

Another new skill necessary for functional health literacy is computer literacy,[14] which is defined as "an understanding of the concepts, terminology and operations that relate to general computer use ... (and) the essential knowledge needed to function independently with a computer. This functionality includes being able to solve and avoid problems, adapt to new situations, keep information organized and communicate effectively with other computer literate people."[17] This skill is needed for accessing, understanding, and applying health information because so much health information is now available on the Internet and through clinical and community-based computer programs (eg, health kiosks). People who lack computer literacy skills are likely to face profound barriers when trying to access essential health information, let alone understand or apply computer-based information.[14]

Another attribute necessary for overall functional health literacy is related to people's beliefs about the health information they receive. In order to effectively access, understand, and apply received health messages, individuals must be motivated to receive and process the information. Lack of motivation to receive or to act on health information can be as much a barrier to functional health literacy as is the lack of cognitive abilities and skills. One predictor of an individual's motivation is his or her perceived personal relevance of the information being presented. Previous research has demonstrated direct positive relationships between an individual's perceived personal relevance of information and the amount of attention and deep thinking that he or she will devote to that information.[18] The cultural factors reflected in the content or format of the presented health information also are strong predictors of personal motivation. The more the information is perceived to be culturally relevant and appropriate, the more attention the receiver is likely to give it.[19]

Physical and/or mental impairment also can affect functional health literacy and influence all other literacy-related skills and abilities. Some impairments may limit one's ability to access, understand, or apply specific types of health messages (eg, visual impairment and printed materials) and other impairments may lead to inadequate health literacy across all necessary skills and abilities. For example, those who suffer from attention deficit hyperactivity disorder may be proficient in all of the aforementioned attributes but may not be able to concentrate long enough to comprehend and apply health information to their benefit. Similarly, victims of traumatic brain injury may have global impairments that lead to inadequate functional health literacy.

Finally, some forms of impairment can be overcome, as can other health literacy skill deficiencies, with the help of another person who provides the patient or message recipient with external assistance. This kind of support can lead to a situation of functional health literacy through a proxy or surrogate who translates and interprets information into another language or to a simpler language, asks questions on behalf of the individual, and provides him or her with reminders and encouragement to increase treatment adherence.

HEALTH LITERACY AND COMMUNICATION MATRIX

Although overall functional health literacy may require that individuals possess a minimum proficiency in all of the aforementioned attributes, functional health literacy in specific communication situations may require a more limited set of situation-specific skills. In these communication situations, functional health literacy will be determined by the strength of the match between an individual's health literacy abilities and the types of abilities required for processing specific types of health messages. In other words, it is this intersection between individual-level health literacy attributes and the characteristics of specific health information being communicated that determines if functional health literacy is achieved. These important intersections are depicted in the *health literacy and communication matrix*, which appears in Figure 1-1. The matrix reveals that functional health literacy is not exclusively a function of an individual's abilities but also a function of the characteristics and qualities of the communication messages that the individual receives.

Just as there are many attributes that together contribute to an individual's functional health literacy, there are many ways for health information to be communicated to individuals and populations. The health literacy and communication matrix depicts four communication channels through which health messages can be presented (ie, print, interpersonal, audio/video, and interactive multimedia) and also acknowledges the role played by the content of health messages. Although any or all health literacy attributes may affect communication for any specific health message, the intersections with darkly shaded cells represent health literacy attributes that are closely connected with channel-specific and content-specific communication, and the cells with the darkest shading represent the most critical intersections.

Some health literacy attributes may be necessary for functional health literacy regardless of the communication channel used. For example, all health messages containing quantitative or statistical information, whether delivered on paper or by a practitioner, require

FIGURE 1-1

Health Literacy and Communication Matrix

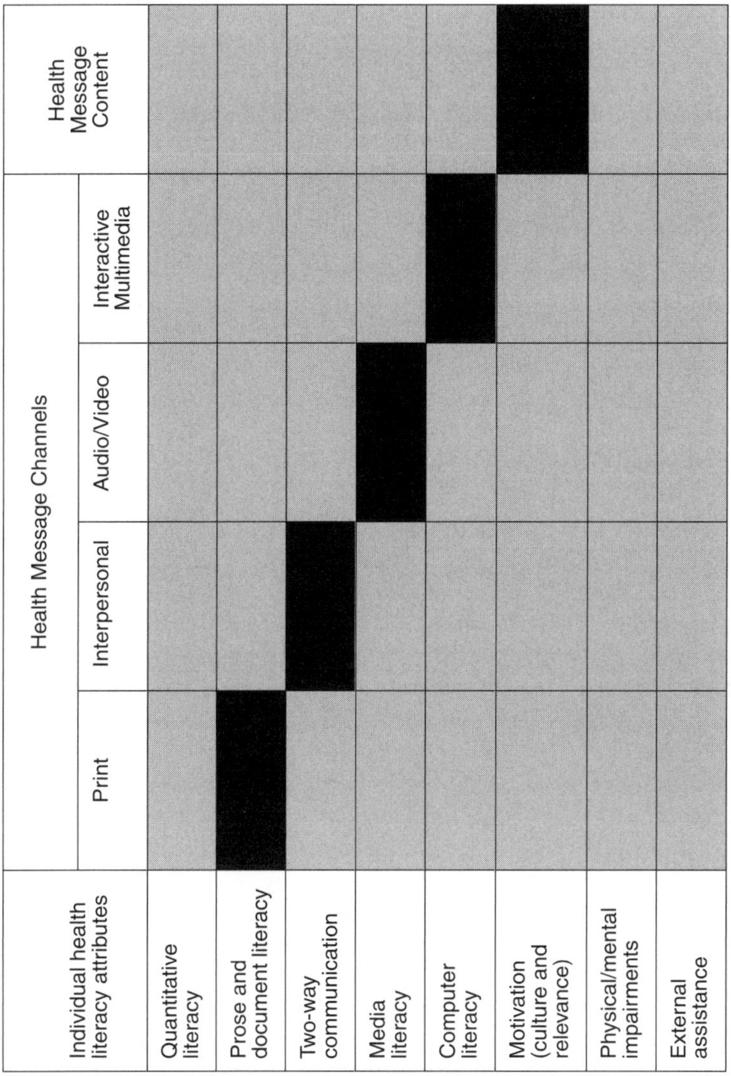

Individual health literacy attributes	Health Message Channels				Health Message Content
	Print	Interpersonal	Audio/Video	Interactive Multimedia	
Quantitative literacy					
Prose and document literacy	■				
Two-way communication		■			
Media literacy			■		
Computer literacy				■	
Motivation (culture and relevance)					■
Physical/mental impairments					
External assistance					

Note: All cells are shaded, indicating that all intersections should be considered. Darker cells represent the most important intersections between the format and content of health messages and the health literacy attributes needed to access, understand, and apply these messages.

that the recipient possess functional ability in quantitative literacy. Similarly, the existence of a physical or mental impairment can lead to inadequate health literacy regardless of message form or format. Whether or not each health literacy attribute is necessary for functional health literacy in any specific communication situation depends on the relationship between the abilities of the individual receiver and both the channel and content of the specific health message in question.

Health Message Channels

Printed health information can include messages that are distributed to individuals using brochures, flyers, and newsletters; messages that are placed in community settings such as on posters, billboards, and bus signs; or messages disseminated to large audiences using articles in newspapers or advertisements in magazines. These messages contain written text messages, graphical depictions, or, most frequently, a combination of both. A positive feature of communicating health information via printed materials is that individual receivers can control the pace at which the information is reviewed and can refer back to it when needed in the future.[20] In addition, graphical depictions may enhance receivers' ability to comprehend and recall message content. However, functional health literacy for accessing print materials that contain text messages may require the message receivers to possess sufficient prose literacy and document literacy (as represented by the dark shaded intersecting cell on the matrix). For example, pharmacists frequently distribute written instructions with prescription medications that describe when and how the medicine should be taken and potential side effects and drug interactions. Also, recipients of this information may not be able to access it for reasons such as the language used or the size of the type or may not be able to understand it because of the difficulty of the words or complexity of the examples. As a result, many people may take their medications incorrectly, which can limit their effectiveness or lead to negative outcomes. There are now more than 300 published studies demonstrating that printed health information is often presented at a readability level beyond that of the target population.[21-24]

Health messages delivered interpersonally can include verbal exchanges between individuals and their health care providers or other health information sources such as family members, peers, lay health advisors, and health insurance administrators. This form of health communication, especially the interactions between physicians and patients, has the potential to be more effective than other channels because two-way conversations allow both parties to be interactive and inquisitive, adjusting their content and presentation style in order to facilitate an effective information exchange.[25] However, many studies have demonstrated that individuals often do not emerge from these interpersonal encounters with a firm understanding of the instructions received.[24] One reason for this failure to communicate may be that individuals lack the two-way communication skills, including speaking and listening abilities, that are necessary to successfully understand health messages or information communicated during these encounters. An additional reason is that health care providers and other information communicators do not understand the abilities and needs of the individuals with whom they communicate. Adequate health literacy implies that the person needing information and the person (or source) providing information share common meaning or understanding. For example, patients with limited communication skills may not know how to express what they are feeling or have the confidence to tell their doctor that they do not understand what they are being told. Practitioners with limited communication training and skills may not give patients the opportunity to ask questions or they may fail to seek appropriate assurances of understanding during clinical encounters. Encouraging the exchange of dialogue with patients may lead to better understanding and patient empowerment.

Health messages using audio or video can be delivered to populations by mass media, such as radio, television, or movies, or to individuals using electronic media, such as compact discs or videos that can be accessed in public or private settings. The major challenge of audio- and video-based health messages is their ubiquitous presence in the media environment, especially in advertisements for health-related products and services that appear on television.[26] Therefore, media literacy is necessary for critically assessing messages and determining their accuracy and relevance. For example, many seniors are frequently exposed to television and radio advertisements for prescription medications for illnesses they have or for illnesses they think they may have, and these ads instruct them to "ask their doctor" for more information. As a result, some people may seek out unnecessary care or request specific medications that are more costly but not necessarily more effective.

Health messages presented through interactive multimedia can be delivered to individuals via Internet-based Web sites and computer-based programs that are accessible in public or private settings where people have computer access and via health-related computer kiosks made available for individual use in public or clinical settings. An advantage of this channel of communication is that it can incorporate the strengths of other channels through its use of audio, video, and interactivity to facilitate communication with people possessing lower literacy skills.[19] However, many individuals and populations may not have access to computers or may lack the computer literacy necessary to use them effectively and efficiently. For example, access to computers and the Internet is unevenly distributed throughout the United States, with higher-income individuals and households having much greater access than lower-income individuals and households.[27] Individuals who do have access must also possess the ability to search for online health information and critically determine if the information received is both relevant and accurate.

Health Message Content

The content of health messages refers to both what and how the health information is being communicated in the message. There are numerous variations in the presentation of the messages including:

- Use of different language or tone
- Use of interactive style, such as items to be checked off or answers to be filled in
- Presence or absence of examples, including statistics, case studies, testimonials, or narratives
- Use of message elements that are designed to elicit an emotional reaction or invoke fear
- Inclusion of message elements designed to appeal to specific audience groups segmented by age, gender, race/ethnicity, and other appropriate characteristics

Because many alternatives are available, message content may interact with any or all health literacy attributes; however, the primary attribute that may be affected is personal motivation. Although an individual may be more or less motivated to pay attention to health messages on any given topic based on its perceived relevance, the content of the message itself is also a powerful determinant of the receiver's motivation to pay attention to it. For example, giving a patient a brochure about smoking cessation is likely to be ignored unless the patient is already motivated to quit. However, the brochure itself may actually help increase a patient's motivation to quit if it incorporates messages that are well suited to the patient's values, beliefs, and experiences. Matching message content to an individual message receiver (message tailoring) or to selected groups of similar message receivers (message targeting) is a frequently used strategy in effective health communication.

APPLYING THE MATRIX

The health literacy and communication matrix can be a useful tool for practitioners and communicators when deciding on the appropriate health communication approach for specific audiences of interest. In an ideal situation, the first step is to determine the health literacy skills, abilities, and beliefs of the people who are to receive the messages. If the health literacy abilities of the intended audience are reasonably homogeneous, the practitioner can use the matrix to select or design health messages that take these abilities and skills into account. For example, if most audience members lack functional prose and document literacy, the dark intersecting cell in the matrix indicates that printed materials may be inappropriate and less effective than health messages delivered through other communication channels. Practitioners who already possess health messages to disseminate can use the matrix to determine what skills and abilities are necessary within an intended audience. For example, if a physician intends to communicate exclusively with patients interpersonally, the physician must determine if each patient has functional two-way communication skills in order for patients to correctly receive, understand, and apply the messages. Practitioners who use the matrix will realize that efforts to improve health literacy require not only improving people's ability to understand but also improving the appropriate development and delivery of health information content.

In many cases, individuals within an intended audience are likely to demonstrate wide variation in their health literacy skills, abilities, and beliefs. In these situations, a more complex communication strategy may be necessary to address the audience's needs. One such approach would be to segment the audience into groups based on their health literacy attributes. Different messages are then created using multiple channels that can be matched and distributed to individuals based on their abilities and needs. For example, a clinical practice that must regularly present health messages to its diverse patients on recommended dietary restrictions can select or create a set of materials that uses different communication channels (eg, brochures, pictograms, videos, Web sites) to present the same educational information in different formats. In this scenario, patients can be invited to select the material format they most prefer.

CONCLUSION

This chapter defines health literacy and identifies and describes the primary individual-level attributes that collectively determine people's ability to function successfully within the health care system. This chapter also introduces the health literacy and communication matrix, which demonstrates the intersecting relationships between specific attributes of health literacy and specific approaches for communicating health information. The two-dimensional matrix also suggests that the responsibility of engaging in effective communication with people who lack functional health literacy is not restricted to individual patients or receivers alone but extends to the practitioners and communicators who select, design, and present individuals with health messages.

Although health literacy is a relatively new concept in the fields of medicine and public health, it is rapidly gaining the attention it deserves. It is hoped that the information presented in this introductory chapter and the rest of this important book will give the reader a solid foundation for understanding health literacy. It is also hoped that the reader will receive ideas and directions for communicating in a manner sensitive to health literacy so that, in the future, all people can get where they want to go, even if they sometimes need to stop and ask for directions.

REFERENCES

1. Simonds SK. Health education as social policy. *Health Educ Monogr.* 1974;2:1–25.

2. Selden CR, Zorn M, Ratzan SC, Parker RM. *Current Bibliographies in Medicine 2000–1: Health Literacy.* Available at www.nlm.nih.gov/pubs/cbm/hliteracy.html. Accessed June 25, 2003.

3. Parker RM, Ratzan SC, Lurie N. Health literacy: a policy challenge for advancing high-quality health care. *Health Aff.* 2003;22:147–153.

4. Ad Hoc Committee on Health Literacy for the Council on Scientific Affairs, American Medical Association. Health literacy: report of the Council on Scientific Affairs. *JAMA.* 1999;281:552–557.

5. US Department of Health and Human Services. Health Communication (Chapter 11). *Healthy People 2010.* 2nd ed. *With Understanding and Improving Health* and *Objectives for Improving Health.* 2 vols. Washington, DC: US Government Printing Office, November 2000.

6. Williams MV, Parker RM, Baker DW, et al. Inadequate functional health literacy among patients at two public hospitals. *JAMA.* 1995;274:1677–1682.

7. Parker RM, Baker DW, Williams MV, Nurss JR. The test of functional health literacy in adults: a new instrument for measuring patients' literacy skills. *J Gen Intern Med.* 1995;10:537–541.

8. US Congress. *National Literacy Act of 1991.* Public Law 102–73, 1991.

9. National Center for Education Statistics. *The 1992 National Adult Literacy Survey: Overview.* Available at http://nces.ed.gov/naal/design/about92.asp. Accessed June 15, 2003.

10. National Center for Education Statistics. *Defining Literacy and Sample Items: Prose Literacy and Sample Items.* Available at http://nces.ed.gov/naal/defining/measprose.asp. Accessed June 15, 2003.

11. National Center for Education Statistics. *Defining Literacy and Sample Items: Document Literacy and Sample Items.* Available at http://nces.ed.gov/naal/defining/measdoc.asp. Accessed June 15, 2003.

12. National Center for Education Statistics. *Defining Literacy and Sample Items: Quantitative Literacy and Sample Items.* Available at http://nces.ed.gov/naal/defining/measquant.asp. Accessed June 15, 2003.

13. Kirsch I. *The International Adult Literacy Survey (IALS): Understanding What Was Measured. ETS Research Report RR-01-25.* Princeton, NJ: Statistics and Research Division of ETS [Educational Testing Services]. 2001.

14. Bernhardt JM, Cameron KC. Accessing, understanding, and applying health information: The challenge of health literacy. In: Thompson TL, Dorsey AM, Miller KI, Parrott R, eds. *Handbook of Health Communication.* Mahwah, NJ: Erlbaum; 2003:583–605.

15. Zettl H. Contextual media aesthetics as the basis for media literacy. *J Comm.* 1998;48:81–95.

16. Austin EW, Johnson KK. Immediate and delayed effects of media literacy training on third graders' decision making for alcohol. *Health Comm.* 1997;9:323–349.

17. Computer Literacy USA. *The Computer Literacy Initiative.* Available at www.computerliteracyusa.com. Accessed June 17, 2003.

18. Petty RE, Cacioppo JT. Personal involvement as a determinant of argument-based persuasion. *J Pers Soc Psychol.* 1984;41:847–855.

19. Huff RM, Kline MV. Health promotion in the context of culture. In: Huff RM, Kline MV, eds. *Promoting Health in Multicultural Settings: A Handbook for Practitioners.* Thousand Oaks, Calif: Sage; 1999:3–22.

20. Bernhardt JM. Developing health promotion materials for health care settings. *Health Promotion Pract.* 2001;2:290–294.

21. Dollahite J, Thompson C, McNew R. Readability of printed sources of diet and health information. *Pat Educ Couns.* 1996;27:123–134.

22. Hearth-Holmes M, Murphy PW, Davis TC, Nandy I, et al. Literacy in patients with chronic disease: Systemic lupus erythematosus and the reading level of patient education materials. *J Rheumatol.* 1997; 24:2335–2339.

23. Doak CC, Doak LG, Friedell GH, Meade CD. Improving comprehension for cancer patients with low literacy skills: Strategies for clinicians. *CA— A Cancer Journal for Clinicians.* 1998;48:151–162.

24. Williams MV. Adult literacy and health literacy: the link to health communication. Paper presented at: Meeting of the Georgia Public Health Association and the Georgia Federation of Professional Health Educators; August 2000; Athens, Ga.

25. Davis TC, Williams MV, Branch WT, Green KW. Explaining illness to patients with limited literacy. In: Whaley B, ed. *Explaining Illness: Research, Theories, and Strategies for Comprehension.* Mahwah, NJ: Erlbaum; 1999.

26. Brownfield ED, Bernhardt JM, Phan JL, Williams MV, Parker RM. Direct-to-consumer drug advertisements on network television: An exploration of quantity, frequency, and placement. *J Health Commun.* In press.

27. US Department of Commerce. *A Nation Online: How Americans are Expanding Their Use of the Internet.* Available at www.ntia.doc. gov/ntiahome/dn/. Accessed February 5, 2003.

Epidemiology of Low Health Literacy

Barry D. Weiss, MD

Health literacy is increasingly recognized as a crucial factor in health care delivery and health outcomes. This chapter provides an overview of the epidemiology of low health literacy, beginning with the definition and measurement of health literacy and the scope and demographics of low health literacy. Consequences of low health literacy as well as factors that contribute to our nation's health literacy problem are described. The chapter concludes with a discussion of barriers to improved health literacy.

DEFINITION AND MEASUREMENT OF HEALTH LITERACY

Health literacy is defined as the degree to which individuals have the capacity to obtain, process, and understand basic health information and services needed to make appropriate health decisions.[1] More simply, health literacy is the ability to obtain, read, understand, and use health information to make appropriate decisions about one's medical care.

Health literacy differs from *general literacy*, which refers to the basic ability to read, write, and compute, without regard to the context in which the reading and writing occur. Health literacy, on the other hand, implies that the reading and understanding occur in the context of health care. Persons with otherwise acceptable reading skills may find it difficult to understand the concepts and vocabulary used in health-related communications.

Despite the fact that health literacy and general literacy are different, they are also inextricably linked. That is, most individuals with limited general literacy also have limited health literacy. In many of the studies and reports discussed in this chapter, individuals with limited general literacy are assumed to have difficulty reading, understanding, and using health care information, ie, they are assumed to have limited health literacy.

Several well-validated instruments have been used to measure literacy in health care settings.[2] The two most widely used instruments are the Rapid Estimate of Adult Literacy in Medicine (REALM)[3] and the Test of Functional Health Literacy in Adults (TOFHLA).[4] * The REALM is a word-recognition test in which subjects read from a list of progressively more difficult medical words; the maximum difficulty level at which words can be read and pronounced correctly defines their health literacy. The TOFHLA is a more complex test that involves reading appointment slips, interpreting prescriptions, and filling in missing words on a consent form. The REALM is available only in English; there are both Spanish and English versions of the TOFHLA.

SCOPE AND DEMOGRAPHICS OF LIMITED HEALTH LITERACY

No nationwide studies have used health literacy assessment instruments, such as the REALM or TOFHLA, to estimate the health literacy skills of the US population. Rather, much of what we know about the prevalence of limited health literacy in America is based either on studies that measured health literacy in selected groups of subjects or on data derived from studies that measured general literacy. Some general literacy studies evaluated specific patient groups, while others, such as the National Adult Literacy Survey (NALS), estimated general literacy in the overall adult population.[5]

These various studies have identified a number of population subgroups in which literacy skills in general, and health literacy skills in particular, are poor. These groups include the elderly, racial and ethnic minority groups, persons with limited education, and immigrants. Other groups include the poor or homeless, prisoners, and military recruits. In some groups, the prevalence of limited general literacy is as high as 80% (Table 2-1).

The list of groups cited in the previous paragraph and in Table 2-1 might create an impression or reinforce a stereotype that individuals with limited literacy skills, as defined by NALS levels 1 and 2, are mostly minority group members and/or immigrants to the United States. There is, in fact, some truth to this stereotype, in that minority group and immigrant populations have disproportionately higher

---

* These tests are described in greater detail in Chapter 10.

Percentage of Adult Population Groups with Literacy Skills at National Adult Literacy Survey (NALS) Level 1 or Level 2

| | Percentage | | |
Group	Level 1	Level 2	Total Level 1–2
All NALS respondents	22	28	50
Older adults (age ≥ 65 years)	49	32	81
Racial/ethnic group			
White	15	26	41
American Indian/Alaska Native	26	38	64
Asian/Pacific Islander	35	25	60
Black	41	36	77
Hispanic (all groups)	52	26	78
Persons with limited education			
0–8 years	77	19	96
9–12 years (no high school graduation)	44	37	81
High school diploma/GED (no college study)	18	37	55
Immigrants to United States (various countries of origin)			
0–8 years of education prior to arrival in United States	60	31	91
9+ years of education prior to arrival in United States	44	27	71

Source: Unadjusted averages of prose and document literacy scores on the NALS as reported in Tables 1.1A, 1.1B, 1.2A, and 1.2B in Kirsch I, Jungeblut A, Jenkins L, Kolstad A. *Adult Literacy in America: A First Look at the Results of the National Adult Literacy Survey.* Washington, DC: National Center for Education Statistics, US Department of Education; September 1993, and on Table B3.13 in US Department of Education. National Center for Education Statistics. *English Literacy and Language Minorities in the United States,* NCES 2001–464, by Greenberg E, Macías RF, Rhodes D, Chan T. Washington, DC: 2001.

rates of limited literacy. It is important to keep in mind, however, that the majority of individuals in the United States with limited literacy skills are white, native-born Americans.

The following paragraphs discuss some of the population groups in which limited literacy is most common. The discussion includes comments on the prevalence, when known, of limited general and health literacy in these groups, along with the evidence on which the prevalence estimates are based.

The Elderly

The NALS shows that close to half of individuals older than 65 years of age scored at level 1, and another third at level 2, on assessment of prose and document literacy, which measured the ability of adults to locate and use information in texts (such as news stories) and documents (such as transportation schedules), respectively (Table 2-1). In total, about 80% of these older subjects demonstrated low-level skills.[5] These figures indicate substantial limitations in general literacy skills among the current population of older Americans.

Studies that specifically evaluated health literacy also found high rates of limited health literacy skill among older adults. In a study involving more than 3,200 Medicare enrollees in Ohio, Florida, and Texas, 34% of English-speaking subjects and 53% of Spanish-speaking subjects demonstrated poor or marginal health literacy when tested with the short version of the English or Spanish TOFHLA, respectively.[6] These subjects with lower literacy had limitations in their health knowledge[7] and use of preventive services.[8] An association between limited health literacy and age has been found even after adjusting for measures of cognitive dysfunction.[9]

The findings from the Medicare study have been corroborated by smaller studies of older adults in both upper and lower socioeconomic strata. In a study of low-income older adults (mean age of 72 years) living in public-assistance housing, one third of subjects had reading skills at or below the fourth grade level and one fourth of the subjects reported difficulty understanding information provided by their physicians.[10] Most subjects in this study reported obtaining health information from television rather than from the health care system. Another study, this one conducted in an affluent retirement community with subjects whose mean age was 70 years, found that one third of subjects were unable to adequately understand written health information.[11]

Thus, data from multiple sources indicate that older Americans, regardless of their socioeconomic status, have a higher rate of limited health literacy. This has important implications for the US health care system, considering the growing size of the geriatric population and its disproportionately high need for medical care. Current estimates are that, within 25 years, one in every five persons living in the United States will be over the age of 65.[12] As discussed later, limited health literacy appears to be associated with poor health outcomes and higher health care costs. Costs for health care of the geriatric population are already staggering, totaling $240,000,000 in 2001.[13] As the older population grows and its health care needs and expenses increase further, improvements in health literacy could be an important target for interventions aimed at improving the health of the older population and decreasing health care costs.

Minority Groups

As indicated by the NALS, a large proportion of the Hispanic and African-American populations has limited general literacy. Specifically, more than half of Hispanics scored at level 1 on the NALS, as did 41% of African Americans; this is compared to only 22% of the general US adult population.[5] Other minority groups with high rates of limited literacy include Pacific Islanders and Native Americans (Table 2-1).

The high prevalence of limited literacy among members of minority groups appears to translate into poor health literacy for these groups as well. Studies have shown that minority-group patients have limited knowledge and less awareness of healthy behaviors for a variety of health issues ranging from breast cancer risk,[14] to cervical cancer screening,[15] to treatment of human immunodeficiency virus (HIV) infection[16] and stroke prevention.[17]

Persons with Limited Education

Not surprisingly, individuals with limited education also have high rates of limited general literacy. More than 80% of individuals who did not finish high school have reading skills at NALS level 1 or 2.[5] The number of high school dropouts is large, with nearly 500,000 students dropping out of school every year in the United States—thus adding 5 million dropouts to the US population every 10 years.[18] Although health literacy has not been specifically studied in this group, the high rate of limited general literacy may correspond with limited health literacy skills as well.

Immigrants

No large-scale studies have specifically measured the health literacy skills of immigrant populations. Rather, studies have focused on immigrants' acquisition of English language skills[19,20] and their health knowledge and health behaviors.[21,22] Other studies have evaluated health literacy among non-English speakers (usually Spanish speakers), but the subjects in these studies may or may not have actually been immigrants.[23]

To estimate the health literacy skills of immigrant populations, it is necessary to draw estimates from the NALS data. According to the NALS, more than half the immigrants who enter the United States after childhood have level 1 literacy skills.[5] With such limited literacy skills, it is likely that most of these individuals also have limited health literacy.

Of course, the NALS tested only English language literacy, and adult immigrants from non–English-speaking nations might, in theory, be highly literate in their native language. However, research indicates otherwise. Most individuals who immigrate to the United States from non–English-speaking nations are from nonindustrialized countries where educational opportunities are limited.[24] As an example, more than half of adults immigrating to the United States from Spanish-speaking countries did not complete high school in their country of origin.[25] Thus, based on NALS data, the conclusion that health literacy levels are low among immigrants to the United States is probably valid.

The Poor

Poverty is closely intertwined with many other sociodemographic factors that are associated with literacy, including advanced age, membership in a racial or ethnic minority group, limited education, and immigration to the United States. It is not clear whether limited literacy in these individuals contributes to poverty or whether individuals in the aforementioned socioeconomic groups have limited literacy because they have had fewer educational opportunities.

Regardless of the reason, there is strong evidence that limited skills in both general and health literacy are common in low-income populations. One study, which used Medicaid enrollment as a marker for low income, tested the general literacy skills of more than 400 Medicaid enrollees. The study found that the average reading skill was at the fifth-grade level and nearly one in five patients had reading levels at or below the second-grade level.[26] Another study tested the health literacy skills of more than 2,600 low-income patients receiving acute care at two urban public hospitals. It was found that 35% of English-speaking patients and 62% of Spanish-speaking patients had inadequate or marginal functional health literacy when tested with the English and Spanish versions of the TOFHLA, respectively.[27] Nearly half of the patients could not understand directions for taking their medications, and 60% could not understand a standard informed consent document.

The Homeless

Although there are no national data on the prevalence of low literacy among homeless individuals, the rate is thought to be high. Indeed, governmental and social service agencies have long targeted homeless populations for literacy training interventions.[28] The reasons why limited literacy skills are common among homeless individuals are complex, but they likely represent an interaction of poverty, learning and language disabilities,[29] and mental illness,[30] all of which are common among homeless populations. Among individuals receiving mental health services through homeless shelters, in particular, the rate of low health literacy is very high, with three quarters of these individuals having below-average health literacy skills when tested with the REALM.[31]

Prisoners

The NALS investigators reported on the general literacy skills of 1,150 inmates in 80 federal and state prisons that had been selected to represent penal institutions across the United States.[32] Limited general literacy skills were found in about 70% of prisoners. Although no data are available on health literacy of prisoners, it is likely that most prisoners with limited general literacy also have limited health literacy.

Many prison inmates have some of the same socioeconomic characteristics already discussed, such as membership in a minority ethnic group, poverty, and limited education. It is not clear which of these factors makes the largest contribution to literacy skills. Nonetheless, the high rate of limited literacy among prisoners is noteworthy, given that there are currently about 2 million individuals in US jails and prisons—about 1 in every 142 US residents.[33]

MILITARY RECRUITS

While military officers are often well educated and possess high-level literacy skills, military recruits (ie, enlisted military personnel) appear to have high rates of limited literacy. Few quantitative data about the literacy skills of military personnel are available through easily accessible public documents, and no data are available specifically on their health literacy skills. Nonetheless, reports indicate that many soldiers cannot perform the high school level reading tasks required of them in the military.[34] As a result, all branches of the US military operate education programs to bring soldiers up to the level of literacy skill needed to adequately function in military service. Most soldiers requiring this remedial education probably possess limited health literacy skills.

CONSEQUENCES OF INADEQUATE HEALTH LITERACY

With large segments of the population—the elderly, minority groups, immigrants, the poor, and others—demonstrating limited literacy, it is important to examine its consequences on health. These consequences have been the focus of much research; findings from various studies demonstrate that individuals with limited literacy have less health knowledge, lower health status, higher utilization of health services, and higher health care costs than their more literate

TABLE 2-2

Consequence of Inadequate Health Literacy

- Less health knowledge
- Poorer health status
- Higher rates of health services utilization
- Higher health care costs

counterparts (Table 2-2). There is also concern that limited health literacy is a threat to patient safety, because limited literacy skills may lead to errors in the self-administration of medications.

Health Knowledge

Numerous studies have shown that individuals with limited literacy skills have limited knowledge about their medical problems. To cite just a few examples, hypertensive patients with limited literacy, as measured by the TOFHLA, are less likely to know that exercise and weight loss can lower blood pressure, and diabetic patients with limited literacy are less knowledgeable about the symptoms of hypoglycemia.[35] Similarly, pregnant women with limited literacy, as determined by the REALM, are less likely to know about the harmful effects of cigarette smoking than are women with better literacy skills.[36] Other studies show that asthma patients with limited literacy are less likely to know how to correctly use an inhaler,[37] and that many low-literacy patients do not understand the meaning of commonly used medical phrases such as screening test, blood in the stool, and mammogram.[38,39]

Health Status

Not surprisingly, several studies have indicated that persons with limited literacy, either general or health literacy, report poorer health than their more literate counterparts, even after adjusting for other sociodemographic variables that are known to influence health status. Some studies have used patients' self-reports to determine health status and found that individuals with limited literacy are more likely to report their health as being poor. For example, limited health literacy, as measured with the TOFHLA, has been associated with poor self-reported health status in the overall population[40] as well as in those with specific medical problems such as HIV infection.[41]

Other studies have used specific health-status measures and also found an association between literacy and health. For example, one study found that, among a socioeconomically homogenous group of Medicaid patients with diabetes, those with limited literacy skills were less likely to have good diabetes control than those with better literacy skills.[42] Another study of adults attending general educational development (GED) diploma classes and adult basic education (literacy) classes used a standardized health status assessment instrument and found that subjects with the lowest reading levels had higher degrees of both physical and mental illness than their more literate counterparts.[43] Poor health literacy, as measured with the REALM, is also associated with a more advanced stage of disease upon diagnosis among low-income patients with prostate cancer.[44]

Utilization of Health Services

Research has shown a relationship between limited health literacy and rates of hospitalization. Medicare managed-care enrollees are 29% more likely to be hospitalized if they have limited health literacy skills.[45] Furthermore, 2-year hospitalization rates are 69% higher for patients with low health literacy who receive care at public hospitals, even when potentially confounding variables such as age, gender, race, self-reported health, socioeconomic status, and health insurance status are considered.[46]

Health Care Costs

The poorer health status and higher use of health services by patients with limited literacy appear to translate into higher costs for these patients, although research on this issue is limited. One small study of medically indigent and needy Medicaid managed-care enrollees found that enrollees with limited literacy skills (reading level at or below third-grade level) generated health care costs averaging $10,688 per year, in comparison to only $2,891 per year for those with higher literacy skills.[47] The disparity was largely due to difference in costs for inpatient care ($7,038 for subjects with limited literacy vs $824 for those with higher literacy skills).

Similar results were found in a study of Medicare enrollees. Those with limited health literacy had average annual costs for emergency room care, prescription drugs, and inpatient care that were $86, $137, and $1,107 higher, respectively, than for subjects with adequate health literacy, even after adjusting for a number of potentially confounding variables.[48]

Experts have estimated that the poorer health status and higher use of health care services by persons with limited health literacy may result in as much as $50 billion to $73 billion per year in excess costs to the US health care system.[49] According to the Center for Health Care Strategies, this amount equals Medicare's annual expenses for physician services, dental services, home health care, drugs, and nursing home care combined.[50]

Patient Safety

Although there is little published research on the issue, it is widely assumed that limited literacy skills contribute to medicine-dosing errors by patients. Indeed, there is much theoretical work on which to base this assumption. First, patient education brochures and handouts are typically written at readability levels that the majority of adults cannot comprehend, leading to poor understanding of the concepts surrounding diagnosis and treatment.[51–56] Second, when patients are provided with standard medication instructions, such as ones that they might receive from a pharmacy, a large proportion of patients demonstrates an inability to correctly follow the instructions.

For example, one recent study found that more than 75% of patients, when asked to follow directions for preparing an oral rehydration solution for a child with diarrhea, were unable to correctly do so. Half of the patients in that study also could not determine the correct dosage from the label on a bottle of their child's cough medicine.[57] Another study demonstrated errors in dosing albuterol inhalers for children, due to inadequate parental attention to or inaccurate interpretation of written instructions for dosing the medication.[58] Yet another study, this one conducted at a county hospital in which the prevalence of limited literacy was likely quite high, demonstrated that a large percentage of patients with diabetes made errors in dosing and administering insulin.[59]

The potential for harm due to such dosing errors is substantial. Several authors have described real-life dosing errors, some serious, by patients who had difficulty reading and understanding medication labels.[60] The problem is particularly serious for individuals who are nonnative English speakers. A recent survey by a language-translation firm found that one third of 592 respondents whose first language was Spanish, Russian, Chinese, or Hindi said they left their physician's office without understanding how to take their medication and 28% stated that they ended up guessing about their medication dose.[61] An example of a potentially serious error cited in the study is that Spanish-speaking patients easily confuse the instructions to take medications "once" daily; they interpret this instruction to mean they should take the medication 11 times per day, because the Spanish word for 11 is *once*.

FACTORS CONTRIBUTING TO LIMITED HEALTH LITERACY

A variety of factors contribute to the problem of limited health literacy in the United States. While these factors are complex and often intertwined, for purposes of discussion, they can be grouped as system factors, provider factors, and patient factors.

System Factors

System factors include medications, time, self-care, fragmentation of care, and insurance and paperwork.

Medications

Progress in the development of new and effective medications has been of great benefit to patients, but it has also made medical care more complex. The number of available medications has grown from several hundred in the 1960s and to more than 11,000 at present,[62] and many patients now take multiple daily medications—sometimes 5 to 10 or more each day—creating potential for confusion in dosing and administration.

To add to the problem, to take these medications properly, patients must follow instructions that are sometimes complex. Indeed, dosing instructions often include specifics about time of day, relationship to meals and other medications, and even the posture one must assume when taking medications. For example, bisphosphonates for osteoporosis therapy must be taken on an empty stomach immediately upon rising in the morning on the same day each week, with a large glass of water. In addition, the patient must be in an upright position when taking the medication and remain upright for at least 30 minutes after taking the medication. Failure to follow these instructions can lead to ulceration with perforation of the esophagus, which is a potentially fatal complication.

Instructions for other drug regimens, such as those for adjusting insulin dosages based on fluctuating blood glucose levels, are even more complex. These tasks are sometimes difficult even for the most educated and organized individuals, but they may be impossible for an individual with third-grade reading skills.

Time

Just as medical treatment regimens are becoming more complex and require more explanation, health providers have less time to spend with patients. The median time that office-based primary care physicians spend with patients during office visits is only about 17 minutes.[63] Even for patients over 85 years of age, who often have a high rate of complex medical problems and are prescribed multiple medications, the average time is only about 22 minutes.[64] Most of this time is devoted to biomedical questions, physical examination, and paperwork. Little time—only 8% according to one study— remains for answering patients' questions and educating patients about the details of their medical conditions and treatments.[65]

Self-Care

Another system factor that creates difficulty for low-literacy patients is that hospital stays have become shorter and more medical treatments are given outside the hospital. Patients are sent home from the hospital only days after a myocardial infarction. Patients with newly diagnosed diabetes, who typically require extensive patient education, are usually managed and treated as outpatients. Even after surgical procedures, many of which are performed in same-day outpatient surgical centers, patients frequently recuperate and care for themselves at home.

Patient self-care usually requires the ability to follow instructions that are typically in a written form that many cannot understand.[66] However, effective home-care instructions, even for complicated medical problems or procedures such as organ transplantation, can be provided to patients with limited literacy skills using appropriately designed personalized education programs.[67] Unfortunately, such personalized education programs are not available to most patients.

Fragmentation of Care

Despite attempts to give patients a primary care "home" that can provide and coordinate most of their care, only about half of the 880 million annual visits to office-based physicians in the United States are to a patient's primary care physician. Furthermore, large numbers of patients do not receive care from office-based primary care physicians. During 2001, patients made 84 million visits to hospital-based outpatient departments[68] and 108 million visits to emergency departments.[69] The result is that patients with chronic medical illnesses see multiple physicians with different specialties in different locations. These physicians frequently do not communicate with one another, and it often becomes the patient's de facto responsibility to relay information and treatment plans between the various physicians. The role of "inter-physician messenger" is not easy for patients with limited literacy skills and a poor understanding of medical concepts.

Insurance and Paperwork

Finally, for patients to receive care, they must be registered properly with insurance companies, health plans, government agencies, and office practices. Appropriate registration often requires an understanding of eligibility rules and completion of application forms, many of which are presented in complex, legalistic language. Persons with limited literacy skills may find it difficult to deal with or even understand the often-confusing regulations and forms with which they must comply, the result being that many patients are unable to or do not obtain appropriate insurance coverage.

However, it is not just insurance and registration forms that are difficult for patients to understand. Research consistently shows that discharge instructions,[70] procedure consent forms,[71,72] and research consent forms[73] are generally written at a level of complexity that most patients do not understand. In fact, the average readability level of research consent forms, even those approved by institutional review boards assigned to protect the rights of human research subjects, is at nearly the eleventh-grade level, which is far above the eighth-grade reading level of the average American.[74]

Provider Factors

Health care providers also contribute significantly to the difficulties experienced by patients with limited literacy. First and foremost, physicians often have a poor grasp of what patients do and do not know about medical concepts and information. For example, many physicians use terms such as *mammogram* or *screening test*, assuming that patients are familiar with these terms. But as noted earlier, patients with limited literacy may not understand such terms.[39] More complex information, such as terms used to describe surgical procedures and chronic diseases or medication instructions, may be even more difficult for patients to understand.

Furthermore, physicians are often rushed and do not take the time needed to ensure that patients understand what they have been told. Although there is limited high-quality research on physician–patient interactions,[75] studies show that, when compared to physicians in other countries, American physicians tend to "control" the physician–patient encounter by asking directive questions, rather than focusing communication on the patients' needs and understanding.[76,77]

It is possible that these factors could be remedied by educating health care providers about how to deliver information effectively and promote patients' understanding. In fact, there are some efforts to provide this type of education.[78,79] As a rule, however, most communication courses taught to physicians and medical students emphasize empathy, listening skills, dealing with difficult patients, and other aspects of communication; few such courses focus on enhancing patients' understanding of critical health information.[80–82]

Patient Factors

Many patient factors that contribute to limited literacy (eg, limited education, difficulty with written communication, or lack of familiarity with medical terms) have already been discussed, but several others deserve mention. In particular, patients who have limited literacy skills often possess characteristics that impair their ability to successfully interact with the health care system. Specifically, patients with limited literacy tend to lack a sense of self-empowerment, creating a situation in which they accept what the health care system offers them instead of seeking and obtaining what they want from the health care system.[83] Self-empowerment is essential to successful patient education and to negotiating the complexities of today's health care system.[84,85] Lack of self-empowerment increases the likelihood that patients will not learn what they need to know and, therefore, will not receive all the care they need. Indeed, research shows that most patients taking medications, regardless of their literacy skills, do not ask their physicians any questions about those medications.[86] The rate of asking such questions is likely to be very low among persons with low literacy levels.

A related problem is shame. Patients who are aware of their limited literacy skills often report that they are ashamed of this limitation and do not readily tell others about it. In fact, most individuals with limited literacy have not disclosed their reading difficulty to their spouses and children, and few have ever told a health care provider.[87] When these patients do not understand what their health provider tells them, they may be hampered by shame and lack of self-empowerment and fail to ask for the clarifications and explanations needed to understand what they should do for prevention and care of disease.[60]

BARRIERS TO IMPROVED HEALTH LITERACY

There are numerous barriers to improving health literacy in the American population. The two most obvious barriers are the education system and the health care system itself.

The Education System

One of the most important barriers—the American education system—is largely out of the control of health professionals. As noted earlier, millions of students drop out of school every decade and, of those who complete school, many have limited literacy. Indeed, some 25% of NALS level 1 readers are high school graduates. These statistics tell us that the US education system is not always effective at teaching its students to read; without adequate general reading skills, it will be very difficult for these individuals to achieve health literacy.

Contributing to this lack of academic success is the fact that some 35% of American children enter kindergarten without the language

TABLE 2-3

Ranking of Science Knowledge of High School Students Around the World

Ranking	Country	Ranking	Country
1	South Korea	15	Hungary
2	Japan	16	Iceland
3	Finland	17	Belgium
4	United Kingdom	18	Switzerland
5	Canada	19	Spain
6	New Zealand	20	Germany
7	Australia	21	Poland
8	Austria	22	Denmark
9	Ireland	23	Italy
10	Sweden	24	Greece
11	Czech Republic	25	Russia
12	France	26	Portugal
13	Norway	27	Mexico
14	United States	28	Brazil

Data from: US Department of Education, National Center for Education Statistics. *Outcomes of Learning: Results From the 2000 Program for International Student Assessment of 15-Year-Olds in Reading, Mathematics, and Science Literacy*, NCES 2002–115, by Lemke M, Calsyn C, Lippman L, et al. Washington, DC: 2001.

skills needed to acquire adequate general literacy.[88] The parents of these children often have limited literacy themselves and do not expose their children to reading in the home. Attempts are being made to overcome this barrier through programs like Reach Out and Read, an intervention in which primary care clinicians encourage parents to read to their children.[89]

Another educational prerequisite for good health literacy is a basic knowledge of science concepts. At present, the US educational system does not adequately teach these concepts to its students. The US ranks only 14th among nations of the Organisation for Economic Co-operation and Development on scores that compare science knowledge of high school–aged students from different countries (Table 2-3).[90] Only 75% of American students take more than one science course in high school, and while biology is the most popular science course, basic biology courses do not typically focus on health and disease concepts.[91,92] Only one in six high school students takes a higher-level biology course in which these advanced concepts might be taught.[91] The result is that many, if not most, students who graduate from high school do not have a sound understanding of the anatomy, physiology, and etiology of the diseases that they are likely to encounter in the course of their own or their family's health care, such as heart disease, diabetes, and cancer.

The Health Care System

It would be a mistake to conclude that all problems with health literacy are attributable to the US education system. Indeed, the health care system itself is often a barrier to improving health literacy.

As discussed earlier, physicians and others who interface with patients are often unaware of the challenges associated with limited health literacy. Even if they are aware, they may lack the skills needed to communicate effectively and in a time-efficient manner. Furthermore, any efforts to enhance patient understanding may be hindered by the scarcity of coordinated efforts to adapt delivery of health information and health care to patients' health literacy skills. When such efforts are made, there is often no clear system for implementing changes efficiently and cost effectively.

These issues will not be resolved until the challenges of health literacy are viewed as a health system concern as well as a patient burden. Efforts are needed to increase the health care community's awareness of health literacy as a factor in patient care. In addition, research is needed to develop educational curricula for health care providers on effective communication and to determine what factors will motivate providers to put this education into practice. Health information materials should be developed and tested with patients' literacy skills and preferences in mind, and systems should be put into place to encourage their widespread use.

CONCLUSION

Limited general literacy and limited health literacy are common among patients in the United States and they are particularly common in certain demographic populations. These populations include the elderly, minority groups, persons with limited education, immigrants, the poor, and several other groups. Limited general literacy and limited health literacy are associated with limited health knowledge, lower health status, higher utilization of health services, and higher health care costs.

Many factors contribute to the poor health outcomes associated with limited health literacy. These include characteristics of the health system plus patient factors and provider behaviors, all of which pose barriers to the effective delivery of health care. By addressing these barriers, we can begin to bridge the gap between the literacy demands of the health care environment and the literacy skills of the average American.

REFERENCES

1. US Department of Health and Human Services. Health Communication (Chapter 11). *Healthy People 2010*. 2nd ed. *With Understanding and Improving Health* and *Objectives for Improving Health*. 2 vols. Washington, DC: US Government Printing Office, November 2000.

2. Davis TC, Michielutte R, Askov EN, Williams MV, Weiss BD. Practical assessment of adult literacy in health care. *Health Educ Behav*. 1998; 25:613–624.

3. Davis TC, Crouch MA, Long SW, et al. Rapid assessment of literacy levels of adult primary care patients. *Fam Med*. 1991;23:433–435.

4. Parker RM, Baker DW, Williams MV, Nurss JR. The test of functional health literacy in adults: a new instrument for measuring patients' literacy skills. *J Gen Intern Med*. 1995;10:537–541.

5. Kirsch I, Jungeblut A, Jenkins L, Kolstad A. *Adult Literacy in America: A First Look at the Results of the National Adult Literacy Survey*. Washington, DC: National Center for Education Statistics, US Department of Education; September 1993.

6. Gazmararian JA, Baker DW, Williams MV, et al. Health literacy among Medicare enrollees in a managed care organization. *JAMA*. 1999;281:545–551.

7. Gazmararian JA, Williams MV, Peel J, Baker DW. Health literacy and knowledge of chronic disease. *Patient Educ Couns*. 2003; 51:267–275.

8. Scott TL, Gazmararian JA, Williams MV, Baker DW. Health literacy and preventive health care use among Medicare enrollees in a managed care organization. *Med Care*. 2002;40:395–404.

9. Baker DW, Gazmararian JA, Sudano J, Patterson M. The association between age and health literacy among elderly persons. *J Gerontol B Psychol Sci Soc Sci*. 2000;55:S368–S374.

10. Weiss BD, Reed RL, Kligman EW. Literacy skills and communication methods of low-income older persons. *Pat Educ Couns*. 1995; 25:109–119.

11. Gausman BJ, Forman WB. Comprehension of written health care information in an affluent geriatric retirement community: use of the test of functional health literacy. *Gerontol*. 2002;48:93–97.

12. Fowles D, Greenberg S. *A Profile of Older Americans*. Washington, DC: Administration on Aging, Department of Health and Human Services, 2001. Available at www.aoa.gov/aoa/stats/profile. Accessed December 29, 2003.

13. Medicare Program Spending. Centers for Medicare and Medicaid Services, Office of the Actuary, June 2002. Available at www.cms.hhs.gov/charts/default.asp. Accessed December 29, 2003.

14. Jones AR, Thompson CJ, Oster RA, et al. Breast cancer knowledge, beliefs, and screening behaviors among low-income, elderly black women. *J Natl Med Assoc*. 2003;95:791–797, 802–805.

15. Sharp LK, Zurawski JM, Roland PY, O'Toole C, Hines J. Health literacy, cervical cancer risk factors, and distress in low-income African-American women seeking colposcopy. *Ethn Dis*. 2002;12:541–546.

16. Van Servellen G, Brown JS, Lombardi E, Herrera G. Health literacy in low-income Latino men and women receiving antiretroviral therapy in community-based treatment centers. *AIDS Patient Care STDS*. 2003;17:283–298.

17. Pratt CA, Ha L, Levine SR, Pratt CB. Stroke knowledge and barriers to stroke prevention among African Americans: implications for health communication. *J Health Commun*. 2003;8:369–381.

18. Young BA. Public High School Dropouts and Completers from the Common Core of Data: School Years 1998–1999 and 1999–2000. National Center for Education Statistics. US Department of Education. Office of Educational Research and Improvement. *Educ Tab*. August 2002. NCES 2002-382. Available at http://nces.ed.gov/pubs2002/2002382.pdf. Accessed December 29, 2003.

19. Westermeyer J, Her C. Predictors of English fluency among Hmong refugees in Minnesota: a longitudinal study. *Cult Divers Ment Health*. 1996;2:125–132.

20. Sanders LM, Gershon TD, Huffman LC, Mendoza FS. Prescribing books for immigrant children: a pilot study to promote emergent literacy among the children of Hispanic immigrants. *Arch Pediatr Adolesc Med*. 2000;154:771–777.

21. Sohng KY, Sohng S, Yeom HA. Health-promoting behaviors of elderly Korean immigrants in the United States. *Public Health Nurs*. 2002;19:294–300.

22. Clark L. Mexican-origin mothers' experiences using children's health care services. *West J Nurs Res*. 2002;24:159–179.

23. Williams MV, Parker RM, Baker DW, et al. Inadequate functional health literacy among patients at two public hospitals. *JAMA*. 1995;274:1677–1682.

24. Schmidley D. The foreign born population in the United States, March 2002. Population characteristics. Population Reports. US Department of Commerce. US Census Bureau. February 2003. Available at www.census.gov/prod/2003pubs/p20-539.pdf. Accessed December 29, 2003.

25. Greenberg E, Macias RF, Rhodes D, Chan T. US Department of Education. National Center for Education Statistics. *English Literacy and Language Minorities in the United States*. NCES 2001-464. Washington, DC: 2001.

26. Weiss BD, Blanchard JS, McGee DL, et al. Illiteracy among Medicaid recipients and its relationship to health care costs. *J Health Care Poor Underserved*. 1994;5:99–111.

27. Williams MV, Parker RM, Baker DW, et al. Inadequate functional health literacy among patients at two public hospitals. *JAMA*. 1995;274: 1677–1682.

28. *Profiles of State Programs: Adult Education for the Homeless*. Division of Adult Education and Literacy, US Department of Education, 1990. Available at: http://ericae.net/ericdb/ED327730.htm. Accessed December 29, 2003.

29. O'Neil-Pirozzi TM. Language functioning of residents in family homeless shelters. *Am J Speech Lang Pathol*. 2003;12:229–242.

30. Goering P, Tolomiczenko G, Sheldon T, Boydell K, Wasylenki D. Characteristics of persons who are homeless for the first time. *Psychiatr Serv*. 2002;53:1472–1474.

31. Christensen RC, Grace GD. The prevalence of low literacy in an indigent psychiatric population. *Psychiatr Serv*. 1999;50:262–263.

32. Haigler KO, Harlow C, O'Connor P, Campbell A. *Literacy behind Prison Walls. Profiles of the Prison Population from the National Adult Literacy Survey*. Washington, DC: US Government Printing Office. 1994.

33. US Department of Justice. Office of Justice Programs, Bureau of Justice Statistics. Prison and jail inmates at midyear 2002. Report number NCJ 198877, April 2003. Available at www.ojp.usdoj.gov/bjs/abstract/pjim02.htm. Accessed December 29, 2003.

34. Hegerfield M. Reading, Writing and the American Soldier: A Study of Literacy in the American Armed Forces. Fort Wayne, Ind: Department of Education, Purdue University at Fort Wayne, 1999. Available at: http://ericae.net/ericdc/ED429281.htm. Accessed December 29, 2003.

35. Williams MV, Baker DW, Parker RM, Nurss JR. Relationship of functional health literacy to patients' knowledge of their chronic disease: a study of patients with hypertension or diabetes. *Arch Intern Med*. 1998;158:166–172.

36. Arnold CL, Davis TC, Berkel HJ, Jackson RH, Nandy I, London S. Smoking status, reading level, and knowledge of tobacco effects among low-income pregnant women. *Prev Med*. 2001;32:313–320.

37. Williams MV, Baker DW, Honig EG, Lee TM, Nowlan A. Inadequate literacy is a barrier to asthma knowledge and self-care. *Chest*. 1998;114:1008–1015.

38. Davis TC, Arnold C, Berkel HJ, Nandy I, Jackson RH, Glass J. Knowledge and attitude on screening mammography among low-literate, low-income women. *Cancer*. 1996;78:1912–1920.

39. Davis TC, Dolan NC, Ferreira MR, et al. The role of inadequate health literacy skills in colorectal cancer screening. *Cancer Invest*. 2001;19:193–200.

40. Baker DW, Parker RM, Williams MV, Clark WS, Nurss J. The relationship of patient reading ability to self-reported health and use of health services. *Am J Public Health*. 1997;87:1027–1030.

41. Kalichman SC, Rompa D. Functional health literacy is associated with health status and health-related knowledge in people living with HIV-AIDS. *J Acquir Immune Defic Syndr*. 2000;25:337–344.

42. Schillinger D, Grumbach K, Piette J, et al. Association of health literacy with diabetes outcomes. *JAMA*. 2002;288:475–482.

43. Weiss BD, Hart G, McGee D, D'Estelle S. Health status of illiterate adults: relation between literacy and health status among persons with low literacy skills. *J Am Board Fam Pract*. 1992;5:257–264.

44. Bennett CL, Ferreira MR, Davis TC, et al. Relation between literacy, race, and stage of presentation among low-income patients with prostate cancer. *J Clin Oncol*. 1998;16:3101–3104.

45. Baker DW, Gazmararian JA, Williams MV, et al. Functional health literacy and the risk of hospital admission among Medicare managed care enrollees. *Am J Public Health*. 2002;92:1278–1283.

46. Baker DW, Parker RM, Williams MV, Clark WS. Health literacy and the risk of hospital admission. *J Gen Intern Med*. 1998;13:791–798.

47. Weiss BD, Palmer R. Relationship between health care costs and very low literacy skills in a medically needy and indigent Medicaid population. *J Am Board Fam Pract*. 2004;17:44–47.

48. Howard DH. The Relationship between Health Literacy and Medical Costs. In: Institute of Medicine. *Health Literacy: A Prescription to End Confusion*. Nielsen-Bohlman LT, Panzer AM, Hamlin B, Kindig DA, eds. Committee on Health Literacy, Board on Neuroscience and Behavioral Health. Washington, DC: National Academies Press; 2004.

49. Friedland RB. *Understanding Health Literacy: New Estimates of the Costs of Inadequate Health Literacy*. Washington, DC, National Academy on an Aging Society; 1998.

50. Anonymous. Fact sheet: Low health literacy skills increase annual health care expenditures by $73 billion. Lawrenceville, NJ: Center for Health Care Strategies; 1998.

51. Davis TC, Mayeaux EJ, Frederickson D, Bocchini KA Jr, Jackson RH, Murphy PW. Reading ability of parents compared with reading level of pediatric patient education materials. *Pediatr*. 1994;93:460–468.

52. Glazer HR, Kirk LM, Bosler FE. Patient education pamphlets about prevention, detection, and treatment of breast cancer for low literacy women. *Patient Educ Couns*. 1996;27:185–189.

53. Estrada CA, Hryniewicz MM, Higgs VB, Collins C, Byrd JC. Anticoagulant patient information material is written at high readability levels. *Stroke*. 2000;31:2966–2970.

54. Wilson FL. Are patient information materials too difficult to read? *Home Health Nurse*. 2000;18:107–115.

55. Wallace LS, Lennon ES. American Academy of Family Physicians patient education materials: Can patients read them? *Fam Med*. In press.

56. Wilson FL, Williams BN. Assessing the readability of skin care and pressure ulcer patient education materials. *J Wound Ostomy Continence Nurs*. 2003;30:224–230.

57. Patel VL, Branch T, Arocha JF. Errors in interpreting quantities as procedures: the case of pharmaceutical labels. *Int J Med Inf*. 2002;65:193–211.

58. Simon HK. Caregiver knowledge and delivery of a commonly prescribed medication (albuterol) for children. *Arch Pediatr Adolesc Med*. 1999;153:615–618.

59. Newman KD, Weaver MT. Insulin measurement and preparation among diabetic patients at a county hospital. *Nurse Pract*. 1994;19:44–45, 48.

60. Baker DW, Parker RM, Williams MV, et al. The health care experience of patients with low literacy. *Arch Fam Med*. 1996;5:329–334.

61. Anonymous. Nearly one in ten children have been given medication incorrectly due to poor translation. New York, NY: Transperfect Translations. April 2, 2003. Available at www.transperfect.com/tp/eng/rxepidemic.html. Accessed December 29, 2003.

62. Klasco RK, ed. USP DI. Drug Information for the Healthcare Professional. Thomson Micromedex, Greenwood Village, Co; 2003.

63. Cherry DK, Burt CW, Woodwell D. National Ambulatory Medical Care Survey: 2001 Summary. *Advance Data from Vital and Health Statistics*. No 337. Hyattsville, Md: National Center for Health Statistics; 2003.

64. Mann S, Sripathy K, Siegler EL, Davidow A, Lipkin M, Roter DL. The medical interview: differences between adult and geriatric outpatients. *J Am Geriatr Soc*. 2001;49:65–71.

65. Roter DL, Stewart M, Putnam SM, Lipkin M Jr, Stiles W, Inui TS. Communication patterns of primary care physicians. *JAMA*. 1997;277:350–356.

66. O'Shea HS. Teaching the adult ostomy patient. *J Wound Ostomy Continence Nurs*. 2001;28:47–54.

67. Blanchard WA. Teaching an illiterate transplant patient. *ANNA J*. 1998;25:69–70, 76.

68. Hing E, Middleton K. National Hospital Ambulatory Medical Care Survey: 2001 Outpatient Department Summary. *Advance Data from Vital and Health Statistics;* no 338. Hyattsville, Md: National Center for Health Statistics; 2003.

69. McCaig LF, Burt CW. National Hospital Ambulatory Medical Care Survey: 2001 Emergency Department Summary. *Advance Data from Vital and Health Statistics*; no. 335, Hyattsville, Md: National Center for Health Statistics; 2003.

70. Spandorfer JM, Karras DJ, Hughes LA, Caputo C. Comprehension of discharge instructions by patients in an urban emergency department. *Ann Emerg Med*. 1995;25:71–74.

71. Hopper KD, TenHave TR, Tully DA, Hall TE. The readability of currently used surgical/procedure consent forms in the United States. *Surgery*. 1998;123:496–503.

72. Hopper KD, TenHave TR, Hartzel J. Informed consent forms for clinical and research imaging procedures: how much do patients understand? *Am J Roentgenol*. 1995;164:493–496.

73. Grossman SA, Piantadosi S, Covahey C. Are informed consent forms that describe clinical oncology research protocols readable by most patients and their families? *J Clin Oncol*. 1994;12:2211–2215.

74. Paasche-Orlow MK, Taylor HA, Brancati FL. Readability standards for informed-consent forms as compared with actual readability. *N Engl J Med*. 2003;348:721–726.

75. Beck RS, Daughtridge R, Sloane PD. Physician-patient communication in the primary care office: a systematic review. *J Am Board Fam Pract*. 2002;15:25–38.

76. Ohtaki S, Ohtaki T, Fetters MD. Doctor-patient communication: a comparison of the USA and Japan. *Fam Pract*. 2003; 20:276–282.

77. Bensing JM, Roter DL, Hulsman RL. Communication patterns of primary care physicians in the United States and the Netherlands. *J Gen Intern Med*. 2003;18:335–342.

78. Weiss BD. *Health Literacy: A Manual for Clinicians*. Chicago, Ill: American Medical Association Foundation; 2003.

79. Health Literacy: Help Your Patients Understand. Chicago, Ill: American Medical Association and American Medical Association Foundation; 2003.

80. Wagner PJ, Lentz L, Heslop SD. Teaching communication skills: a skills-based approach. *Acad Med*. 2002;77:1164.

81. Roth CS, Watson KV, Harris IB. A communication assessment and skill-building exercise (CASE) for first-year residents. *Acad Med*.2002;77: 746–747.

82. Ang M. Advanced communication skills: conflict management and persuasion. *Acad Med*. 2002;77:1166.

83. Wallerstein N. Health and safety education for workers with low-literacy or limited-English skills. *Am J Ind Med*. 1992;22:751–765.

84. Wallerstein N. Empowerment to reduce health disparities. *Scand J Public Health*. 2002;59(suppl):72–77.

85. Roter DL, Stashefsky-Margalit R, Rudd R. Current perspectives on patient education in the US. *Patient Educ Couns*. 2001;44:79–86.

86. Sleath B, Roter D, Chewning B, Svarstad B. Asking questions about medication: analysis of physician-patient interactions and physician perceptions. *Med Care*. 1999;37:1169–1173.

87. Parikh NS, Parker RM, Nurss JR, Baker DW, Williams MV. Shame and health literacy: the unspoken connection. *Patient Educ Couns.* 1996;27:33–39.

88. Boyer EL. *Ready To Learn: A Mandate for the Nation.* Princeton, NJ: The Carnegie Foundation for the Advancement of Teaching; 1991.

89. High PC, LaGasse L, Becker S, Ahlgren I, Gardner A. Literacy promotion in primary care pediatrics: can we make a difference? *Pediatr.* 2000;105(suppl):927–934.

90. Lemke M, Calsyn C, Lippman L, et al. Outcomes of Learning: Results from the 2000 Program for International Student Assessment of 15-Year-Olds in Reading, Mathematics, and Science Literacy. NCES 2002-115. Washington, DC: National Center for Education Statistics, US Department of Education; September 1993. Available at http://nces.ed.gov/pubsearch/ pubsinfo.asp?pubid=2002115. Accessed December 29, 2003.

91. National Center for Education Statistics. *The 1998 High School Transcript Study Tabulations: Comparative Data on Credits Earned and Demographics for 1998, 1994, 1990, 1987, and 1982 High School Graduates.* US Department of Education, Office of Educational Research and Improvement. NCES 2001-498. May 2001. Available at http://nces.ed.gov/pubsearch/pubsinfo.asp?pubid=2001498. Accessed December 29, 2003.

92. Schmidel DK, Wojcik WG. Biology Guide. High School Hub Interactive Learning Center, 2003. Available at http://highschoolhub.org/hub/biology.cfm. Accessed December 29, 2003.

The Patient Perspective

Editor: Rima E. Rudd, MSPH, ScD

INTRODUCTION

The patient's perspective in health literacy combines the patient's experience of the literacy-related demands he or she confronts in health care settings and the sense of adequacy or inadequacy in the face of these demands. This takes on new significance when considered in light of what has been measured and what is known about adult literacy in the United States.

This section begins with an explication of the findings from the National Adult Literacy Survey (NALS), undertaken by the US government in 1992. NALS measured adults' ability to use the written word for everyday tasks and focused on three of five widely accepted functional literacy skills: reading, writing, and arithmetic. As described by Comings and Kirsch in Chapter 3, NALS findings indicate that relatively few adults in the United States are truly illiterate, but *nearly half* are at a disadvantage when faced with the literacy demands of 21st century life.

In Chapter 4, Strucker and Davidson offer an explanation of how this might occur in an industrialized nation with required schooling. After describing the component skills of reading and the stages of developing these skills, Strucker and Davidson present findings from their Adult Reading Components Study. These findings offer insight into how family resources, schooling, and learning abilities/disabilities may stall reading development at any given stage. This chapter concludes with suggestions to health care providers, from an educational perspective, on how to optimize interactions with adults who have limited literacy skills.

These discussions lay the foundation for an exploration of the literacy-related demands faced by adults in health care settings. In Chapter 5, Rudd, et al explore the literacy demands of materials and tasks encountered in various health contexts, such as the home, the workplace, the community, and the health care setting itself. After describing the underlying assumptions that shape these materials and tasks, they highlight a mismatch between the literacy skills of the average adult and the demands reflected in health information and in health care settings.

Literacy Skills of US Adults

John P. Comings, EdD, and Irwin S. Kirsch, PhD

THE NATIONAL ADULT LITERACY SURVEY AND SIMILAR EFFORTS

Few adults in the United States have no literacy skills at all, but the literacy skills of the population range from extremely limited to completely competent. In 1992, the US government undertook the National Adult Literacy Survey (NALS) to describe this range of skills and determine how many US adults have skills sufficient to function effectively as workers, parents, and citizens. NALS defined literacy as:

> Using printed and written information to function in society, to achieve one's goals, and to develop one's knowledge and potential.[1]

Under this broad definition, Educational Testing Service (ETS), which develops and manages such tests as the Scholastic Aptitude Test (SAT) used for college admissions, developed NALS to test literacy skills as applied to various text types instrumental for accomplishing specific tasks. The literacy skills tested were reading, writing, and quantitative literacy (arithmetic skills).

NALS was preceded by several attempts to gauge the literacy skills of adults in the United States. Sticht and Armstrong[2] identified four assessments of military personnel and six assessments of civilians that took place between 1917 and 1986. The military tests were developed to determine which recruits should be inducted into military service and which jobs would be appropriate for them. The civilian tests were developed to gauge the impact of participation in the school system and the capacity of the workforce. There were two other assessments in the United States: a 1985 US Department of Education survey of 21- to 25-year-olds and a 1989–1990 US Department of Labor survey of job seekers.[1] NALS drew on the findings of these latter two surveys.

Shortly after the findings from NALS were published, Statistics Canada (the Canadian government's central statistics unit) and ETS developed the International Adult Literacy Survey (IALS), which follows the same format as the NALS and applies the same definition of literacy. Between 1994 and 1999, 20 countries participated in the IALS. The Organisation for Economic Co-operation and Development (OECD), which is a membership organization of 30 industrialized countries, published the IALS findings.[3–5]

In 2003, the US Department of Education began collecting data for a second national survey, the National Assessment of Adult Literacy (NAAL), which employs a test developed by the American Institute of Research. The NAAL follows the same format and includes many of the same items as the NALS but expands the number of background questions related to health and includes additional health-related tasks as part of the item pool. Therefore, the analysis, with its completion anticipated for 2005, should provide more insight into the relationship between health and literacy.[*]

At the same time that NAAL was initiated, the OECD began collecting data for a second survey, the Adult Literacy and Lifeskills (ALL) Survey, developed by Statistics Canada and ETS. This survey follows the format of the IALS but includes a new test of problem-solving ability as well as a broader measure of math skills. In addition, the US Department of Education is funding a new literacy survey of participants in federally sponsored adult education programs. This assessment, which is referred to as the Adult Education and Literacy (AEL) Survey, uses measures of literacy and math from ALL and will report results on the same scales as the NAAL, allowing direct comparisons between the survey populations. The reports of these efforts will be available in 2005.

At present, NALS provides the most current and comprehensive information about the literacy skills of adults in the United States. This chapter describes features of NALS (with some comparison to IALS), including the literacy domains assessed and findings from the survey. This chapter also describes characteristics of adults with low literacy skills and concludes with a brief discussion of health communication approaches based on NALS level.

---

* Of note, Rudd et al.[6] coded all health-related items and tasks from the 1985 Department of Education assessment, the 1989 Department of Labor assessment, NALS, and IALS and used these to create the Health Activities Literacy Scale (HALS). Their analysis of NALS using the HALS instrument can be found in a report published by ETS in 2004.

FEATURES OF NALS

Survey Participants and Methods

NALS tested 26,000 Americans who were 16 years of age or older. Survey participants were randomly selected to demographically represent the adult population in the country as a whole, and additional participants were selected to provide enough data for 11 states that were conducting their own assessment[†] and to assess the prison population.[‡] Each participant was tested for reading, writing, and math skills in a 90-minute session, using materials that simulated the literacy demands of everyday life. These materials and tasks were drawn from six domains of everyday life: home and family, health and safety, community and citizenship, consumer economics, work, and leisure and recreation.[1] Each participant was also interviewed about demographic, employment, education, and other personal characteristics.

NALS Scoring

The NALS assessment measured literacy on three scales. The first scale measured *prose literacy*, which includes the knowledge and skills needed to locate and use information contained in texts such as editorials, news stories, poetry, and fiction. The second measured *document literacy*, which includes the knowledge and skills needed to locate and use information contained in job applications, payroll forms, transportation schedules, maps, tables, graphs, and other common documents. The third was *quantitative literacy*, which includes the knowledge and skills needed to apply arithmetic operations to tasks such as balancing a checkbook, computing a tip, completing an order form, and determining the amount of interest from a loan advertisement.

NALS measured each of the three skills on a continuous scale of 0 to 500 points, with 0 points representing the lowest level of skill and 500 points representing the highest level. The points were then divided into five ranges, or levels: level 1 (0 to 225 points), level 2 (226 to 275 points), level 3 (276 to 325 points), level 4 (326 to 375 points), and level 5 (376 to 500 points). Adults with a level 1 aggregate score were considered to have very limited literacy and math skills, while adults scoring at level 5 were considered capable of managing almost any reading or math task.

[†] The states were California, Illinois, Indiana, Iowa, Louisiana, New Jersey, New York, Ohio, Pennsylvania, Texas, and Washington. In addition, Mississippi and Oregon, using the same measures of literacy, conducted and reported their results independently of the NALS evaluation.

[‡] NALS tested 1100 inmates in 80 federal and state prisons.

NALS levels not only represent the individual's skill level but also an increasing complexity of tasks based on both the difficulty of the text and the difficulty of the operation being performed. Certain tasks have been placed along the NALS scale (levels 1, 2, 3, 4, and 5) as a result of how well a nationally representative sample of adults performed these tasks. For example, a task that requires reading a simple text and finding one piece of information within it is considered a level 1 task; a level 2 task requires reading a simple text, finding two pieces of information, and using them to answer a question. Research has shown that successful performance of such tasks is related to a combination of features relating to both the text and the kind of processing or operation that must be performed with that text.[7]

NALS Levels 1 and 2

Only people who scored in the very lowest point range of level 1 could be considered illiterate, in the sense that they could not accomplish even simple reading and math tasks. Most people performing at level 1 can locate a single piece of information in a short and simple piece of text, but they have difficulty with tasks requiring them to locate several pieces of information in moderately complicated text. Level 1 adults can solve simple math problems when the numbers and the operations are provided, but they find it difficult to solve the same problems when they must locate the numbers and the operations in a piece of text.

In comparison, NALS level 2 adults can locate information in moderately complicated text and solve simple math problems when the numbers and operations must be found in a piece of text. However, they find it difficult to perform these operations in difficult text and to perform operations that are complicated by distracting information and complex forms. Level 2 adults can use their literacy skills, but they are not fluent and competent readers of the kinds of text and documents that are common in everyday life. Considered in the context of everyday literacy needs, adults in level 1 are at a severe disadvantage, and those in level 2 are disadvantaged, in relation to the demands of 21st century life.

NALS Level 3

NALS level 3 adults are better equipped to face the demands of everyday life. They are able to locate several relevant pieces of information in complicated and lengthy text and solve problems that require locating several numbers in a text and determining which operation to use. Other examples of level 3 tasks include using a flight schedule to plan travel arrangements, writing a brief letter explaining an error made on a credit card bill, and identifying information from a bar graph that depicts sources of energy and years of production. The mean NALS score for high school graduates (who terminate their education at this point) is in the range between level 2 and level 3 on each of the literacy scales.

NALS level 3 tasks are common in most jobs and many aspects of everyday life. For that reason, NALS level 3 is becoming broadly recognized as a minimum performance standard for jobs that pay a good salary and benefits. Competence in level 3 tasks is also required for success in postsecondary education institutions; in fact, only 17% of degree-seeking postsecondary students scored in levels 1 and 2 in the NALS survey, while the rest scored in level 3 or higher. Both the National Governors' Association and the National Educational Goals Panel have identified NALS level 3 as the minimum standard for the 21st century.[8]

NALS Levels 4 and 5

NALS level 4 adults are able to synthesize information drawn from complex and lengthy text. An example of a level 4 task might be contrasting the different positions of two editorials. Level 5 adults have the ability to perform even more complex literacy tasks. They are able to contrast complex information drawn from dense text that might draw from specialized domains. For example, level 5 adults can summarize and contrast two ways that lawyers can challenge prospective jurors or they can calculate the correct dose of a pediatric medicine based on height and weight of a child. Adults in levels 4 and 5 are well equipped for the demands of 21st century life.

Features of IALS

The IALS followed the same format as NALS in every way, but its population was limited to 16- to 65-year-olds. Sample sizes varied by country, and studies that compare NALS and IALS findings adjust for this difference. IALS reports have been published for Australia, Belgium (Flanders), Canada (English and French), Chile, Czech Republic, Denmark, Finland, Germany, Hungary, Ireland, Italy, the Netherlands, New Zealand, Norway, Poland, Portugal, Slovenia, Sweden, Switzerland (French, German and Italian), the United Kingdom, and the United States.[9]

Criticisms of NALS

Like most standardized tests and national surveys, NALS (and IALS by extension) has received criticism.[10] Critics suggest that the way in which NALS data were analyzed placed too many people in levels 1 and 2. The basis for this argument is that an individual had to demonstrate an 80% probability of being able to accomplish the tasks in a level to be placed in it. Some people in NALS level 2, for example, were able to accomplish some but not all of the NALS level 3 tasks.

The other argument is that NALS used tasks (balancing a checkbook, for example) that might be unfamiliar to some people (in the preceding example, those who do not have checking accounts). People who have never had a checking account might have been able to complete a task that required similar mathematical operations had they been familiar with that particular type of task.

Despite these criticisms, NALS findings are considered applicable to medical and public health contexts. After all, the kinds of tasks required of adults using the health care system are similar to those used in NALS. Often, adults must apply their literacy skills to unfamiliar texts and operations with accuracy and speed in order to fully function in the health care setting.

NALS FINDINGS

NALS data were analyzed to determine the percentage of adults in the United States that scored in each level. Figure 3-1 presents the percentage of adults that scored in levels 1 to 5 for each of the three skills measured (prose, document, and quantitative literacy).

Depending on the type of literacy skill, 21% to 23% of NALS participants scored in level 1; 25% to 28% scored in level 2; 31% to 32% scored in level 3; 15% to 17% scored in level 4; and 3% to 4% scored in level 5. Between 46% and 51% of all adults in the sample, therefore, scored in levels 1 and 2. Because the adult population was around 190

FIGURE 3-1

Percentage of US Adults in Each National Adult Literacy Survey (NALS) Level by Test Component

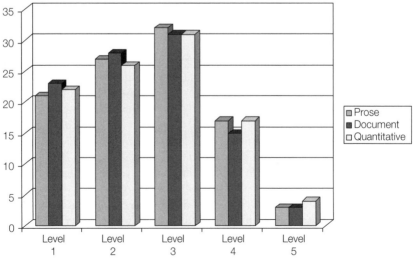

million at the time the data was collected, it is calculated that almost 90 million adults scored in levels 1 or 2 on at least one of the components of the test.[1] Within each level, scores among the three tests are in a narrow range.

Nonwhites, immigrants, the disabled, school dropouts, and those over 65 were more likely to score in NALS level 1 than those who did not fit into one of these categories. Nonetheless, in terms of total numbers, the majority of all survey participants scoring in levels 1 and 2 were white, US-born English speakers.[1] Reder[11] looked at the geographic distribution of NALS level 1 adults and found that the District of Columbia had the highest rate at 37%, followed by Mississippi (30%), Louisiana (28%), and Alabama, Florida, and South Carolina at 25%. Alaska, Utah, and Wyoming had the lowest rates of NALS level 1 at 11%, followed by New Hampshire and Vermont at 12%, and Colorado, Idaho, Iowa, Minnesota, Montana, and Nebraska at 13%. Within states, urban areas and poor rural counties had the highest rates of NALS level 1, and a state could have counties that had very low and very high rates of NALS level 1 adults. For example, Utah's San Juan County, which is in the rural southeast corner of the state, had an NALS rate of 33%, while Summit County, which is a suburb east of Salt Lake City, had a rate of only 7%. Clay County in Florida's northeast had a NALS level 1 rate of 14%, while Miami-Dade County had a rate of 42%. Some urban and poor rural areas had NALS level 1 rates above 50%.

When Tuijnman[12] compared the NALS and IALS data, he found that the United States performed below the Nordic countries and the Netherlands but was at par with Australia, Canada, and Germany. The United States outperformed Ireland, Switzerland, and the United Kingdom and was far ahead of Chile, the Czech Republic, Hungary, Poland, Portugal, and Slovenia. Tuijnman also found that the United States had a wide inequality in its population. Only Sweden had a higher mean score for the group accounting for the top 25% of their population, while Sweden, Norway, Finland, the Netherlands, and Canada all had higher mean scores for the bottom 25% of their population. More recently, Sum et al.[13] suggested that the United States' mediocre performance on NALS and IALS, as well as the high degree of inequality within its population, may place it at a competitive disadvantage in the world economy.

CHARACTERISTICS OF ADULTS WITH LOW LITERACY SKILLS

Kirsch and colleagues[1] describe some characteristics of adults who scored in NALS level 1. Around 25% of NALS level 1 adults were immigrants who probably do not speak English well. Some of these adults may have strong literacy skills in another language, but all have limited skills in English. Age-related decline in cognitive function could also play a role, since 33% of NALS level 1 adults were over the age of 65. In addition, 26% of NALS level 1 adults reported a physical, mental, or health condition (such as visual and hearing impairment, learning disability, and mental and emotional conditions). The largest group within NALS level 1, however, was composed of adults who had not completed high school or a high school equivalency program, such as passing the general educational development (GED) test. This group made up 62% of the total. Although these groups overlap, they suggest various reasons why adults scored in NALS level 1. NALS level 1 adults may not have had sufficient education in English to develop strong reading and math skills or they may have had an age, physical, mental, or health-related factor in their literacy skills.

NALS level 2 adults differed from those in levels 3, 4, and 5 primarily in terms of education. Only 4% of level 2 adults completed 4 years of college, while 10% of level 3, 22% of level 4, and 30% of level 5 adults completed 4 years of college. Only 25% of level 2 adults had any education beyond high school, while 44% of level 3, 55% of level 4, and 51% of level 5 adults had at least some postsecondary education. For the most part, there is no specific reason why the skills of level 2 adults are low, but these adults probably did not use their literacy skills enough to develop strong vocabularies and adequate speed and accuracy in their reading.

NALS did not look directly at the relationship between literacy and health, although this relationship is well documented.[14] However, health is related to socioeconomic status and NALS level is related to income. Between 41% and 44% (depending on the test component) of those in level 1 lived in a household with income below the poverty line, as did 20% to 23% of those in level 2. In comparison, poverty rates were 7% to 8% and 4% to 6% for adults in levels 4 and 5, respectively.

NALS LEVELS AND THE COMMUNICATION OF HEALTH INFORMATION

Communication Approaches for Adults in NALS Levels 3, 4, and 5

More than 50% of US adults scored in NALS levels 3, 4, and 5. While these adults may possess the skills to function in most jobs and other aspects of everyday life, they may still encounter difficulties in health care settings. Their literacy skills may be less effective in a health context that includes unfamiliar vocabulary and background knowledge. In addition, most of this group is in NALS level 3 and, although they are competent at reading and math, they may make mistakes when attempting difficult tasks, such as those that require drawing inferences from complex texts. Advocates of the plain language approach—an approach for planning, writing, editing, and designing reader-friendly materials—provide guidelines on how to make difficult materials easier to read.[14,15] Application of these guidelines could help adults at or above NALS level 3 accomplish the tasks demanded by the health care system.

Communication Approaches for Adults in NALS Level 2

The plain language efforts that help more accomplished readers can also help NALS level 2 adults, but reader-friendly materials alone may not meet their communications needs. Sometimes rewriting materials in simpler language significantly lengthens the amount of information that must be read and processed which, in turn, can cause problems for adults with limited or poor reading strategies. In addition, some health care tasks are too complex to be broken down into a reasonable number of simple operations supported by simple written materials. Other forms of communications such as oral dialogue, telephone help lines, and media-based materials (eg, audiotapes, videotapes, or computer software or Internet access) might increase the likelihood of successful task accomplishment for NALS level 2 adults.

Communication Approaches for Adults in NALS Level 1

NALS level 1 adults are most in need of assistance to cope with the literacy and math demands of the health care system. For example, adults who do not speak English require translators for interpersonal communication in the health care setting. Older adults may need assistance to follow complex directions and remember treatment regimens. Adults with disabilities (those with poor vision or hearing, for example) may require assistance with barriers related to their disability. The NALS level 1 adults who do not fall into any of these categories most likely failed to develop strong literacy skills in school. Some in this group may have learning disabilities, and all of them are in fact reading-disabled. It can be argued that all NALS level 1 adults—more than 20% of the US adult population—should be identified as having a disability in relation to understanding health-related literacy and math tasks, and thus be provided with an accommodation to ensure their equal access to health care.

CONCLUSION

Findings from NALS, undertaken by the US government in 1992, indicate that nearly half of the US adult population may not be able to meet the literacy demands of 21st century life. Not only are these individuals challenged by the literacy-related tasks of everyday life, but they may struggle even more in the health context, which involves unfamiliar vocabulary, operations, and background knowledge.

An investment in improving health communications for adults who score in NALS levels 2, 3, 4, and 5 will probably provide a solid and immediate return, both in terms of lower health care costs and improved indicators of health. Such improvements should focus on making the communications tasks (both the text and the operations) less demanding and employing media and technology in creative ways. Helping NALS level 1 adults use the health care system effectively is significantly more difficult and will require an investment in research and development and in the provision of communications services.

REFERENCES

1. Kirsch I, Jungeblut A, Jenkins L, Kolstad A. *Adult Literacy in America: A First Look at the Results of the National Adult Literacy Survey.* Washington, DC: National Center for Education Statistics, US Department of Education; September 1993.

2. Sticht T, Armstrong W. *Adult Literacy in the United States: A Compendium of Quantitative Data and Interpretive Comments.* Washington, DC: National Institute for Literacy; 1994.

3. Organisation for Economic Co-operation and Development and Statistics Canada. *Literacy, Economy and Society: Results of the First International Adult Literacy Survey.* Paris and Ottawa: OECD; 1995.

4. Organisation for Economic Co-operation and Development and Human Resources Development Canada. *Literacy Skills for the Knowledge Society: Further Results from the International Adult Literacy Survey.* Paris: OECD; 1997.

5. Organisation for Economic Co-operation and Development and Statistics Canada. *Literacy in the Information Age: Final Report of the International Adult Literacy Survey.* Paris: OECD; 2000.

6. Rudd R, Kirsch I, Yamamoto K. *Literacy and Health in America.* Princeton, NJ: Educational Testing Services; 2004.

7. Kirsch I. *The International Adult Literacy Survey: Defining What Was Measured.* ETS Research Report RR-01-25. Princeton, NJ: Statistics and Research Division of ETS [Educational Testing Services]. 2001.

8. Comings J, Reder S, Sum A. Building a level playing field: The need to expand and improve the national and state adult education and literacy systems. National Center for the Study of Adult Learning and Literacy Occasional Paper, Harvard University Graduate School of Education, December 2001. Available at www.gse.harvard.edu/~ncsall/research/op_comings2.pdf. Accessed July 16, 2003.

9. Tuijnman A, Boudard E. *Adult Education Participation in North America: International Perspectives*. Ottawa: Statistics Canada; 2001.

10. Sticht T. The international adult literacy survey: how well does it represent the literacy abilities of adults? *Can J Stud Adult Educ*. 2001; 15:19–36.

11. Reder S. *The State of Literacy in America: Estimates of the Local, State and National Levels*. Washington, DC: National Institute for Literacy; 1998.

12. Tuijnman A. *Benchmarking Adult Literacy in America: An International Comparative Study*. Washington, DC: US Department of Education; 2000.

13. Sum A, Kirsch I, Taggart R. *The Twin Challenges of Mediocrity and Inequality: Literacy in the United States from an International Perspective*. A Policy Information Center Report. Princeton, NJ: Educational Testing Service; February 2002.

14. Rudd R, Moeykens B, Colton T. Health and literacy: A review of medical and public health literature. In: Comings J, Garner B, Smith C, eds. *The Annual Review of Adult Learning and Literacy*. Vol. 1. San Francisco, Calif.: Jossey-Bass; 2000.

15. Doak LG, Doak CC. (1987). Lowering the silent barriers to compliance for patients with low literacy skills. *Promoting Health*, 1987;8(4):6–8.

4

What Does Low Literacy Mean?

John Strucker, EdD, and Rosalind Davidson, EdD

The 1992 National Adult Literacy Survey (NALS)[1]—described in greater detail in Chapter 3—estimated that 46% to 51% of the US adult population fell into the lowest two levels of literacy: from 21% to 23% in level 1 and from 25% to 28% in level 2.* A few newspaper headlines of the day shouted: "46% of Americans Illiterate," but such interpretations were untrue and irresponsible. In fact, most people in levels 1 and 2 were not illiterate. Most adults in level 1 could be characterized as having primary-to-early middle school skills, and only a few were completely unable to read. Level 2 adults ranged upward from people with middle school abilities to those with literacy abilities approaching that of high school. In addition, 25% of the adults in level 1 were foreign born, and it is probable that they possessed at least some literacy skills in their native languages.** The real message of the NALS for US educational policymakers was not about *illiteracy* but *low literacy*—what Chall referred to as the problem of "under-education" among significant pockets of people in the developed and highly literate societies.[2]

Even though most level 1 and 2 adults are not illiterate, their low literacy and low levels of education can make it difficult for them to interact with a health care system that increasingly requires patients to play an informed and active role in their own care. Such difficulties are a subset of the general range of problems in other areas of life described by Comings and Kirsch,[3] including problems with employment, lifelong learning, and civic participation. Many low-literacy adults lack the English reading and math skills required to take a basic computer course at a community college, be retrained when their jobs change, understand a ballot referendum, or, in the case of

---

* The range represents the scores across the three literacy scales (prose, document, and quantitative literacy).

** Non-English speaking foreign-born adults are discussed separately at the end of this chapter.

health literacy, be able to complete a typical patient health questionnaire accurately.

From the vantage point of reading researchers and clinicians, we
address two related questions in this chapter:

1. What different forms does low literacy take among US adults?
2. What are the implications of these different forms of low literacy
for health care professionals?

THE READING PROCESS

We start with some background on the actual reading process. Good
readers, by definition, experience reading as a seamless event—
almost as if the book were speaking to them. However, reading teachers
and researchers have found it helpful to break down the reading
process into its constituent parts or components. Noted researcher
Gough offered a useful simplifying assumption that divides reading
comprehension into two primary domains: decoding the written symbols into the sounds of real words (also called "print skills") and
knowing what those words mean (also called "meaning skills").[4]
This commonsense formulation forms the cornerstone of most modern
research on reading and reading difficulties.[5-9] It is also the best
starting point in understanding the range of problems low-literacy
adults may have with the health care system.

The domain of decoding or print skills includes knowledge of
letter-sound correspondences (phonics), recognition of English
spelling patterns at the syllable level, and automatic and fluent word
recognition. Automatic and fluent word recognition is a critical print
skill. If a reader must expend large amounts of conscious mental energy decoding print, insufficient mental energy will be available for
efficient comprehension.[6] In fact, good readers decode so effortlessly
and automatically that they are usually not even aware of it, except
when they encounter an unusual or foreign word in print.

The domain of meaning skills involves more than "having a good
vocabulary" in the conventional sense. In fact, having strong meaning
skills includes both knowing the meanings of numerous words (called
"breadth of vocabulary knowledge") and knowing the multiple meanings and nuances assumed by these words in different contexts
(called "depth of vocabulary knowledge").[10] It is not simply a matter
of possessing a large mental dictionary of definitions and usages. As
vocabulary words move beyond simple everyday nouns and verbs (eg,
"cat" or "jump"), they come to resemble organized knowledge and concepts, what we mean by being educated (eg, "metaphor," "oligarchy," or
"photosynthesis").[11] Most people acquire such knowledge and concepts
through formal schooling in middle school and high school—schooling

that also involves reading in the subject areas of literature, social studies, and science.

STAGES OF READING DEVELOPMENT

Because many low-literacy adults had difficulties with reading during their kindergarten through 12th-grade years, it is important to understand the normal development of children's reading. Harvard's Chall[2,5] demonstrated that children do not acquire all of the skills of mature readers at once. Instead, they acquire reading skills in clearly defined stages, with attainment of more advanced skills contingent on the successful mastery of earlier stages of development.[5,7] Chall's Stages of Reading Development is referred to in the following discussion of the various patterns of adult low literacy and undereducation.

Methodology

Our typology of adult reading problems is based on the Adult Reading Components Study (ARCS) that was recently conducted by Davidson and Strucker.[12] In that study, 955 adult basic education (ABE) and English as a second language (ESL) students in seven US states were interviewed and given an extensive battery of diagnostic reading tests in English. Spanish speakers were also given comparable tests in Spanish reading. Cluster analysis was applied to the ABE and ESL students' test profiles separately. Among ABE students, 10 profile clusters emerged, ranging from beginning readers up through those with strong high school abilities. Among Spanish-speaking ESL students, six clusters emerged, based on their reading skills in both Spanish and English.

The goal of this study was to identify instructionally relevant groups of readers that adult education and ESL teachers should consider when planning their teaching approaches. For the purposes of this chapter, the cluster of strongest ABE readers was eliminated, because it is less likely that they would encounter literacy-related problems with the health care system. The remaining nine clusters were then collapsed into three large groups based on shared characteristics that would be most relevant for health care professionals. The discussion of ESL adults and the health care system was based on insights gained from Spanish-speaking ESL students. The ESL adults' six profiles were collapsed into two broad categories based on their Spanish literacy and educational attainment.

Note that the student participants in the study were enrolled in adult education programs at the time that they were interviewed, which raises the question of whether or not their skills are typical of adults in the unenrolled population. Surprisingly little investigation of this question has been performed. However, a large-scale longitudinal study underway[13] comparing the literacy skills and distributions of enrolled and unenrolled adults from the same community suggests that the literacy skill distributions between the two populations are very similar.

Patterns of Adult Low Literacy

We now take a closer look at the adults in NALS levels 1 and 2, beginning with those who are native speakers of English. First, we focus on adults who have not acquired basic print skills. Next, we turn our attention to adults who have not become fluent and automatic readers. Finally, we discuss adults in NALS levels 1 and 2 who did not acquire high school levels of knowledge and vocabulary. These three groups and their risk factors are summarized in Table 4-1. When we turn our attention to those who are not native speakers of English, we address issues related to those adults who are literate and reasonably well educated in their native languages and those who are not.

Adults Who Have Not Acquired Basic Print Skills

In US schools, the basic print skills are usually acquired from kindergarten through third grade,[14,15,8] when children are in stage 1—the stage Chall called *Learning to Read*.[5] This term is not as tautological or prosaic as it sounds. In this stage, schools typically give children books containing familiar words and familiar subjects because they want them to concentrate on the difficult task of mapping printed language to the oral language they mastered in infancy. At this beginning stage, children are not expected to gain new information from print; their main "job" and the organizing principle of their instruction is learning to read.

A small number of children do not easily acquire the sound-symbol correspondences that are the basic building blocks of reading in alphabetic languages. According to the National Research Council (NRC) and National Reading Panel (NRP), those who are at risk for not learning these basic decoding skills include children from low-literacy homes.[14,15] Such children are not read to often as young children, and they may not be exposed to sufficient oral language from adult caregivers during early childhood. Lack of exposure to oral language in early childhood may affect more than simply how many words these children know when they arrive at school. It may also reduce the rate at which they are able to acquire vocabulary throughout their lives.[16]

The NRC and NRP reports also note that some at-risk children have grown up in homes where languages other than English are spoken.[14,15] These children arrive at school faced with learning to read

TABLE 4-1

Reading Profiles and Risk Factors for Adults with National Adult Literacy Survey (NALS) Levels 1 and 2 Literacy Skills

Reading Profiles for NALS Levels 1 and 2 Adults (Native Speakers of English)	Risk Factors for Low Literacy
Adults who have not acquired basic print skills	A combination of any of the following during childhood: ■ Living in poverty ■ Coming from a family with low literacy skills ■ Coming from a family with limited English proficiency ■ Dyslexia ■ Attending schools where compensatory help is both limited and of poor quality
Adults who have not become fluent and automatic readers	A combination of any of the following during childhood: ■ Moderate dyslexia ■ Failure to master phonic principles in primary school ■ Reading problems experienced in primary grades ■ Attending schools where compensatory help is not available after the primary school grade levels
Adults who did not acquire high school levels of knowledge and vocabulary	A combination of any of the following during childhood: ■ Somewhat slower reading rate ■ Poor spelling abilities ■ Coming from a family that does not speak English ■ Having parents who do not encourage reading ■ Attending poor-quality schools ■ Presence of behavioral and emotional problems in childhood ■ Immigration to the United States as an adolescent

in a language they have not yet learned to speak fluently. Although their spoken English usually develops well, they are completely dependent on out-of-home experiences for acquiring literate vocabulary. This is especially true if their parents have limited native-language education, because the children are not exposed to a more literate vocabulary in their native languages either.

A few children may be dyslexic. That is, despite adequate teaching, they have an underlying difficulty in the area of phonological awareness—the ability to analyze speech as a sequence of sounds—that is critical for acquiring the letter-sound relationships. Dyslexia is neurologically based, usually inherited, and appears to vary in severity from mild to moderate to severe. Early identification and intervention by trained teachers can mediate its severity and hence its negative effects on school success.[17,18]

Most children with the above risk factors do learn to read. US schools are increasingly successful at identifying and treating children at risk for early reading failure. Trained reading specialists provide children who have dyslexia and other learning disabilities with the specific instruction they need through Special Education and Title I programs. Bilingual and ESL children also receive special attention in literacy acquisition. But when various risk factors such as poverty, family low-literacy, limited English proficiency, and dyslexia aggregate, the overall probability of early reading failure increases dramatically.

For example, dyslexia by itself need not preclude academic success. Many dyslexic children from middle-class literate families go on to complete college and graduate degrees. This is usually because their parents and schools help them strengthen their print skills, while ensuring that their decoding problems do not prevent them from acquiring academic skills and knowledge. On the other hand, children from poor, low-literacy families are more likely to attend schools where compensatory help is both limited and of poor quality. In addition, their parents may not understand the need for this extra support and the need to advocate for aggressive remediation.[13,14] For these children, the academic consequences of even moderate dyslexia can be disastrous. Their inability to decode prevents them from acquiring knowledge and concepts from school classes or books. As a result, their knowledge of the world may remain at the level of the familiar and conversational.

Fortunately, relatively few US adults are in this category of having failed to acquire the most basic early reading skills. In the ARCS study, only about 10% of the adult education students fit this reading-impaired profile.[19] These adults show signs of severe dyslexia and other learning disabilities in the areas of memory and processing speed. Their working or easily accessible memory, for example, appears so severely impaired that they often have difficulty understanding two- or three-step directions or parsing embedded grammatical constructions in spoken language (eg, "The cat that ate the rat was frightened by the dog."). Their oral vocabulary is at the second- to third-grade level, below the first percentile on norm-referenced tests, and at a concrete, day-to-day conversational level. Interestingly, these very impaired adults are considerably older than the average adult education students in the ARCS study population, suggesting that the US education system has, over time, improved its ability to identify and treat children at risk for catastrophic early reading failure.

Health care professionals should bear in mind that adults who fit this profile not only cannot read any printed material or fill out the simplest forms but also may have difficulty understanding the spoken language used in many routine health care interactions. Not only do these adults struggle with the medical and scientific jargon that patients from all backgrounds can find challenging but they may not even understand general vocabulary words that are not at all health-specific (eg, "annual," "seldom," or "frequent") and basic math concepts such as decimal place (eg, 1,000 versus 10,000), much less fractions or percentages.

Adults Who Have Not Become Fluent and Automatic Readers

The next Stage of Reading Development described by Chall is *Fluency*.[2,5] Around second and third grade, most children not only become accurate decoders, they become fluent and automatic decoders as well. This means that they are able to pronounce (or decode silently) the words they see in texts quickly and effortlessly. They have progressed from beginners who must sound out and blend each letter-sound or syllable into readers who are no longer even aware of the decoding process when they read text of the appropriate level of difficulty. For most children, this shift takes place somewhat naturally if they receive sufficient opportunities to read aloud with feedback from adults and if they are stimulated with interesting material at the appropriate level of reading challenge. For the at-risk categories of children described in the NRC and NRP reports, however, fluency may not develop naturally.[14,15] To achieve fluent, automatic reading, these children may require the most expert classroom teaching, at times supported by specialist-teacher interventions.

Reading theorists assert that, if children do not become fluent and automatic decoders before fourth grade, a cascade of related problems may occur.[7,20] First, because these children read slowly and dysfluently, their working memory is overtaxed, especially by the longer sentences they encounter in fourth grade and beyond. Such readers find themselves having to read longer sentences over and over again until they can chunk their phrases into meaningful linguistic units and understand how those relate to each other. This in turn impairs their ability to "read to learn" because so much effort is applied toward decoding they have little left for understanding and analysis. To make matters worse, children who do not become fluent readers often find reading exhausting and boring. They respond by reading less, rather than more, both in and out of school.

Children who fail to develop into fluent readers never receive the full benefit of the subjects studied in middle school and later in high school (eg, math, science, social studies, and literature). Thus, they also fail to develop the vocabulary and concepts that can support learning in adult life.[7,20] What begins as a print skill breakdown now undermines the domain of meaning skills.

The ARCS data suggest that these adults who can decode "a little," but who lack the all-important fluency needed for effortless reading, were probably moderately dyslexic as children. Testing shows that they have learned some phonics principles but have not mastered them to the point of fluency. Many of these adults reported that their early reading problems were recognized when they were in first and second grades, and that they received extra help in early reading. However, the help did not continue, and they received little or no support as they moved into middle school and none at all in high school.[12,20]

The prognosis for these adults is good if they are able to attend adult education programs that recognize their fluency problems and the accompanying vocabulary deficits. Fortunately, in recent years, the kindergarten through 12th-grade educational system has begun to pay closer attention to the needs of students whose reading skills fail to develop completely after third grade. Reading teachers are helping these students strengthen their print skills so that they can receive the full benefit of subject-area learning in middle and high school.

We estimate this group of nonfluent adult readers to be fairly significant, comprising about 30% of the students in adult education programs.[12] In functional terms, these adults can manage the literacy demands of street signs and advertisements, the TV program guide, and some simple work-related materials and forms. Their print skills (the words they can decode easily) and their meaning skills (vocabulary and background knowledge) are relatively even at approximately the fourth- to fifth-grade equivalent. However, on oral vocabulary tests, their supplied definitions of words they "know" are often imprecise and fuzzy (eg, "destination" means "going somewhere"; "humiliation" means "someone upsets you"). They may not know relatively common words such as "exposure," "vague," and "efficient," along with syntactic "signal words" that occur frequently in print but not in conversation (eg, "despite," "nevertheless," and "moreover"). Adults who fit this profile do not enjoy reading for pleasure, and it is nearly impossible for them to acquire new information from extended texts.

Health professionals should be aware that these adults are able to read and understand familiar texts such as newspaper sports stories if they are given enough time to compensate for their lack of fluency. However, if a topic is unfamiliar (eg, how to treat a chronic illness), no amount of extra time is likely to be sufficient for comprehension. Although these adults can read, it would be a mistake for health care professionals to rely on printed materials that are not supplemented by oral interactions to convey details of their conditions or treatments. Great care should also be taken with the vocabulary and concept load in these oral interactions. For this reason, even videotaped health educational materials, if used without support and face-to-face follow-up, may not be effective with these adults.

Adults Who Did Not Acquire High School Levels of Knowledge and Vocabulary

Chall's next Stage of Reading Development is *Reading to Learn the New*, or using reading skills to learn "new information, ideas, attitudes, and values. Growth takes place in background knowledge, meaning vocabulary, and cognitive abilities."[5]

Based on estimates from ARCS data, about 40% of adults in adult basic education seem stalled in this stage; that is, these adults have made a start on "learning the new" but they have some distance to go. Although their print skills enable them to decode with adequate fluency and read at the ninth-grade level or higher, their vocabulary and background knowledge lag far behind, often at early middle school levels. Most of the adults who fit this profile show few signs of the neurologically based decoding problems that are associated with dyslexia, although a small percentage appear to be "partially compensated dyslexics."[21–23] These adults received effective primary school help with reading, and the only signs of their early print skills difficulties are somewhat slower reading rates and poor spelling.

Why do the vocabulary and background knowledge (meaning skills) of these adults fail to keep pace with their decoding ability (print skills)? There are many possible reasons for this. In some cases, these individuals' vocabulary deficits may have begun to develop in early childhood, perhaps because their parents did not speak English or because their parents spoke English but were not very literate and did not encourage reading or use more literate styles of oral language with their children.[20] In other cases, these individuals attended schools where expectations were low and resources were diverted to more academically and emotionally needy children.[24] Others may have themselves been the children with behavioral and emotional problems, leading school officials to focus on these areas to the exclusion of their academic needs. And, finally, some may have been ESL students who immigrated to the United States when they were adolescents. Their US high school careers were over before their English developed sufficiently for them to learn math, science, social studies, and literature in English.

Adults at this level of literacy can decode extended text fairly effortlessly but, because they are undereducated, they may not fully understand everything they read. It can be difficult for health care professionals to detect these individuals because they are able to fill out forms correctly and may be seen avidly reading magazines and newspapers in waiting areas.

For these adults, printed materials about their health care can be useful if they are explicitly written and do not rely on the reader's general science or health background knowledge. These adults probably know that the lungs are responsible for breathing and they may recognize the word "respiration" as a synonym for "breathing" but they may not be aware of how the lungs function in respiration or how they are related to the rest of the cardiorespiratory system.

At the upper reaches of this group, adults manifest levels of vocabulary and knowledge associated with high school function. Health care professionals should keep in mind, however, that even for these somewhat stronger readers, their science and math background knowledge often lags behind their general knowledge. Typically, they may not be able to identify the shape of a hexagon on a picture vocabulary test or know that a frog is an example of an amphibian.

Nonnative Speakers of English

The percentage of nonnative English speakers living in the United States has been increasing rapidly, even in states such as North Carolina and Maine that are not traditional ports-of-entry for newcomers. According to the 1990 Census, 13.9% of the US population reported speaking a language other than English at home.[25] By the time of the 2000 Census, the number had risen to 17.9%, with 23% of this group reporting that they spoke English "not well" or "not at all."[26] About 70% of the nonnative speakers of English are native speakers of Spanish, but the language diversity is astounding among the remaining 30% of nonnative speakers of English.[27]

It may be helpful for health care professionals to divide this heterogeneous group of nonnative speakers of English into two broad categories: those who are literate and reasonably well-educated in their native languages and those who are not.

People who have completed or nearly completed high school in their native country generally possess adequate native language vocabulary and background knowledge to understand basic health concepts. Cultural beliefs aside, they simply need to have the English words for those concepts translated quickly and accurately into their native languages. Hospital and community-based translators are usually capable of meeting these needs.

Those who are not literate and well-educated in their native languages pose a different set of challenges. For these individuals, it is not enough to simply translate a phrase such as *high blood pressure* into their native language. They may also need to have the concept itself explained, along with related background information about the heart and blood vessels. In other words, the medical translator must possess the skills of a teacher to know when more explanation is needed, even if the patient does not ask. Translators must also have sufficient knowledge of the patient's home culture to know which areas of modern medicine might conflict with traditionally held concepts of health and disease. Like undereducated native English speakers, undereducated non-English speakers lack the background knowledge to understand what can appear to be routine aspects of medical care and health.

"TEACHING" INTERACTIONS WITH LOW-LITERACY PATIENTS

Health care professionals have long understood, implicitly or explicitly, that teaching is a critical part of their responsibilities. With well-educated patients, it may be reasonably sufficient to explain a condition or treatment completely yet succinctly and then ask if the patient has any questions. This approach can work well if the patient possesses or can create some underlying schema for organizing the new information—a sort of "cognitive Velcro" to which new facts can be attached, remembered, and analyzed. Educated adults may be more adept at actively processing new information; furthermore, they may feel confident enough to interrupt the health care professional with questions of their own, aimed at confirming how they are organizing the new information (eg, "This new drug you're prescribing—is it a type of antihistamine?").

For many of the low-literacy adults discussed in this chapter, presenting a single, uninterrupted explanation may not be the most effective approach. It may be more effective to present information in smaller chunks, stopping after each chunk to ask very specific questions to verify what the patient understands (eg, "So, Paul, what do we mean by an 'asthma trigger'?" or "What are your 'asthma triggers'?"). In these examples, the health care professional can verify that the patient understands that the familiar word "trigger" is being used in an extended or metaphorical sense to mean "precipitating cause," rather than familiarly and concretely as a part of a firearm. In using such "check-back" questions, the health care professional should ask direct and specific questions, (eg, "How many times a day should you use your new inhaler?") rather than open-ended questions (eg, "Any questions so far?").

While it appears that such interactions will consume more of a physician's time, they may ultimately be worth the increased time spent. Some policymakers have suggested that health maintenance organizations (HMOs) allow physicians more time per patient when working with low-literacy and undereducated adults, because this would prove more efficient in the long run. Another widely used approach has been the use of specially trained paraprofessionals who spend whatever time is needed to ensure that patients understand their care and treatment regimens.

CONCLUSION

Because of the cumulative nature of reading development, most adults who have weak or unreliable print skills (decoding) also have weak-to–very weak meaning skills (vocabulary and background knowledge). Three general reading profiles can be identified among the NALS levels 1 and 2 English-speaking populations:

- A small group, comprising about 10% of the total, can be considered virtually illiterate. They experience failure at the earliest stages of learning to read. They have almost no ability to decode print and extremely low levels of vocabulary and background knowledge. Special care should be taken to ensure that they understand even the most basic oral language interactions.

- A larger group, about 30% of the total, has the ability to read most everyday print and fill out very basic forms, but their failure to become fluent decoders makes reading even simple texts laborious, slow, and unreliable. Because of this, these individuals tend to avoid reading. Their vocabulary and background knowledge, while somewhat stronger than that of the previous group, is still primarily limited to the familiar and conversational. Care should be taken to ensure that they understand oral language interactions with health care professionals, especially if familiar words are used in an unfamiliar or metaphoric way.

- About 40% of the population have relatively strong print skills (up to high school decoding ability in some cases), but their reading comprehension is limited by their meaning skills. They have only middle school levels of general vocabulary and significant gaps in their background knowledge, especially in the areas of science and math. They are capable of obtaining information from written material, provided that it is explicit and requires minimal background knowledge.

Nonnative speakers of English can be divided into two categories:

- Those with adequate native language education. Cultural issues aside, these individuals may require only the translation of English words and terms into their native language.

- Those with limited native language education. These individuals may require not only translation but also careful explanation of the concepts and background knowledge they have not acquired.

In their all-important roles as teachers, health care professionals should analyze their oral interactions with patients carefully. For many low-literacy adults, it may not be enough simply to avoid medical jargon; even words that are not strictly medical in nature can pose problems.[28] What can be considered basic background knowledge about science and health among educated adults may be missing or only partly developed for low-literacy adults.

These skills and sensitivities are not new to the health professions. It is likely that they have always been a part of the repertoires of successful practitioners. A hundred years ago, physicians may have encountered a much higher percentage of illiterate and low-literate patients than do physicians today. A barrier to change today is the pressure of increasing health care costs and larger patient panels that have limited the amount of time physicians spend with patients, even as medicine becomes increasingly complex, and patient interactions require as much time as ever before.

REFERENCES

1. Kirsch I, Jungeblut A, Jenkins L, Kolstad A. *Adult Literacy in America: A First Look at the Results of the National Adult Literacy Survey.* Washington, DC: National Center for Education Statistics, US Department of Education; September 1993.

2. Chall JS. Developing literacy in children and adults. In: Wagner D, ed. *The Future of Literacy in a Changing World.* New York, NY: Pergamon; 1987:65–80.

3. Comings J, Kirsch I. Literacy skills of US adults. In: Schwartzberg JG, VanGeest JB, Wang CC, eds. *Understanding Health Literacy: Implications for Medicine and Public Health.* Chicago, Ill: American Medical Association Press; 2004.

4. Gough PB. One second of reading. In Kavanagh JF, Mattingly IG, eds. *Language by Ear and Eye.* Cambridge, Mass: MIT Press; 1972:331–358.

5. Chall JS. *Stages of Reading Development.* New York, NY: McGraw-Hill; 1983.

6. Perfetti CA (1985). *Reading Ability.* New York, NY: Oxford University Press; 1985.

7. Stanovich KE. Matthew effects in reading: some consequences of individual differences in the acquisition of literacy. *Reading Res Q.* 1986; 21:360–406.

8. Adams MJ. *Beginning to Read: Thinking and Learning about Print.* Cambridge, Mass: MIT Press; 1990.

9. Carver RP. Reading for one second, one minute, or one year from the perspective of rauding theory. *Sci Stud Reading.* 1997;1:3–43.

10. McKeown MG, Curtis ME. *The Nature of Vocabulary Acquisition.* Hillsdale, NJ: Lawrence Erlbaum Associates; 1987.

11. Hirsch ED. Reading comprehension requires knowledge—of words and the world: scientific insights into the fourth-grade slump and stagnant reading comprehension. *Am Edu.* Summer 2003.

12. Davidson RK, Strucker J. Patterns of word-recognition errors among adult basic education native and nonnative speakers of English. *Sci Stud Reading*. 2002;6:267–299.

13. The First Five Years: National Center for the Study of Adult Learning and Literacy, 1996–2001. NCSALL Report 23, October 2002, p 44. Cambridge, Mass: NCSALL.

14. Snow CE, Burns S, Griffin P. Preventing Reading Difficulties in Young Children. A report of the National Research Council. Washington, DC: Academy Press; 1998.

15. Report of the National Reading Panel: Teaching Children to Read. NIH Publication No. 00-4769. Washington, DC: NIH; 2000.

16. Hart B, Risley TR. *Meaningful Differences in the Lives of Young American Children*. Baltimore, Md: Paul H. Brookes Publishing Co.; 1995.

17. Shaywitz SE. Dyslexia. *Sci Am*. November 1996;98–104.

18. Lyon GR. Reading disabilities: why do some children have difficulty learning to read? What can be done about it? *Perspectives*, Spring 2003; 29:2.

19. The First Five Years: National Center for the Study of Adult Learning and Literacy, 1996–2001. NCSALL Report 23, October 2002, pp 19–22. Cambridge, Mass:NCSALL

20. Snow C, Strucker J. Lessons from preventing reading difficulties in young children for adult learning and literacy. In: Comings J, Garner B, Smith C, Eds. *Annual Review of Adult Learning and Literacy*, vol. 1. San Francisco, Calif: Jossey Bass; 2000.

21. Bruck M. Word-recognition skills of adults with childhood diagnoses of dyslexia. *Dev Psychol*. 1990;26(3):439–454.

22. Bruck M. Persistence of dyslexic's phonological awareness deficits. *Dev Psychol*. 1992;28(5):874–886.

23. Fink RP. Literacy development in successful men and women with dyslexia. *Ann Dyslexia*. 1998;48:311–342.

24. Jencks C, Phillips M. America's next achievement test: closing the black-white score gap. *The American Prospect*, September–October 1998;44–53.

25. US Census Abstracts. Washington, DC: US Census Bureau; 1990.

26. US Census Bureau, Census 2000, summary File 3. (2003). Available at: http://www.census.gov/population/socdem/language/table1txt. Accessed July 16, 2003.

27. Strucker J. NCSALL's adult reading components study: Spanish speakers in ESL classes. Paper presented at: Annual Meeting of the International Dyslexia Association; June 27, 2002; Washington, DC.

28. Santos M. (2003). *The Vocabulary Knowledge of Language Minority Community College Students* [dissertation]. Cambridge, Mass: Harvard Graduate School of Education; 2003.

Literacy Demands in Health Care Settings: The Patient Perspective

Rima E. Rudd, MSPH, ScD; Diane Renzulli, MSPH;
Anne Pereira, MD, MPH; and Lawren Daltroy, DrPH[†]

Functional literacy assessments, as discussed in the previous chapters, measure an adult's ability to use the written word to accomplish specific tasks. Materials used in these assessments are drawn from many different contexts to represent the types of tasks adults might be expected to perform in everyday life. Findings from the 1992 National Adult Literacy Survey (NALS) indicate that 90 million adults, almost all of whom can read, have difficulty using the written word to accomplish everyday tasks with consistency and accuracy.[1,2]

Nonetheless, our industrialized nation is an environment that assumes the population has high levels of literacy. Signs and billboards are ubiquitous and include place markers, advertisements, and warnings. Streets, public squares, buildings, agencies, and institutions are named and numbered. The inside hallways and offices of government programs and service agencies are replete with signs and postings. US adults are surrounded by the written word in public locations and within public and private institutions. They are expected to use reading, writing, and mathematical skills to locate places, follow posted and oral directions and instructions, and complete needed forms.[3] For example, consider the demanding environment of a community-based social security office:

> The Social Security Office is located on a very large and busy street. The waiting room, which has no social security professionals except for a security guard who occasionally chats with visitors, is one large rectangular room with 8 windows facing the entrance. Each window has a number above it. In the middle of this wall of windows, messages run across a computerized sign

---

[†] Dr Daltroy died in September 2003.

directing visitors to take a number, fill out a form before heading to a window, or to call a toll free Social Security number for help. The messages, written fairly simply, would be easy to understand if they were not sweeping so rapidly across the screen. At the entranceway, a standing sign meant to direct visitors to the appropriate line fails to tell visitors where to get Medicare information. No other flyers or posters indicate that this office serves to provide Medicare information. While a rack with various types of forms contains a Medicare application, it has no further information on the service itself.

Alice Kuo, ScM, Student, Health Literacy Graduate Course at the Harvard School of Public Health; 2002; Boston, Mass.

The ability to read quickly is critical in this case. However, print is irrelevant for people with significant literacy problems. Purcell-Gates[4] captures the experience of Jenny, a married woman with children living in a Midwestern city, who cannot make use of the postings, the packaging, or the tools of modern society. Jenny is a nonreader. A native-born English speaker with a seventh-grade education, Jenny is able to recognize some words but only in context. Thus, she relies on what she knows and has experience with and uses people as well as location tools, such as color and shape, to help her navigate the world of print. While Jenny's total lack of reading skills is unusual, she has developed the kinds of coping mechanisms that are used by many adults in our society, including those who can read.

Any number of coping strategies may work, on average. However, these strategies can also result in errors, inconveniences, and limitations. Errors become more than inconvenient when they occur in health-related settings and health activities. When a person's literacy skills are limited and/or when the demands exceed the skills of the average person, results can be harrowing and may directly affect a person's health.

This chapter focuses on the mismatch between the average functional literacy skills of US adults and the literacy-related demands of the health care setting. It begins with a description of health contexts and the literacy demands encountered within various settings, including health care settings. Next, health literacy is examined from the perspective of patient rights and patient-provider interaction. The chapter concludes with a discussion of implications and needed actions.

HEALTH CONTEXTS

Functional literacy always takes place within a particular context. However, there are multiple health activities and the contexts vary. Throughout any given day, adults engage in a wide variety of health-related activities such as promoting and protecting health, preventing disease, or seeking care and treatment. These activities take place at home, in the workplace, in the community, and in health care settings.

In the home, mundane activities may include reading nutrition labels or directions for household products, following instructions for cleaning agents or equipment, taking care of ill children or elders, monitoring symptoms of a chronic disease, following instructions for follow-up care, and, increasingly, completing paperwork for government or private insurance. Furthermore, adults read, watch, and listen to news stories and discuss health issues with family and friends. At work, employees rely on right-to-know information about a wide variety of substances and on postings and specialized equipment for safety. They make health and safety decisions alone and with friends and colleagues. Other health-related activities are linked to actions for disease prevention or early detection measures. Public health announcements in the news or letters from schools to parents about available screening tests are meant to be useful tools and guides for action. In addition, adults take action in the voting booth and contribute to health policy and the formation of regulations. Of course, adults may also be patients and, in this role, they are expected to engage in dialogue and discussion with health care providers and follow up with recommended action. Thus, the home, the workplace, the community, and various health care settings are all "health contexts."[5]

A cacophony of voices surrounds and invades these contexts. Health, after all, is a topic of critical concern and holds high interest for the general public. People share stories and both give and receive advice. This interest in health is reflected daily on television and radio, in newspapers and magazines, within Internet chat rooms, through government and private sector Web sites and print materials, as well as in multitudes of visual, oral, and print commercials.

Materials on the Internet, in the Media, and in Health Care Settings

Some studies have examined the accessibility of health-related messages and information delivered through various media. Approximately 6 million US adults go online for medical advice on a typical day—more people than actually visit health professionals.[6] Yet research to date suggests the average person will have difficulty understanding health information on the Web because it is often written at very high reading levels (tenth grade or higher).[7] For example, the Children's Partnership study of 1000 Web sites related to education, family, finance, government, health, housing, jobs, and personal enrichment found only 10 (1%) that were appropriate for adults with literacy skills below the high school level.[8]

Graber and colleagues,[9] in a study of privacy policies on Internet health sites, found that the average readability level of sites with privacy statements required 2 years of college education. Croft and

Peterson[10] examined asthma education information on the Web and found a mean reading grade level of 10.3, as scored by the Flesch-Kincaid formula. Overall, initial inquiries indicate that information on many Web sites is not necessarily any more readable than the information printed in booklets and brochures.[11]

Although advertisements successfully sell health-related products, important health-related details are often not clearly communicated or easily understood. Bell and colleagues,[12] for example, found that many direct-to-consumer magazine advertisements only provided superficial coverage of medical conditions and their treatments. Kaphingst[13] noted that some risk statements in direct-to-consumer advertisements lacked important contextual information, that the readability scores of referenced text materials were in the high school–level range, and that the brief summary sections of print advertisements were in the college-level range.

A substantial body of literature yields consistent findings that the reading level of health education materials far exceeds the reading skills of the public for whom they were developed.[14] Some researchers assessed the readability of materials targeted at specific diseases, such as cancer, diabetes, asthma, or HIV, and other materials that examined a specific type of material and documents needed for actions involved in medications, self-care, or consent. More than 250 studies indicate that materials are written at grade-level equivalents far above the eighth or ninth grade reading skills of the average US adult.[14]

This documented mismatch between available materials, whether on the Internet or in text, serves to limit access to information and, ultimately, to inhibit action.[15–17] Consequently, the average adult is challenged to differentiate among various sources of information as well as various solutions to health problems. Health researchers have not yet fully examined the match between the skills of the average person and the cognitive demands placed on individuals by all of these information sources. However, researchers are starting to look more closely at literacy demands in formal health care settings such as hospitals, health care centers, and health professionals' offices and to reexamine the underlying assumptions that shape these demands.

Prevailing Assumptions

Expectations and assumptions about average skills may account for a mismatch between people's actual skills and health system processes and procedures. For example, public health campaigns often rely on an understanding of complex concepts such as risk and probability.[18] Many health professionals assume that the average person knows the names, locations, and functions of various organs and systems of the human body, although this information is not uniformly part of any curriculum in kindergarten through 12th-grade state educational systems. Private insurance and public beneficiary programs shape procedures and forms that are based on assumptions about people's familiarity and ease with forms, legal and bureaucratic language and procedures, and arithmetic calculations. For the most part, these assumptions are faulty.

Findings from the first national literacy assessment of adults were published in 1993, and in-depth analyses of US and international findings were published in 2000 and 2001.[1,2,19] The mean score for US adults falls at the cusp of the NALS levels 2 and 3. As noted in Chapter 3, educators and education economists agree that NALS level 3 skills are needed for full participation in the economic and civic life of the US in the 21st century.[20,21] However, diffusion of information across disciplines is often slow, and many of those responsible for crafting health-related signs, messages, informational booklets, patient brochures, forms, and documents may not be aware of these findings or their implications.

Consequences

NALS analysis indicated that people with limited literacy skills rarely identify themselves as struggling with literacy issues.[1] Consequently, people who need help may not actively seek it. Indeed, health literacy research indicates that limited reading skills may be accompanied by feelings of embarrassment or shame.[22]

Health literacy research studies conducted since the NALS have identified additional consequences or associations for patients with low or limited literacy skills. Patients with inadequate reading skills (as measured by the Test of Functional Health Literacy in Adults [TOFHLA] or the Rapid Estimate of Adult Literacy in Medicine [REALM], described in Chapter 10) are more likely than are patients with adequate skills to report their health as poor,[23] to be hospitalized,[24] to have less knowledge of their chronic disease and how to manage it,[25-28] or to have more advanced disease when they are first seen by their doctor.[29] These and other findings are addressed in greater depth in subsequent chapters. Overall, research indicates that health professionals must consider the implications of low or limited literacy skills for patients' health outcomes.

HEALTH CARE SETTINGS AND THEIR LITERACY-RELATED DEMANDS

In its broadest sense, navigating the health care system includes a range of activities that involves accessing information and resources, participating in decisions and actions, and implementing needed procedures and protocols. People may encounter difficulties finding and entering a health or dental care facility, using materials or tools for navigation, filling in needed forms, offering consent for procedures, and finding the vocabulary to describe feelings and experiences.[30]

Physical Navigation

Tools such as maps, directions, signs, and schedules are posted or readily available to help the traveler or the visitor navigate the physical pathways of health care environments. However, both the postings and the tools that infuse our health care environments require literacy skills that many of us take for granted. Some materials contain dense or cumbersome prose, and many document formats and design elements pose additional difficulties that require sophisticated skills and keen eyesight. Postings and directional signs on buildings, hospital lobbies, and hallways often include sophisticated words and phrases that are difficult to read or pronounce. For example, hospitals frequently have multiple entrances named with terms such as "admitting," "receiving," "ambulatory care," or "emergency entrance." The use of "ambulatory" in place of "walk-in" can easily lead to confusion because, after all, ambulances have an entrance as well. Also, many hospital signs are topped, in headline fashion, by the name of a donor. The average person might not be able to differentiate between proper names and medical terms.[30,31] Subsequent errors and accompanying costs, lost time, and feelings of inadequacy are rarely documented.

Overall, settings with an array of signs and postings have a high literacy demand. People entering such settings might feel overwhelmed by print. This is captured in the following vignette:

> Before getting to the pediatric radiology department, a patient must first navigate the public areas of this large private hospital. Imagine a dense and busy environment, with directional signs both overhead and mounted on walls, posters on easels, display cases filled with flyers, and many plaques on the walls identifying rooms, highlighting donors, or giving historical information. Symbols announce toilets, payphones, and ATMs; arrows are used to indicate directions and turns; and hallways are color-coded. While an information desk directly opposite the main entrance could help people with limited literacy, it is not always staffed.
>
> ***Paul Gilbert***, ScM, Student, Health Literacy Graduate Course at the Harvard School of Public Health; 2002; Boston, Mass.

Settings dense with the written word can confuse the best reader. So too might the use of esoteric terms. For example, an observer noted the use of the word *triage* on an entry post to a hospital emergency department:

> As a parent enters an emergency department waiting room, a glass wall stands in front of her, next to a seating area filled with chairs, a fish tank,

and other child-friendly paraphernalia. On the glass, the word TRIAGE is written sideways along the left edge. No other cues suggest to the parent that this is the first place where she should stop. Many parents walk past this reference point and migrate deeper in the room, noticing a sign announcing REGISTRATION with desks and staff sitting at computers. Along the way, human interceptors—a security guard, the triage nurse, or the registration secretary—may redirect the parent back to the TRIAGE sign.

> *Stephen C. Porter*, MD, Student, Health Literacy Graduate Course at the Harvard School of Public Health; 2002; Boston, Mass.

The word *triage*, borrowed from another language and difficult to pronounce, carries a meaning that may be foreign to the general public. As a result, the sign does not serve to simplify a process but instead requires vigilance on the part of staff and possible embarrassment for the visitor.

Those working in medical care facilities understand the terms used for specific practices and tests; the general public, however, may rarely encounter these terms in the outside world. Thus, medical jargon and abbreviations used on directional signs and place postings, such as "Nuclear Medicine," "EEG," "EKG," "EMG," "Pulmonary Diseases," "Nephrology," or "Rheumatology," add to the burdens of navigation.[31] Educators suggest that the literacy skills of the audience, the context of the communication, the tasks people need to perform, and the difficulty of the text itself must all be considered. Adequate communication takes place only when all these components match.[2,4] While such matching is not possible on an individual level, health care systems and the text produced could incorporate everyday language and aim for a match with "average skills," often calculated at approximately the eighth-grade reading level.

Documents and Open Entry Forms

Documents (ie, short forms or graphical displays of information, such as job applications, transportation schedules, and maps) can be more difficult to use than materials presented in prose format, partly because documents do not use full sentences and paragraphs. NALS findings indicate that adults have less proficiency with documents than with prose.[1] Nonetheless, documents and open entry forms, in particular, which contain blank spaces to be filled in by users, are critical and ubiquitous within health care settings.

> When you have medical forms and stuff, I don't think it should be complicated for a person to not understand what it's saying. I think it should be ... more cut and dry.
>
> *Margarite Smith*, parent, *In Plain Language* video transcript, 2002.

Access to care may be limited by the ritual-like requirement of filling in forms. These can include insurance forms, Medicaid or Medicare forms, and medical or dental history forms.[32,33] In addition, follow-up information and test results are often presented in document format without prose discussion and explanation. Consider the forms and follow-up letters patients encounter at a hospital mammography department:

> Each patient must complete a mammography questionnaire, available in English and Spanish, written at a post high school reading level (SMOG reading assessment). After the exam, test results are mailed to patients. While state and federal regulations require mammography facilities to provide patients with written mammography results using "lay terms," the mammography report reads at a post high school level (SMOG reading assessment). The report contains many unexplained technical terms and words that could be substituted with simpler language. Neither the questionnaire nor the mammography report was developed with feedback from the intended audience, as is recommended by health literacy researchers.
>
> **Rosemary Frasso Jaramillo**, ScM, Student, Health Literacy Graduate Course at the Harvard School of Public Health; 2002; Boston, Mass.

Oddly, the burdensome structure, format, and language used in forms as well as in mailed letters and test results often necessitate staffing dedicated to helping people understand, manage, and respond appropriately. Consequently, those who can turn to community resources, including librarians, adult educators, and social service agency staff, to help them interpret materials and complete needed forms. This level of assistance is invisible and unpaid.[34,35]

Written Directions

Health care systems rely on printed materials to convey directions and instructions related to procedures, medicines, side effects, and self-care. These materials are often written at readability levels that exceed the reading ability of the average adult. Several researchers found that package inserts from pharmaceutical companies, nonprofit organizations, and commercial vendors had an average readability score of grade 10.[36,37] Emergency department discharge instructions have been assessed at readability levels that range from grade 6 to above grade 13.[38,39] National guidelines for asthma management plans set a goal of grade levels at or below fifth grade reading; however, researchers found that none of the plans in 2002 achieved this goal.[40] While written directions are developed to supplement oral communication, materials written above the eighth-grade level do not adequately serve the average US adult nor do they serve people with limited or low literacy skills.

PATIENT RIGHTS

Few studies have examined health literacy from the perspective of social justice and rights. US adults may regularly come across health-related information that is not clearly presented, but this obstacle may pale in comparison to limitations on access to information related to their rights. Patients' rights and responsibilities are posted in hospital and health center entrances or are available as handouts. This important information speaks to critical issues of dignity and autonomy and can be prepared in a variety of ways. Some hospitals and health care facilities draft the information legally with formal language and complex sentence format. For example, the wording below is taken from a hospital posting of patients' rights (calculated with a SMOG score of grade level 21):

■ Upon request to obtain from the facility in charge of his care the name and specialty if any, of the physician or other person responsible for his care or the coordination of his care.

■ To have all reasonable requests responded to promptly and adequately within the capacity of the facility.

■ To prompt lifesaving treatment in an emergency without discrimination on account of economic status or source of payment and without delaying treatment for purposes of prior discussion of the source of payment unless such delay can be imposed without material risk to his health, and this right shall also extend to those persons not already patients or residents of a facility if said facility has a certified emergency care unit.

In contrast, the same listing of rights, rewritten for parents (calculated at SMOG grade-level 12) is posted in the entrance of a children's hospital:

■ There are many people who take care of your child in the hospital. You have the right to know who they are and what they do.

■ You can ask what is happening to your child and why. We will do our best to explain information to you, in ways you can understand, and in your own language.

■ Your child has the right to emergency, lifesaving treatment whether or not there is a source of payment. This applies to children who are already patients of the hospital, as well as new patients.

The two postings make very different demands. The first erects an unreasonable barrier and compromises rights. After all, posted information that is not intelligible is technically not available.[30,31]

Privacy Rights

The federal privacy standards of the Health Insurance Portability
and Accountability Act of 1996 (HIPAA) went into effect in April 2003.
Originally designed to give patients more control over how their
medical records are used and disseminated, the regulations require
that health care providers disclose to their patients how the providers
may use personal medical information. Patients' rights must also be
specified. What is not required, however, is evidence that patients
comprehend their new rights. The law requires that patients sign
off noting that they *received* a description of the new rules and
regulations. Nothing in the regulations mandates a statement of
understanding, nor do the regulations suggest an appropriate readability grade level for the text or propose a writing style and format.
Consequently, language used in the forms may well obfuscate statements of rights. Consider, for example, how one health clinic chose
to inform patients that they have the right to change their mind when
it comes to sharing their health information with outside interests:

> You may revoke your authorization or any written authorization obtained
> in connection with your "Highly Confidential Information," except to the
> extent that we have taken action in reliance upon it, by delivering a written
> revocation statement to the Privacy Officer identified below.

In contrast, one hospital's notice of privacy practices states:

> You may cancel your permission in writing at any time.

Informed Consent

Whenever adults participate in a research project, they must sign
an informed consent form.*[1] Federal law requires formal research
consent statements to describe research, tests and procedures, and
possible outcomes. The purpose of informed consent for research is to
ensure participants' autonomy as they consider whether or not to
take part in a study. Thus, the formal aspect of consenting is a critical
aspect of health literacy and requires comprehension. However,
over the past three decades, published reports have highlighted
difficulties with the highly technical vocabulary in informed consent
documents.[41-45] Cumbersome sentences and scientific terms obscure
meaning. Consequently, US adults may not be in a position to truly
offer informed consent.

> They had tons and tons of papers for me to sign . . . I signed them, but . . .
> I wasn't knowing what I was signing.
>   ***Karen Rivera***, parent and patient, In *Plain Language* video tran-
> script; 2002.

---

* Informed consent is discussed in greater detail in Chapter 8.

Cox's[46] research of patients in nine clinical trials found that all of the patients in the study felt that some of the information was too difficult to understand and that half indicated that the information was useless. Paasche-Orlow and associates[47] found that the mean readability scores for sample text provided by Institutional Review Boards (IRBs) exceeded the IRB's stated standards by 2.8 grade levels. The legal ramifications of an adult's inability to comprehend the technical language of informed consent documents have yet to be fully explored.

PATIENT-PROVIDER COMMUNICATION

An analysis of patient-provider communication is offered in Section 3 this book. However, it is noted in this chapter that health care professionals use their own language, provide unusual services, and require people to engage in technical procedures with which they are not familiar and may not fully understand:[48]

> Sometimes the doctors and pharmacy use the type of words that, you know, they're sometimes hard. ... They be using those fine words, those college words, that's hard for people like me to understand and read.
> **Miguel Cruzado, Sr,** Public Works Department Employee. *In Plain Language* video transcript; 2002.

Reading is only one part of a complex phenomenon. As people develop literacy skills, they develop a number of other skills, including reading for meaning (vs decoding of individual words), the ability to describe with accuracy, and ability to give and understand instructions without relying on face-to-face interaction and shared context, a large working vocabulary, and an understanding of abstract concepts.[49] Linguists and reading experts have established links among a variety of skills such as reading, verbal presentation, and oral comprehension.[50] Thus, the relationship between health outcomes and patients' skills and competencies is not limited to reading but may instead be related to the full spectrum of literacy skills.

Medical, nursing, dental, and mental health encounters rely on patients' oral skills. Patients are expected to describe experiences and symptoms so that a practitioner can complete a diagnosis. Auditory skills, better known as oral comprehension skills, are critical as well. The practitioners' talk and commentary, presentation of findings, and advice for action are important components of care and self-care. Consequently, patients' oral presentation and comprehension abilities can enhance or limit their experiences.

Patients with high levels of oral presentation and comprehension abilities may still experience problems when they communicate with their health care providers, because status and power differentials shape discussions and interactions. In addition, a patient may be physically or cognitively impaired due to illness, stress, fear, or discomfort. Shame or feelings of embarrassment, as noted earlier, might diminish a person's capacity to express his or her concerns in a health care setting's highly literate environment.[51,52] Patients' weak or strong literacy skills are further affected by the scientific language and jargon used by health professionals in writing and in speech. While the literacy skills of patients are of critical importance, so too are vocabulary and communication skills of those in the health fields.

Health practitioners need to continuously improve the clarity of their written and spoken health information. Reading, writing, and presentation skills, finely tuned in institutions of higher learning, are geared for dialogue and discussion among members of highly educated and often specialized audiences. Plain-language communication should be considered a critical skill, along with other professional competencies for those in health professions.

IMPLICATIONS AND NEEDED ACTIONS

As illustrated in Chapter 1, health literacy is a dynamic skill that ebbs and flows in response to other factors, including health materials, communication skills of those delivering the message, changes in life experience, education, and the presence of comorbid conditions such as functional status, mental illness, stress, or depression. Health literacy must also be understood in terms of having multiple antecedents and/or confounders. They include not only such obvious factors as educational attainment but also such factors as dyslexia or social deprivation. Further exploration of these issues is needed.[3]

The 1998 Socioeconomic Status and Health Chartbook summarizes a wide array of research findings linking education, income, and health status.[53] Family income increases with each higher level of education. Life expectancy is related to family income. Death rates for chronic diseases, communicable diseases, and injuries are all inversely related to education. Health-damaging activities such as smoking, sedentary lifestyle, and heavy alcohol use are associated with lower income and lower education. Dental visits, screening, and avoidable hospitalization are associated with higher income and higher levels of education.[53] Of course, the cited research uses education and/or income as markers of socioeconomic status and not as variables to be examined. Until recently, few inquiries had looked more closely at factors associated with education such as literacy. The National Institutes of Health began to support explorations of possible pathways from education to health in 2003.

Health literacy is still a new field of inquiry. Innovative and rigorous research inquiries will contribute to the pool of knowledge, while well-tested interventions that incorporate the needs and perspectives of the patient can improve health care and health outcomes. First, however, faulty assumptions about health literacy skills of adults entering the health care system must be corrected.

REFERENCES

1. Kirsch IS, Jungeblut A, Jenkins L, Kolstad A. *Adult Literacy in America: A First Look at the Results of the National Adult Literacy Survey.* Washington, DC: National Center for Education Statistics, US Department of Education; September 1993.

2. Kirsch I. *The International Adult Literacy Survey: Defining What Was Measured. ETS Research Report RR-01-25.* Princeton, NJ: Statistics and Research Division of ETS [Educational Testing Services]; 2001.

3. Rudd R. Literacy implications for health communications and for health. In: Murray M, ed. *Conference Report: Health and Literacy Action Conference.* Newfoundland, Canada: Memorial University of Newfoundland Division of Community Health; 2001:11–24.

4. Purcell-Gates V. *Other People's Words: The Cycle of Low Literacy.* Cambridge, Mass: Harvard University Press; 1995.

5. Rudd R. Literacy and Health: Recalibrating the Norm. Oral Session 3292 Presented at 130th Annual Meeting of the American Public Health Association; November 11, 2002; Philadelphia, Pa.

6. Fox S, Raine L. *Vital Decisions: How Internet Users Decide What Information to Trust When They or Their Loved Ones Are Sick.* Washington, DC: Pew Internet & American Life Project; 2000.

7. Hochhauser M. Patient education and the web: what you see on the computer screen isn't always what you get in print. *Patient Care Manag.* 2002;17(11):10–12.

8. Lazarus W, Mora F. *Online Content for Low-Income and Underserved Americans: The Digital Divide's New Frontier.* Santa Monica, Calif: The Children's Partnership; 2000.

9. Graber MA, D'Alessandro DM, Johnson-West J. Reading level or privacy policies on Internet health web sites. *J Fam Pract.* 2002; 51(7):642–645.

10. Croft DR, Peterson MW. An evaluation of the quality and contents of asthma education on the World Wide Web. *Chest.* 2002; 121(4):1301–1307.

11. Zarcadoolas C, Blanco M, Boyer J. Unweaving the web: an explanatory study of low-literate adults' navigation skills on the World Wide Web. *J Health Commun.* 2002;7:309–324.

12. Bell RA, Kravitz RL, Wilkes MS. Direct-to-consumer prescription drug advertising, 1989–1998: a content analysis of conditions, targets, inducements and appeals. *J Fam Pract.* 2000;49(4):329–335.

13. Kaphingst KA. *Examining the Educational Potential of Direct-to-Consumer Prescription Drug Advertising* [dissertation]. Boston, Mass: Harvard School of Public Health; 2002.

14. Rudd RE, Moeykens BA, Colton TC. Health and literacy: a review of medical and public health literature. In Comings J, Garner B, Smith C, eds. *The Annual Review of Adult Learning and Literacy*. San Francisco, Calif: Jossey-Bass; 2000:158–199.

15. Meade CD, Diekmann J, Thornhill DG. Readability of American Cancer Society patient education literature. *Oncol Nurs Forum*. 1992;19(1):51–55.

16. Davis TC, Crouch MA, Willis G, Miller S, Abdehou DM. The gap between patient reading comprehension and the readability of patient education materials. *J Fam Pract*. 1990:31(5);533–538.

17. Alexander RE. Readability of published dental educational materials. *J Am Dent Assoc*. 2000;131(7):937–942.

18. Rudd R, Comings J, Hyde J. Leave no one behind: improving health and risk communication through attention to literacy. *J Health Commun*. 2003;8 [Suppl 1]:104–15.

19. Sum A, Kirsch I, Taggart R. *The Twin Challenges of Mediocrity and Inequality: Literacy in the United States from an International Perspective*. A Policy Information Center Report. Princeton, NJ: Educational Testing Service; February 2002.

20. Comings J, Sum A, Uvin J. *New Skills for a New Economy: Adult Education's Key Role in Sustaining Economic Growth and Expanding Opportunity*. Boston, Mass: MassINC, The Massachusetts Institute for a New Commonwealth; December 2000.

21. Comings J, Reder S, Sum A. *Building a Level Playing Field*. Cambridge, Mass: National Center for the Study of Adult Learning and Literacy, Harvard University; December 2001.

22. Parikh NS, Parker RM, Nurss JR, Baker DW, Willams MV. Shame and health literacy: the unspoken connection. *Patient Educ Couns*. 1996;27:33–39.

23. Baker DW, Parker RM, Williams MV, Clark WS, Nurss J. The relationship of patient reading ability to self-reported health and use of health services. *Am J Public Health*. 1997;87(6):1027–1030.

24. Baker DW, Parker RM, Williams MV, Clark WS. Health literacy and the risk of hospital admission. *J Gen Intern Med*. 1998 Dec.;13(12):791–798.

25. Kalichman SC, Rompa D. Functional health literacy is associated with health status and health-related knowledge in people living with HIV-AIDS. *J Acquir Immune Defic Syndr*. 2000 Dec;25(4):337–344.

26. Williams MV, Baker DW, Parker RM, Nurss JR. Relationship of functional health literacy to patients' knowledge of their chronic disease: a

study of patients with hypertension and diabetes. *Arch Intern Med.* 1998;158(2):166–172.

27. Williams MV, Baker DW, Honig EG, Lee TM, Nowlan A. Inadequate literacy is a barrier to asthma knowledge and self-care. *Chest.* 1998;114(4):1008–1015.

28. Schillinger D, Grumbach K, Piette J, et al. Association of health literacy with diabetes outcomes. *JAMA.* 2002;288(4):475–482.

29. Bennett CL, Ferreira MR, Davis TC, et al. Relation between literacy, race, and stage of presentation among low-income patients with prostate cancer. *J Clin Oncol.* 1998;16(9):3101–3104.

30. Rudd R. When words get in the way: problems navigating health care. In: Program & Abstracts, 128th Meeting of the American Public Health Association; November 12–15, 2000; Boston, Mass. Abstract 6695.

31. Rudd R, Bruce K. *Navigation Study, Report to NCSALL, 1999.* Cambridge, Mass: National Center for the Study of Adult Learning and Literacy, Harvard University; 1999.

32. Pereira A, Zobel E, Rudd R. Literacy demand of Medicaid applications. Paper presented at The 129th Meeting of the American Public Health Association; October 23, 2001; Atlanta, Ga.

33. Friedman R, Barclay G, Rudd RE. A case study for oral health: assessment of literacy barriers. In: Program & Abstracts, 129th Meeting of the American Public Health Association; October 23, 2001; Atlanta, Ga. Abstract 31357.

34. Molnar C. Addressing challenges, creating opportunities: fostering consumer participation in Medicaid and children's health insurance managed care programs. *J Ambul Care Manage.* 2001;24(3):61–68.

35. Sofaer S. *A Classification Scheme of Individuals and Agencies Who Serve as Information Intermediaries for People on Medicare.* New York, NY: School of Public Affairs, Baruch College; May 2000.

36. Basara LR, Juergens JP. Patient package insert readability and design. *Am Pharm.* 1994;34(8):48–53.

37. Ledbetter C, Hall S, Swanson JM, Forrest K. Readability of commercial versus generic health instructions for condoms. *Health Care Women Int.* 1990;11(3):295–304.

38. Powers RD. Emergency department patient literacy and the readability of patient-directed materials. *Ann Emerg Med.* 1988;17(2):124–126.

39. Williams DM, Counselman FL, Caggiano CD. Emergency department discharge instructions and patient literacy: a problem of disparity. *Am J Emerg Med.* 1996;14(1):19–22.

40. Forbis FG, Aligne CA. Poor readability of written asthma management plans found in national guidelines. *Pediatrics.* 2002;109(4):52.

41. Morrow GR. How readable are subject consent forms? *JAMA.* 1980;244:56–58.

42. Baker MT, Taub HA. Readability of informed consent forms for research in a Veterans Administration medical center. *JAMA*.1983;250(19):2646–2648.

43. Hammerschmidt DE, Keane MA. Institutional Review Board (IRB) review lacks impact on the readability of consent forms for research. *Am J Med Sci*. 1992;304(6):348–351.

44. Philipson SJ, Doyle MA, Gabram SG, Nightingale C, Philipson EH. Informed consent for research: a study to evaluate readability and processability to effect change. *J Investig Med*. 1995;43(5):459–467.

45. Davis TC, Holcombe RF, Berkel HJ, Pramanik S, Divers SG. Informed consent for clinical trials: a comparative study of standard versus simplified forms. *J Natl Cancer Inst*. 1998;90(9):668–674.

46. Cox K. Informed consent and decision-making: patients' experiences of the process of recruitment to phases I and II anti-cancer drug trials. *Patient Educ Couns*. 2002;46(1):31–38.

47. Paasche-Orlow MK, Taylor HA, Brancati FL. Readability standards for informed-consent forms as compared with actual readability. *N Engl J Med*. 2003;348:721–726.

48. Williams MV, Davis T, Parker RM, Weiss BD. The role of health literacy in patient-physician communication. *Fam Med*. 2002;34(5):383–389.

49. Rudd R. *How to Create and Assess Print Materials*. Available at www.hsph.harvard.edu/healthliteracy/materials.html. Accessed June 24, 2003.

50. Snow CE. The theoretical basis for relationships between language and literacy in development. *J Res Child Educ*. 1991;6(1):5–10.

51. Rudd R, DeJong W. *In Plain Language* [videotape]. Available at www.hsph.harvard.edu/healthliteracy/video.html. Accessed June 30, 2003.

52. AMA Foundation. *Low Health Literacy: You Can't Tell By Looking* [videotape]. Available at www.kumc.edu/service/acadsupt/edtech/gjames/amaliteracy/amafoundationstreams.htm. Accessed June 30, 2003.

53. Pamuk E, Makuc D, Heck K, Reuben C, Lochner K. *Socioeconomic Status and Health Chartbook. Health, United States, 1998*. Hyattsville, Md: Center for Health Statistics; 1998.

Health Literacy and Communication

Editor: Debra L. Roter, DrPH

INTRODUCTION

The role of communication as medicine's primary therapeutic vehicle has been well recognized throughout the history of medicine. In this day and age, medical communication can take a variety of forms, including direct exchange between patients and providers, as well as exchanges through text, audiovisual aids, and the Internet.

This section begins with a discussion of health literacy and the patient-provider relationship. In Chapter 6, I present a framework for understanding the impact of low health literacy on patient-provider communication and how, in turn, the medical dialogue can shape the nature of the patient-provider relationship. This framework is constructed around a three-step communication continuum in which patients become increasingly involved in the health care process as physicians foster patients' engagement and collaboration by using certain communication strategies.

Focusing on medical communication specifically related to decision-making, Cooper and associates in Chapter 7 explore the association between health literacy and the propensity of physicians to involve patients in treatment decisions. Because few studies have directly investigated the association between participatory decision-making and low literacy, the authors review a variety of social factors (eg, age, ethnicity, or socioeconomic status) closely linked to low literacy that are also related to participatory decision-making. After expanding on the potential impact of literacy on patient involvement in care, the authors conclude by identifying directions for future research.

In Chapter 8, Paasche-Orlow provides a critical review of the challenges that the informed consent process presents for low literate populations. The author elucidates the purpose of informed consent and explains how, in practice, informed consent processes frequently fail to fulfill their intended purpose. In particular, Paasche-Orlow describes elements of the informed consent process, notes specific barriers to each element for patients with low literacy, and addresses the readability of consent forms.

The Internet and computer technologies present new communication perils—and opportunities—to individuals with low health literacy. In Chapter 9, Baur completes this section by examining the accessibility and utility of medical information on the Internet to low literate users. After describing potential obstacles for low-literate persons, including access issues, the need for technical skills, and the dominance of print information, the author proposes strategies for overcoming these obstacles. In conclusion, Baur explains how the Internet can progress from an agent in the health and social disparities that characterize low-literate populations into a vehicle for optimizing the delivery of health information to all.

chapter 6

Health Literacy and the Patient-Provider Relationship

Debra L. Roter, DrPH

The delivery of medical care is a complex process under the most straightforward of circumstances. It is far more complicated when patients and physicians do not share similar experiences, expectations, and assumptions regarding the nature and processes of the medical exchange. The recent Institute of Medicine report on racial and ethnic disparities in health care drew national attention to the challenges and health consequences of providing high-quality medical care and culturally sensitive communication to an ethnically diverse and vulnerable patient population.[1] While less well studied than racial and ethnic diversity in relation to health disparities, there are other factors that characterize vulnerable populations that may have consequences for interpersonal dynamics and the quality of health care delivery. These include aspects of an individual's psychological and sociological environment, such as age, social class, education, and gender, that act to shape the way in which someone sees himself or herself or is seen by others.[2] It is within this context that the effect of patient's health literacy on medical communication may be viewed.

While we tend to think of the physician as the active agent directing the content and tone of communication during a medical visit, influence does not simply flow from the physician to the patient. Interaction is a highly reciprocal process, and it is clear that both patients and physicians have a powerful influence on one another and the nature of their medical exchange.

This chapter provides a framework through which the effects of low health literacy on patient-physician communication may be considered and explores how this communication may shape the nature of the patient-provider relationship.

FRAMEWORK FOR UNDERSTANDING THE IMPACT OF LOW LITERACY ON PATIENT-PHYSICIAN COMMUNICATION

Many investigators suspect that impaired medical communication may be a primary vehicle through which low literacy affects the nature of the patient-provider relationship, patients' health-related behaviors, and, consequently, poor health status.[3,4] However, the interpersonal dynamics of low literacy in medical encounters has not been well studied and few attempts have been made to provide a framework for understanding the pathways by which health literacy may affect communication. In developing such a framework, the work of Freire provides a helpful starting point.[5]

While Freire's methods were originally developed to teach literacy skills to adults, his ideas have been useful in attaining broader community-based health education goals, including community development, health and social advocacy, and adoption of preventive health behaviors.[6] Freire sees the economic, political, and social relations that often characterize vulnerable populations as mirrored in traditional educational experiences that reinforce powerlessness by treating learners as passive objects. In contrast, adult learning strategies recognize the need for learners to be active agents in their own learning so that educational experiences act to foster the competence and confidence necessary for personal transformation and the realization of "critical consciousness." This transformation is attributed to three key adult education experiences: relating and reflecting on experience, engaging in critical dialogue, and taking conscious action.[5]

In this light, parallels to the social context of the medical visit may be considered. A physician's use of certain communication strategies can reinforce patient passivity and dependence or foster full engagement and active collaboration in the medical dialogue.[7] Figure 6-1 presents a framework for conceptualizing the communication continuum within the medical visit, which parallels Freire's key empowering experiences. Using this framework, the dynamics of medical communication with low-literate patients may be explored and its consequences ameliorated.[7–9]

The first communication step is *patient participation in the medical dialogue* through the telling of the patient's story. The process of narrative construction and delivery may be considered a vehicle for patient affirmation of self-worth and self-knowledge. This is similar to Freire's process of disclosure and reflection to affirm the value of life experiences for an adult learner. For low-literate patients with limited descriptive and organizational skills related to oral expression, the articulation of an illness narrative may be particularly problematic. Consequently, physician communication skills that assist a patient in building a history are especially important.[10]

FIGURE 6-1

Framework for Viewing Participatory Social Orientation Approach to Patient-Physician Communication

Freire's Elements of Critical Consciousness

Patient-Physician Communication Continuum

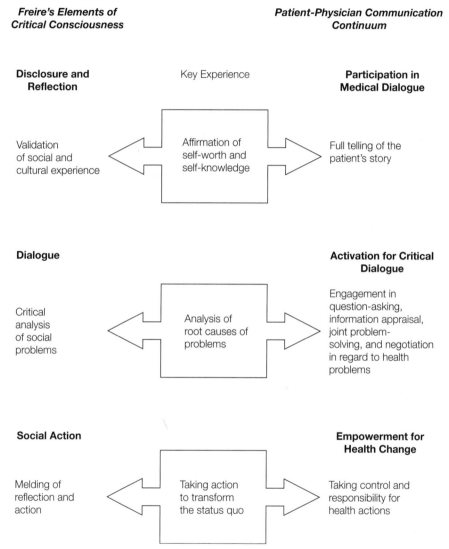

Disclosure and Reflection — Key Experience — Participation in Medical Dialogue

Validation of social and cultural experience — Affirmation of self-worth and self-knowledge — Full telling of the patient's story

Dialogue — Activation for Critical Dialogue

Critical analysis of social problems — Analysis of root causes of problems — Engagement in question-asking, information appraisal, joint problem-solving, and negotiation in regard to health problems

Social Action — Empowerment for Health Change

Melding of reflection and action — Taking action to transform the status quo — Taking control and responsibility for health actions

The second communication step is *activation for critical dialogue* through the use of questions, information appraisal, joint problem-solving, and negotiation skills as they relate to medical decisions. This step is similar to Freire's description of dialogue and critical analysis as a process that encourages examination of one's situation and the core conditions and circumstances that have contributed to it. The cognitive challenges associated with recall and comprehension of complex medical instructions and terminology and the disinclination to ask questions or initiate challenges to physician expertise present particular difficulties for patients with low levels of literacy. These patients may be more dependent on the physician's skillful facilitation of patient engagement in the dialogue than are more literate patients.

Finally, the third step of the communication continuum is *patient empowerment for change* by making informed choices and taking control and responsibility for the social, environmental, and personal context of one's health-related status quo. This last step is closest to the final step in the Freire's process, which transforms an individual from a passive subject to an active participant through recognition of one's ability to control and transform life circumstances through action.

Each communication step and the skills physicians need to assist patients across the communication continuum are discussed in the following paragraphs and displayed in Table 6-1. Where available, evidence to support each step of the communication continuum is also provided.

Participation in the Medical Dialogue

Relating and reflecting on life experiences with all of life's physical, emotional, and social significance are affirming at the most fundamental level in which the self is expressed. As noted by Engel: "... interpersonal engagement required in the clinical realm rests on complementary and basic human needs, especially the need to know and understand and the need to feel known and understood."[11] In affirming the worth and relevance of life experiences, self-reflection is encouraged, and the patient is transformed from a passive reporter of symptoms to an active "co-investigator" of his or her health problems.[6] The issues uncovered in self-reflection may then constitute the agenda of the medical visit.

The critical communication skills that facilitate patient participation in the medical dialogue include those originally derived from the psychotherapy literature and applied to interviewing skills: data gathering, relationship building, and partnering.[12] At its most elementary level, patient participation in the medical visit can be seen as reactive; physicians inquire and patients respond. However, this can

TABLE 6-1

Key Physician Communication Skills for Enhancing Patient Participation across the Communication Continuum

Communication Continuum Skills	Participatory Communication
Participation in medical dialogue	• Data-gathering skills (open questions and probes, particularly in the psychosocial domain) • Relationship skills (emotional responsiveness, including empathy, reassurance, concern, and legitimation; not interrupting) • Partnering skills (indicating interest both verbally and nonverbally, paraphrasing and interpretation; not being verbally dominant)
Activation for critical dialogue	• Patient education and counseling (providing medical and treatment information; providing lifestyle and self-care information; counseling about treatment; counseling about lifestyle and psychosocial issues) • Relationship skills (emotional responsiveness, including empathy, reassurance, concern, and legitimation; not interrupting) • Partnering skills (indicating interest both verbally and nonverbally; paraphrasing and interpretation; asking for patient expectations, opinions, suggestions; joint problem-solving)
Empowerment for health change	• Patient education and counseling (verification of information; counseling about treatment; counseling about lifestyle and psychosocial issues) • Relationship skills (support and reassurance) • Partnering skills (paraphrasing and interpretation; asking for patient opinions and suggestions; brainstorming options; negotiation and joint problem-solving)

be transformed to full participation when the parameters of communication are broadened so that patients can fully and most meaningfully tell their story.

Data-gathering skills reflect a variety of questioning behaviors that encompass variation in both form and content. Opportunities for patient participation during the medical visit are restricted through closed-ended questions to which the patient provides direct answers. Open questions, by their very nature, allow more room for patient discretion in response than closed-ended questions. Questions about things patients know and care about and that are relevant to daily experience and context enhance the parameters and meaning of disclosure. Relationship-building skills, including emotional support, empathy, reassurance, and personal regard create an atmosphere that facilitates open and sensitive disclosure by optimizing rapport and trust. Partnering skills also make it easier for a patient to tell his or her story by actively facilitating patient input through prompts and signals of interest, interpretations, paraphrasing, requests for opinion, and probes for understanding. In addition, a patient may be encouraged to more actively participate in the visit by having the physician assume a less dominating relationship stance. This includes lowered verbal dominance by listening more and talking less and using head nods, eye contact, and forward body lean to signal interest.

Effects of Low Literacy on Oral Expression During Medical Visits

Low-literate patients may face special challenges in the presentation of their illness narrative. There is some intriguing literature linking poor literacy to limitations in expressive language, suggesting that low-literate patients may be less capable than literate patients of spontaneously relating symptoms and medical history in a detailed, organized, and coherent narrative. These communication difficulties have been attributed to differences in the descriptive nature, structure, and complexity of speech used by literate and low-literate individuals. Furthermore, an observation made by low-literate patients participating in focus groups suggests that the conveyance of patient narratives may be complicated by the fact that some patients do not feel listened to when attempting to communicate with their physicians.[13]

Much of the literature on oral language and literacy acquisition focuses on children[14–16] or the social and ideological context and general use of language.[17,18] Especially intriguing is the work of linguistic theorists who distinguish "decontextualized" language that is independent of shared experience from "contextualized" language that assumes common background, knowledge, and experience.[16,18] Decontextualized language conveys abstract ideas or novel use of language or metaphors in sufficient detail to describe an event or an internal state to another person. For example, in the medical context, a decontextualized description of chest pain might be "a dull pain and heaviness like an elephant on my chest," while a nondifferentiated description like "my chest hurts here, I feel bad, I can't explain it" is more typical of low-literate individuals but less helpful to the physician making the diagnosis. It is the more descriptive and nuanced language skills that are necessary for communication in the impersonal world of bureaucracies and professional services,[15] including the relating of one's symptoms or illness experiences to the doctor, yet this kind of language may present special difficulties for low-literate individuals.

Several recent studies have explored the implication of this literature for health communication in developing countries.[15] The authors found that literacy facilitates recall and comprehension of formal spoken language, such as physicians' communications to patients and health communication messages delivered through mass media. Moreover, these researchers demonstrated that literacy skills are linked to an individual's ability to give adequate health-related descriptions. This research suggests that low literacy not only presents barriers to recall of health messages, but restricted expressive language may also characterize low-literate patients as poor medical historians and complicate the processes of gathering data and establishing the primary complaint.

Since the patient's skill as a data historian is an important element of physician satisfaction with a visit, oral language restrictions have implications not only for diagnostic accuracy but for satisfying interpersonal relationships as well.[19]

Activation for Critical Dialogue

The medical dialogue provides the vehicle for agenda-setting, information-seeking, reflection, problem-posing, and joint problem-solving. Active involvement in the dialogue transforms the patient role from reactive to proactive, with patients taking the initiative to present their agenda and have their needs met. Intervention strategies to increase active patient involvement in the medical dialogue include guides or algorithms to help patients identify, phrase, and rehearse questions, concerns, and issues to be included in the agenda of the visit.[9] In addition, physicians can activate patients in a variety of ways.[20] These include the use of relevant information, familiar terms, and plain language as well as direct and unambiguous counseling so that patients know what they are expected to do, when, for how long, and why. Furthermore, probing a patient's explanatory framework and asking directly for patient questions, expectations, and preferences pull patients into the medical discourse and facilitate negotiation and problem-solving related to treatment and lifestyle regimens. Finally, relationship skills are important when responding to patient discussion of feelings and thoughts related to coping with their illness burden and the lifestyle and psychosocial demands of their medical condition and treatment.[21] The use of feedback and checking skills, including a review to ensure the patient has understood the information communicated, is especially critical and necessary for comprehension and recall.[22]

Low Literacy and Compromised Recall
and Understanding

Despite some evidence from the anthropological literature suggesting that nonliterate adults in tribal societies have exceptional abilities to recall epic stories and oral histories, there is little evidence that low-literate adults living in a literate society have particular memorization skills. Similarly, the compensatory strategies used by functionally illiterate adults to cope with their literacy deficits does not appear to extend to an ability to remember rapidly delivered, complex messages. In an early study that addressed these questions, Stauffer and colleagues investigated the abilities of low-literate adults to recall and use information presented in a standard 30-minute televised news program.[23] The investigators found that recall correlated highly with reading levels. Compared with low-literate adults (attending a basic education program), college students scored at least 55% higher on a test of unaided recall immediately after viewing a news program and 63% higher on a multiple-choice test of information gain.[23] The authors suggest that the educational process that develops reading and writing skills also enhances an individual's ability to synthesize and retrieve both oral and visually presented material. It was also noted that the news networks typically used complex sentence structure, multisyllabic words, and specialized vocabulary—all of which challenge a low-literate viewer.

Within the medical context, understanding and remembering complex explanations are difficult for all patients but even more so for patients with poor literacy skills. Williams et al[24] reported that patients with inadequate literacy skills were far less likely to retain even basic knowledge about their chronic disease than more literate patients, even after attending patient education classes. Almost half of the hypertensive and diabetic patients in their study demonstrated inadequate functional health literacy, and these patients scored significantly lower on tests of disease knowledge, related lifestyle risks, and self-management skills. Furthermore, many of the poor readers in the focus group discussions mentioned earlier noted that their physicians could not explain their medical problems and treatments to them in ways they could understand.[13] Despite confusion, the patients remarked that they rarely asked their doctors questions.

Direct examination of the communication dynamics of low-literate patients and their experience in medical visits has been rare and largely limited to small studies.[24,25] An exception is a recent study by Schillinger et al.[26] The functional health literacy levels of more than 400 English- and Spanish-speaking diabetic patients were assessed, and these scores were related to the patients' rating of the quality of communication with their doctors in the past six months using a standard measure of interpersonal communication. The investigators found that inadequate functional health literacy was associated with lower quality of interpersonal processes of care across three of seven communication dimensions, including general clarity, explanation of condition, and explanation of processes of care. The relationship between literacy and these communication quality ratings was even stronger after statistically adjusting for a variety of confounding variables. These variables included whether the patient's primary language was English or Spanish, whether the physician spoke Spanish, the duration of the patient-physician relationship, and a variety of sociodemographic and health status measures.

Because patients' ratings of physicians' elicitation and responsiveness to patient concerns and expectations were not associated with low levels of health literacy, the authors suggest that patients' literacy deficits may influence the cognitive dimensions of communication more directly than the interactive dynamics related to elicitation of patients' problems and responsiveness to concerns. Fortunately, the recall deficits appear to be remediable. In analyzing audiotape data from this study, Schillinger et al.[22] found that when physicians addressed cognitive issues by assessing recall and comprehension of new concepts introduced during the medical visit related to diabetes control, patients were more likely to have glycated hemoglobin (A_{1c}) levels below the mean compared with patients whose physicians missed the opportunity to clarify and reinforce important information.

The recall and organizational problems associated with poor literacy may be especially exacerbated in older individuals who are simultaneously suffering cognitive and physical decline. The dramatically low literacy levels found among many elderly populations are likely a reflection of both actual literacy deficits and cognitive decline associated with procedures such as open heart surgery, chemotherapy, and kidney dialysis as well as common chronic conditions such as hypertension and diabetes.[27] It is reasonable to speculate that the effect of cognitive decline appears earlier and is even more devastating for low-literate patients who are likely to have fewer cognitive compensatory resources than others.

Finally, the aspect of literacy related to poor numeracy skills may act to especially undermine a patient's ability to understand health risks. Schwartz and colleagues[28] found that the one third of their study sample who demonstrated inadequate numeracy skills (for instance, were unable to accurately predict how many of 1000 fair coin flips would land on the same side) misinterpreted risk-reduction data provided to them. The authors conclude that quantitative information about cancer risks and the benefits of screening may be meaningful only to individuals who have facility with basic probability and numerical concepts. In a similar vein, Davis et al[29] found that women with reading skill levels at or below the fifth grade were three times less likely than those reading at or above the ninth-grade level to understand the value of a mammogram in cancer control.

Patient Empowerment for Health-Related Change

Empowerment implies the ability to take thoughtful action to change a detrimental status quo on behalf of one's self, family, and community.[5] Within the health context, patient empowerment implies the ability to take thoughtful action to change aspects of a detrimental health-related status quo on behalf of one's self, family, and community. While medicine has long recognized the importance of patient responsibility for health behaviors, relatively little attention has been given to the extent to which physicians may facilitate the empowerment process.[9]

As discussed in greater detail in Chapter 7 (Participatory Decision-Making in the Medical Encounter and its Relationship to Patient Literacy), participatory decision-making (PDM) style has been used as an indicator of the propensity to involve patients in treatment decisions. The Medical Outcomes Study (MOS) pioneered a measure of PDM in which patients' reports involving choice, control, and responsibility over treatment decisions were assessed.[30] Physician practices and patient experience in terms of shared decision-making was found to vary widely. Most notably, physicians with primary care or interviewing skills training were reported to be more facilitative of patient engagement in the decision-making process and its follow-through than were other physicians. While the MOS study did not identify particular facilitative skills for participatory decision-making, other observational studies have found that trained physicians were more likely to engage in discussion of psychosocial issues, be emotionally supportive, ask questions in an open manner, ask for patient opinion, be skilled in interpersonal communication, be psychologically minded, and be less verbally dominant.[31]

These skills are likely to extend the influence of the therapeutic relationship to building patient confidence and competence to act on one's own behalf.[7] In using these skills for empowerment, the physician's communication role is to provide an atmosphere in which confidence and competence is built and emotional support given, and in which support for choice, control, and responsibility for health behavior is recognized and reinforced. Key skills are those related to relationship building in the provision of emotional support and partnering skills to enhance behavioral competence and confidence in following through on an action plan.

PHYSICIAN RECOGNITION OF LOW-LITERATE PATIENTS

Because low literacy is so widespread, physicians are likely to routinely encounter patients with limited literacy skills. Nevertheless, physicians are largely unaware of their patients' literacy deficits. In one study by Bass and colleagues,[32] patient scores on the Rapid Estimate of Adult Literacy in Medicine-Revised (REALM-R) were compared with primary care residents' ratings of the patient as having or not having a literacy problem. Fewer than 10% of patients reading below the sixth-grade level were identified as having a literacy problem; a full 90% of the patients with a reading deficit were not recognized by their physicians. A second study by Lindau and colleagues,[33] who studied women attending an obstetrics and gynecology clinic or a women's HIV clinic, also found low levels of residents' awareness of their patients' literacy problems, with accurate recognition limited to about one quarter of the patients with inadequate reading skills. It was noted in both studies that residents infrequently misclassify literate patients as lacking literacy skills.

Low levels of recognition are not surprising. Consider the results of Parikh and colleagues[34] who reported that one in three patients who are characterized by the Test of Functional Health Literacy in Adults (TOFHLA) as having low functional health literacy denied any difficulty reading or understanding what they read. This suggests that these patients may not even be aware of the extent of their own limitations or were unwilling to admit these limitations to a researcher. Among those patients in the study who did admit having trouble reading, 40% revealed feelings of shame and more than half of these patients had never told their spouses or children about their difficulties reading. Notably, 75% of the patients with a literacy deficit had never mentioned their limited literacy skills to their physician.

Embarrassment may inhibit some patients from disclosing their literacy problems to their physician, but focus group discussions with poor readers suggest that many patients simply do not think that their physician would be interested in knowing about their literacy difficulties or that this knowledge would be useful to the physician in helping them in any way.[35] Indeed, until recently, there has been little offered in the literature to help physicians better communicate with their low-literate patients. Consequently, it is not surprising that, even when patients with poor literacy skills are recognized, few physicians feel competent to adequately respond to their needs.[3]

Amelioration of the consequences of low patient health literacy, we must conclude, is a communication problem.

CONCLUSION

Almost half a century ago, Pratt and colleagues[36] described a communication-limiting cycle in which reticent patients appear to wait for their doctor to offer explanations while the doctor interprets patient reticence as an indication of disinterest or incompetence. The description is as apt today as it was then:

> . . . When the doctor perceives the patient as rather poorly informed, he considers the tremendous difficulties of translating his knowledge into

language the patient can understand along with the dangers of frightening the patient. Therefore, he avoids involving himself in an elaborate discussion with the patient; the patient, in turn, reacts dully to this limited information, either asking uninspired questions, or refraining from questioning the doctor at all, thus reinforcing the doctor's view that the patient is ill equipped to comprehend his problem. This further reinforces the doctor's tendency to skirt discussions of the problem. Lacking guidance by the doctor, the patient performs at a low level, hence, the doctor rates his capacities as even lower than they are.

With increasing time and productivity pressures plaguing all physicians, many fear that a patient-centered approach to communication may result in an increase in visit length within the context of an already time pressured atmosphere. Indeed, recent reports that the length of the average medical visit has increased by some 10% over the last 10 years are largely attributed to a proliferation of guidelines and expectations regarding preventive and counseling services.[37,38] Ironically, the patient education and counseling efforts that comprise much of this time burden may be falling far short of an optimal effect for a large segment of the patient population.

Finally, of special note is the fact that all patients, not only those with inadequate or marginal literacy skills, will benefit from physician efforts to engage them as active and full partners in the medical dialogue.

REFERENCES

1. Cooper LA, Roter DL. Patient-Provider Communication: The Effect of Race and Ethnicity on Process and Outcomes of Health Care. In Smedley BD, Stitch AY, Nelson AR, eds. *Unequal Treatment: Confronting Racial and Ethnic Disparities in Health Care*. Committee on Understanding and Eliminating Racial and Ethnic Disparities in Health Care. Washington, DC: National Academies Press, 2003, 552–593.

2. Roter D, Hall JA. *Doctors Talking to Patients/Patients Talking to Doctors: Improving Communication in Medical Visits*. Westport, Conn: Auburn House; 1992.

3. Ad Hoc Committee on Health Literacy for the Council on Scientific Affairs, American Medical Association. Health literacy: report of the Council on Scientific Affairs. *JAMA*. 1999;281:552–557.

4. Williams MV, Davis T, Parker RM, Weiss BD. The role of health literacy in patient-physician communication. *Fam Med*. 2002;34:383–389.

5. Freire P. *Education for Critical Consciousness*. New York, NY: Continuum Press; 1983.

6. Wallerstein N, Bernstein E. Empowerment education: Freire's ideas adapted to health education. *Health Educ Q*. 1988;15:379–394.

7. Roter D. The medical visit context of treatment decision-making and the therapeutic relationship. *Health Expect*. 2000;3:17–25.

8. Roter DL, Hall JA. *Doctors Talking with Patients: Patients Talking with Doctors*, 2nd ed. Westport, Conn: Auburn House. In press.

9. Roter DL, Stashefsky-Margalit R, Rudd R. Current perspectives on patient education in the US. *Patient Educ Couns*. 2001;44:79–86.

10. Haidet P, Paterniti D. "Building" a history rather than "taking" one: a perspective on information sharing during the medical interview. *Arch Intern Med*. 2003;163:1134–1140.

11. Engel GL. How much longer must medicine's science be bound by a seventeenth century world view? In: White D, ed. *The Task of Medicine: Dialogue at Wickenburg*. Menlo Park, Calif.: The Henry J. Kaiser Family Foundation; 1988:114–136.

12. Roter D. The enduring and evolving nature of the patient-physician relationship. *Patient Educ Couns*. 2000;39:5–15.

13. Baker DW, Parker RM, Williams MV, et al. The health care experience of patients with low literacy. *Arch Fam Med*. 1996;5:329–334.

14. LeVine R, Dexter E, Velasco P, LeVine S, Joshi A. Maternal literacy and health care in three countries: a preliminary report. *Health Trans Rev*. 1994;4:186–191.

15. Dexter ER, LeVine SE, Velasco PM. Maternal schooling and health-related language and literacy skills in rural Mexico. *Comp Educ Rev*. 1998;42:139–162.

16. Snow C. Linguistic development as related to literacy. In: Eldering L, Leseman P, eds. *Early Intervention and Culture. Preparation for Literacy: The Interface between Theory and Practice*. Utrecht, Netherlands: Netherlands National Commission for Unesco; 1993:133–148.

17. Gee JP. *Social Linguistics and Literacies*. London: Taylor and Francis Ltd; 1996.

18. Street B. *Literacy in Theory and Practice*. Cambridge, Mass.: Cambridge University Press; 1984.

19. Suchman AL, Roter D, Green M, Lipkin M Jr. Physician satisfaction with primary care office visits. Collaborative Study Group of the American Academy on Physician and Patient. *Med Care*. 1993; 31:1083–1092.

20. Roter DL, Hall JA, Kern D, Barker LR, Cole KA, Roca RP. Improving physicians' interviewing skills and reducing patients' emotional distress: a randomized clinical trial. *Arch Intern Med*. 1995;155:1877–1884.

21. Roter D. The enduring and evolving nature of the patient-physician relationship. *Patient Educ Couns*. 2000;39:5–15.

22. Schillinger D, Piette J, Grumbach K, et al. Closing the loop: physician communication with diabetic patients who have low health literacy. *Arch Intern Med*. 2003;163:83–90.

23. Stauffer J, Frost R, Rybolt W. Literacy, illiteracy, and learning from television news. *Commun Res*. 1978;5:221–231.

24. Williams MV, Baker DW, Parker RM, Nurss JR. Relationship of functional health literacy to patients' knowledge of their chronic disease: a study of patients with hypertension and diabetes. *Arch Intern Med*. 1998;158:166–172.

25. Roter DL, Rudd RE, Comings J. Patient literacy: a barrier to quality of care. *J Gen Intern Med*. 1998;13:850–851.

26. Schillinger D, Bindman A, Stewart A, Wang F, Piette J. Health literacy and the quality of physician-patient interpersonal communication. *Pat Educ Couns*. 2004;3:315–323.

27. Baker DW, Gazmararian JA, Sudano J, Patterson M, Parker RM, Williams MV. Health literacy and performance on the Mini-Mental State Examination. *Aging Ment Health*. 2002;6:22–29.

28. Schwartz LM, Woloshin S, Welch HG. The role of numeracy in understanding the benefit of screening mammography. *Ann Intern Med*. 1997;127:966–972.

29. Davis TC, Williams MV, Marin E, Parker RM, Glass J. Health literacy and cancer communication. *CA Cancer J Clin*. 2002;52:134–149.

30. Kaplan SH, Greenfield S, Gandek B, Rogers W, Ware JE. Characteristics of physicians with participatory decision-making styles. *Ann Intern Med*. 1996;124:497–504.

31. Roter D, Larson S, Shinitzky H, et al. Use of an innovative video feedback technique to enhance communication skills training. *Med Educ*. 2004;38(2):145–157.

32. Bass PF III, Wilson JF, Griffith CH, Barnett DR. Residents' ability to identify patients with poor literacy skills. *Acad Med*. 2002;77:1039–1041.

33. Lindau ST, Tomori C, McCarville MA, Bennett CL. Improving rates of cervical cancer screening and Pap smear follow-up for low-income women with limited health literacy. *Cancer Invest*. 2001;19:316–323.

34. Parikh NS, Parker RM, Nurss JR, Baker DW, Williams MV. Shame and health literacy: the unspoken connection. *Patient Educ Couns*. 1996;27:33–39.

35. Baker DW, Parker RM, Williams MV, et al. The health care experience of patients with low literacy. *Arch Fam Med*. 1996;5:329–334.

36. Pratt L, Seligmann A, Reader G. Physicians' views on the level of medical information among patients. *Am J Public Health*. 1957;47:1277–1283.

37. Carr-Hill R, Jenkins-Clarke S, Dixon P, Pringle M. Do minutes count? Consultation lengths in general practice. *J Health Serv Res Policy*. 1998;3:207–213.

38. Yarnall KSH, Pollock KI, Ostbye T, Krause KM, Michener JL. Primary care: is there enough time for prevention? *Am J Public Health*. 2003;93:635–641.

Chapter 7

Participatory Decision-Making in the Medical Encounter and Its Relationship to Patient Literacy

Lisa A. Cooper, MD, MPH; Mary Catherine Beach, MD, MPH; and Sarah L. Clever, MD, MS

Patient participation in medical decision-making has gained widespread attention in the clinical, ethical, and medical education literature over the last several decades. Participatory decision-making (PDM) is ethically grounded in the principle of respect for autonomy, which has been defined as "self-rule that is free from controlling influences and from limitations such as inadequate understanding that prevents meaningful choice."[1] Although this is an inherently important aspect of medical care, it is a relatively unexplored area for patients with limited literacy.

The concept of shared or participatory decision-making between physicians and patients was first introduced as an element of patient-centeredness by Byrne and Long.[2] Subsequently, several models and definitions have been developed in the research and clinical literature.[3–6] While the definitions differ with regard to details, all share, either implicitly or explicitly, value on a holistic approach to the patient as an individual and a collaborative process for developing the meaning of health experiences and prioritizing goals in medical encounters.

In their conceptual framework and review of the empirical literature on patient-centeredness, Mead and Bower[7] identify five conceptual dimensions of patient-centeredness: biopsychosocial perspective, the "patient-as-person," sharing power and responsibility, therapeutic alliance, and the "doctor-as-person." PDM is best reflected by the "sharing power and responsibility" dimension, in which patients are increasingly regarded as active consumers and potential critics with the right to certain standards of information, including the right to full information, to be treated with respect, and to be actively involved in decision-making about treatment.

A physician's PDM style can also be defined as the propensity of a physician to involve patients in treatment decisions. It has been measured by patient report as the aggregate of responses to several items regarding the physician's propensity to give the patient choice, control, and responsibility in making treatment decisions[8]; to discuss pros and cons of each treatment option; to get the patient to state which choice or option he or she prefers; and to take the patient's preferences into account when making treatment decisions.[9]

One definition of involvement in decision-making states that involvement has three elements. First is *information exchange*, in which patients and physicians share information regarding their symptoms and the options for treatment, respectively. Next is *deliberation*, which is the process of expressing and discussing treatment preferences. Finally, there is the *decision on the treatment to implement.* Through the deliberation process, both patient and physician work toward reaching an agreement and both parties have an investment in the ultimate decision made.[10]

For the purposes of this chapter, PDM is defined as a process that considers the input of both patients and physicians to be equally important and involves each of the three elements just described (information exchange, deliberation, and decision-making). In the remainder of this chapter, we discuss the importance of PDM in patient care, review patient factors that are related to both PDM and literacy, and discuss the potential impact of patient literacy on PDM. We conclude with a discussion of strategies to improve PDM and areas for future research.

IMPORTANCE OF PDM IN PATIENT CARE

PDM is important to patients. To the extent that PDM is an element of patient-centered communication, strong evidence links these communication behaviors to valued patient outcomes, including improvements in markers of disease control, such as glycated hemoglobin (A_{1C}) and blood pressure, and enhanced reports of physical and emotional health status, functioning, and pain control.[11–13] In particular, visits in which the physician used a PDM style have been associated with higher levels of patient satisfaction.[14] Studies also link patient ratings of interpersonal care (and PDM in particular) to health service utilization and continuity of care.[14,15]

Lerman and colleagues[16] designed an instrument called the Patient's Perceived Involvement in Care Scale to examine three relatively distinct factors: (1) physician facilitation of patient involvement, (2) level of information exchange, and (3) patient participation in decision-making. Of these factors, physician facilitation and patient decision-making were related significantly to patients' satisfaction with care. Physician facilitation and information exchange related consistently to patients' perceptions of post-visit changes in their understanding, reassurance, perceived control over illness, and expectations for improvement in functioning.

Another study[17] of patients' perceptions about the roles they played during medical visits showed that, after adjusting for age, sex, baseline illness ratings, and physician-rated prognosis, "active" patients reported less discomfort, greater alleviation of symptoms, and more improvement in their general medical condition one week after the visits than did "passive" patients. These differences were not influenced by the roles patients desired to play. Active patients also reported being less concerned about their illnesses, a greater sense of control of their illnesses, and more satisfaction with their physicians one day after the visit. The authors concluded that patients' perceptions about their involvement in care appeared to be related to their attitudes about their illnesses as well as to recovery. The authors recommended that further research be conducted to determine the factors that influence these role perceptions and to define the types of patients, illnesses, and settings in which the benefits of active-role perceptions are most likely to be realized.

PATIENT FACTORS RELATED TO PDM

Several factors that have been related to PDM have also been related to patients' literacy levels. These include low socioeconomic status and educational attainment, older age, cultural factors such as ethnicity and language, and health status. Each factor is described below.

Low Socioeconomic Status/ Low Educational Attainment

Studies of PDM have shown that patients with lower levels of education rate their visits with physicians as less participatory.[8,18] It is also known that physicians give more information, in particular, to patients of higher social class, even though, when asked later, patients of different classes do not differ in how much information they say they want. Pendleton and Bochner,[19] in their videotape study of 79 general consultations in the United Kingdom, found that patients' social class was a significant predictor of how many explanations were volunteered by doctors. Physicians spontaneously offered more explanations during visits to patients of higher social class than to patients of other classes. The investigators suggested that physicians are less likely to volunteer explanations to patients with backgrounds of lower social class because they are perceived as less interested in information and more diffident when asking questions. Waitzkin's large study in the United States found that better-educated patients and patients of higher socioeconomic backgrounds received more physician time, more total explanations, and more explanations in comprehensible language than other patients.[20]

Older Age

Older patients appear to be more passive and less actively engaged in the treatment decision-making process during visits. The Medical Outcomes Study (MOS),[8] based on surveys of more than 8,000 patients sampled from the practices of 344 physicians, found that patients aged 75 and over reported significantly fewer participatory visits with their doctors than all but the youngest age cohorts of patients (those younger than 30 years). Interestingly, the most participatory visits were evident in the scores of only slightly younger patient groups, including those aged 65 to 74 and the middle-aged group ranging from 45 to 64 years. A possible explanation for these findings is that the elderly typically demonstrate lower levels of literacy, have had less exposure to formal education than younger birth cohorts,[21] and may exhibit lower levels of functioning including cognitive function. This, in turn, may discourage physicians from involving the patient in decision-making.

Cultural Factors

Cultural factors such as patients' race, ethnicity, and language and the racial/ethnic concordance between physicians and patients have also been related to PDM.

Ethnic Minority Patients
Studies have found that physicians deliver less information, less supportive talk, and less proficient clinical performance to African-American and Hispanic patients and to patients of lower economic class than they do to more advantaged patients, even in the same care settings.[22-26] In at least two studies of patients attending primary care practices, belonging to an ethnic minority was associated with lower reports of participatory visits.[8,18] An additional example is provided by preliminary data from our ongoing study of primary care physicians and patients in the Baltimore–Washington, DC, metropolitan area.[27] Data show that African-American patients experience shorter visits that are more verbally dominated by the physician than white patients.

Patients with Limited English Proficiency
Patients with limited English proficiency report less satisfaction with interpersonal aspects of care[28] and more difficulties communicating with physicians, including less participation in decisions about their care, than they would like.[29] This may, in part, be attributed to patients' low literacy, because persons with limited English proficiency are also more likely to have poor reading ability.[30] In a cross-sectional acute care survey study of 2,659 predominantly indigent and minority patients presenting for acute care (1892 English-speaking and 767 Spanish-speaking), researchers used the English-language Test of Functional Health Literacy in Adults (TOFHLA) and the Spanish TOFHLA to show that 35% of English-speaking patients and 62% of Spanish-speaking patients had inadequate or marginal functional health literacy in their native language. The prevalence of inadequate or marginal functional health literacy among the elderly (age $\geq$ 60 years) was 81% for English-speaking patients and 83% (57/69) for Spanish-speaking patients and was significantly higher ($P < .001$) than in younger patients.[31]

Ethnic Concordance
In a telephone survey study of 1,816 adult managed-care enrollees attending primary care practices in a large urban area, Cooper-Patrick and colleagues examined the association between race or ethnic concordance and discordance on patient ratings of physicians' PDM style.[18] The patient sample was 43% Caucasian, 45% African-American, and 12% other race/ethnic groups (5% Asian, 5% Latino, and 2% Native American). To study the potential influence of race concordance or discordance between physicians and patients on PDM, patients were stratified according to the race/ethnicity of their physicians and the relationship between PDM style; patient race within each physician race group was measured, adjusting for patient age, gender, education, marital status, health status, and length of the relationship. African-American patients' visits with Caucasian physicians were significantly less participatory than those of Caucasian patients with Caucasian physicians. ($\beta^* = -4.3$; SE = 1.7, $P < .02$, adjusted). Asian and Latino patients' had fewer participatory visits with African-American physicians than African-American patients; however, these results were based on very small sample sizes. There were no significant racial differences in PDM scores among patients seeing Asian or Latino doctors. However, there were only two Latino physicians in the study sample; therefore, reliable conclusions regarding the PDM style of Latino physicians could not be drawn.

---

* The beta coefficient represents the difference in average PDM scores between patients in race-concordant and race-discordant patient–physician relationships.

To explore the overall significance of racial and ethnic concordance in the physician-patient relationship, Cooper-Patrick and colleagues assessed the relationship between race/ethnic concordance between physicians and patients and PDM style. Patients in race-concordant relationships with their physicians rated their physicians as significantly more participatory than patients in race-discordant relationships ($\beta = +2.6$; SE $= 1.1$; $P < .02$, adjusted).[18]

In a recent cross-sectional study using post-visit surveys and audiotape analysis, Cooper et al[32] examined the relationship between race concordance and actual patient and physician communication behaviors (252 adult patients [142 Caucasian, 110 African-American] and 31 primary care physicians [13 Caucasian, 18 African-American]). Race-concordant visits were longer (+2.15 minutes; 95% CI, 0.60-3.71) and had higher ratings of patient positive affect (+0.55 points; 95% CI, 0.04-1.05) than race-discordant visits. Moreover, consistent with previous work,[18] patients in race-concordant visits were more satisfied and rated their physicians as more participatory (+8.42 points; 95% CI, 3.23-13.60).[32]

Patients with Chronic Illness

Relatively little is known about the degree of participation in decision-making that patients with chronic illness actually prefer or experience with physicians. The studies outlined here suggest that patient preferences for PDM and actual PDM vary with health status. At the same time, studies also show that patients with inadequate functional literacy are more likely to have poor physical and mental health status, including depression and poorer cognitive function, than patients with adequate health literacy.[33-36] In the association between health literacy and PDM, chronic illness may be a common factor. To the degree that health literacy and health status are associated, these studies may help improve our understanding of relationships between patient literacy level and participation in medical decisions.

Hypertension

In one study,[37] researchers administered questionnaires about three aspects of decision-making to 210 hypertensive outpatients and to their 50 clinicians, who represented three types of medical practices. The researchers found that 41% of patients preferred more information about hypertension. Clinicians underestimated patient preferences for discussion about therapy in 29% of cases and overestimated it in 11% ($k = 0.22$). Fifty-three percent of patients preferred to participate in making decisions, while clinicians believed that their patients desired to participate in 78% of cases. Many patients who preferred not to make initial therapeutic decisions did want to participate in ongoing evaluation of therapy. Thus, the authors concluded that clinicians treating hypertension underestimate patients' desire for information and discussion but overestimate patients' desire to make decisions and suggested that awareness of this discrepancy may facilitate communication and decision-making.

Variation by Disease Category
Using data from 2,197 patients in the MOS (a 4-year observational study of patients with chronic disease [hypertension, diabetes, myocardial infarction, congestive heart failure, and depression]), Arora and McHorney[38] sought to identify the determinants of patient preferences for participation in medical decision-making. They found that a majority of the patients (69%) preferred to leave their medical decisions to their physicians. Compared with patients who only suffered hypertension that was not severe, those with severe diabetes (OR = 0.62; $P = .04$) and heart disease that was not severe (OR = 0.45; $P = .02$) were less likely to prefer an active role. However, patients with clinical depression were more likely to prefer an active role in decision-making (OR = 1.64; $P = .01$). The authors concluded that, although a majority of patients prefer to delegate decision-making to physicians, preferences vary significantly by patients' disease category.

Asthma
A cross-sectional observational study of 128 adult patients with asthma receiving care in the pulmonary unit of a university teaching hospital identified factors associated with asthma patients' perceptions of the propensity of pulmonologists to involve them in treatment decision-making and the association with asthma outcomes.[39] The researchers found that patients' mean ratings of physicians' PDM style was 72 (maximum = 100) (95% CI, 65-79). PDM scores were significantly correlated ($P < .0001$) with the duration of clinic visits ($r = 0.63$), patient satisfaction ($r = 0.53$), duration of tenure of physician-patient relationship ($r = 0.37$), and formal education ($r = 0.22; P = .023$). Significantly higher PDM style scores were reported when visits lasted longer than 20 minutes and when a patient had a relationship with a particular physician for longer than 6 months. PDM scores were also significantly correlated with possession of a written asthma action plan ($r = 0.54$; $P < .0001$), days affected by asthma ($r = 0.36; P = .0001$), asthma symptoms ($r = 0.23; P = .017$), and preferences for autonomy in asthma management decisions ($r = 0.28; P = .0035$). Those with PDM scores <50 reported significantly lower quality of life for all domains of a disease-specific instrument and the short-form 36 (SF = 36) health survey version 1.0. In multiple regression analysis, PDM style was associated with the length of the office visit and the duration of tenure of the physician-patient relationship ($R^2 = 0.47, P = .0009$). The adjusted

odds ratio, per standard deviation decrease in PDM scores, for an asthma hospitalization was 2.0 (95% CI, 1.2-3.2) and for rehospitalization was 2.5 (95% CI, 1.2-4.2). The authors concluded that patients' report of their physicians' PDM style is significantly associated with health-related quality of life, work disability, and recent need for acute health services, and that organizational factors, specifically longer visits and more time seeing a particular physician, are independently associated with more participatory visits.

Diabetes

Pendleton and House conducted a small study and found that low-income urban diabetic outpatients had little interest in medical decision-making.[40] In a recent survey study of 2,000 patients receiving diabetes care across 25 veterans' affairs facilities, researchers assessed the influence of patients' evaluation of their physicians' PDM style, physician communication (PCOM), and reported understanding of diabetes self-care on their self-reported diabetes management. Results showed that higher ratings in PDM style and PCOM were each associated with higher self-management assessments ($P < .01$ in all models).[9] When modeled together, PCOM remained a significant independent predictor of self-management (standardized $\beta = 0.18$; $P < .001$), but PDM style became nonsignificant. Adding Understanding to the model diminished the unique effect of PCOM in predicting self-management (standardized $\beta = 0.10$; $P = .004$). Understanding was strongly and independently associated with self-management (standardized $\beta = 0.25$; $P < .001$). The authors concluded that for diabetic patients in this setting, ratings of providers' communication effectiveness were more important than a PDM style in predicting diabetes self-management. Reported understanding of self-care behaviors was highly predictive of and attenuated the effect of both PDM style and PCOM on self-management, raising the possibility that both provider styles enhance self-management through increased patient understanding or self-confidence.[9] As discussed in the previous chapter, understanding complex explanations is particularly problematic for patients with poor literacy skills. This study's findings suggest that physician communication is an important tool for enhancing understanding in low-literate patients.

POTENTIAL IMPACT OF PATIENT LITERACY ON PATIENT INVOLVEMENT IN CARE

Although few studies explicitly examine the link between low literacy and PDM, there are many reasons to believe that patients with low literacy would be less involved in their own medical care. Most of these potential mechanisms work by impairing a low-literate patient's ability to exchange information with their health care providers. This impaired information exchange likely occurs in both directions.

First, patients with low literacy report that medical care is intimidating[41] and harbor a deep sense of shame that makes disclosure of their low literacy more difficult.[41,42] Given the inherent differential power dynamics within the patient-physician relationship, any additional feelings of inadequacy on the part of the patient that leads to a greater diminution of patient power would undermine PDM.

Second, patients with low literacy may have difficulty with oral as well as written communication. These difficulties may be due to differences in vocabulary between low-literate patients and their health care providers, as well as to differences in the structure and complexity of speech used by literate and low-literate persons.[43] For example, patients with poor literacy skills may have difficulty providing a detailed history, responding to questions from their physicians, and formulating questions to ask their physicians.

Third, for a myriad of reasons, patients with low literacy report a poorer knowledge of health conditions, which ultimately limits their ability to take an active role in their own self-management. For example, patients with low literacy have been shown to have poorer knowledge of chronic conditions such as hypertension, and diabetes[44] and asthma.[45] Patients with poorer reading skills have also been shown to have less family planning knowledge[46] and cervical cancer prevention knowledge.[47] Not surprisingly, patients with low literacy are less likely to use preventive services.[48] From the diseases that have been studied so far, it is clear that health literacy is vital for self-management.

PATIENT LITERACY AND PDM

Few studies have been conducted to directly relate patient literacy to patient reports of PDM. The Commonwealth Fund 2001 Health Care Quality Survey collected information on the health care experiences of a cross section of adults living in the United States, representing people from a diverse group of racial/ethnic backgrounds.[29] Survey questions covered experiences in the health care system, including usual sources of care and patient-physician communication. In addition, the survey inquired about respondents' demographics, socioeconomic and self-rated health status, health literacy, primary language spoken in the home, and foreign-born status. The descriptive report of the survey findings includes a section showing that low health literacy, as measured by respondent self-assessed ability to read and understand prescription drug labeling, is associated with poor communication with health care providers, including less participation in decisions than the respondent would have liked.[29]

In order to enhance patient recall, comprehension, and adherence, it is often recommended that physicians use PDM communication skills that include eliciting patients' comprehension of new concepts and tailoring subsequent information, particularly for patients with low functional health literacy. Schillinger and colleagues[49] used direct observation to measure the extent to which primary care physicians working in a public hospital assessed patient recall and comprehension of new concepts during outpatient encounters. The researchers used audiotapes of visits between 38 physicians and 74 English-speaking patients with diabetes mellitus and low functional health literacy. They then examined whether there was an association between physicians' application of this interactive communication strategy and patients' glycemic control, using information from clinical and administrative databases. The results showed that physicians assessed recall and comprehension of any new concept in 12 (20%) of 61 visits and for 15 (12%) of 124 new concepts and that patients whose physicians assessed recall or comprehension were more likely to have A_{1C} levels below the mean ($\leq 8.6\%$) vs patients whose physicians did not (OR, 8.96; 95% CI, 1.1-74.9; $P = .02$). After multivariate logistic regression, the two variables independently associated with good glycemic control were higher health literacy levels (OR, 3.97; 95% CI, 1.09-14.47; $P = .04$) and physicians' application of the interactive communication strategy (OR, 15.15; 95% CI, 2.07-110.78; $P < .01$). The authors concluded that primary care physicians caring for patients with diabetes mellitus and low functional health literacy rarely assessed patient recall or comprehension of new concepts and that overlooking this step in communication reflects a missed opportunity that may have important clinical implications.[49]

In a follow-up study that compared the communication patterns of physicians with patients of inadequate health literacy compared to adequate health literacy, the same authors discovered that patients with inadequate health literacy were more likely to report worse communication in the areas of general clarity, explanation of condition, and explanation of processes of care.[50] These domains would certainly impact the ability of a patient to participate in decisions.

USING CLINICAL DECISION AIDS AND OTHER BEHAVIORAL STRATEGIES TO INCREASE PDM

Several interventions have used decision aids (educational media that provide patients with the information and/or structure to make decisions) to improve shared decision-making for patients with cancer and other chronic diseases and for persons facing decisions about screening.[51-56] A recent systematic review concluded that, compared to usual care, decision aids improve knowledge and realistic expectations of the benefits and harms of options, reduce passivity in decision-making, and reduce decisional conflict related to feeling uninformed.[56] However, when simpler aids such as decision boards and illustrated pamphlets are compared to more detailed aids (eg, interactive CD-ROMs and videotapes), patient differences in knowledge are marginal, while there are other benefits for improving realistic expectations and reducing decisional conflicts. Decision aids have shown little effect on anxiety levels or satisfaction (with the decision-making process or with the decision), and the effects of choices vary with the decision.[56]

Few of these interventions have targeted specific populations, such as those of low socioeconomic status (SES), ethnic minorities, or low-literate patients. One intervention conducted among newly diagnosed prostate cancer patients with low SES revealed that, despite high levels of satisfaction with an interactive shared decision-making CD-ROM program, patients with lower literacy scores had lower knowledge after participating in the program than did patients with higher literacy. This suggests that collaborative efforts with the target population are necessary to improve the success of shared decision-making programs among patients with low health literacy.[57]

A new intervention, which uses community health workers as coaches within the health care system and includes a monthly newsletter with a comic book format, is currently being tested on low-income urban ethnic minority patients with hypertension.[58] Provider interventions that focus on improving provider partnership and shared decision-making communication skills with low-literate patients are another promising strategy. The study mentioned above also includes a physician intervention that uses individualized communication skills training via a self-administered CD-ROM tutorial. Because few studies simultaneously intervene with patients and providers, this study may help identify whether interventions that target both providers and patients are necessary to achieve success in shared decision-making, particularly for vulnerable patients such as the elderly, ethnic minorities, and patients with low literacy.

DIRECTIONS FOR FUTURE RESEARCH

We have identified several gaps in knowledge regarding health literacy and its relation to PDM. First, future work should focus on improved measurement of shared decision-making between physicians and low-literate patients, using both provider and patient self-report and direct observation methods.[59,60] In particular, studies of low-income, ethnic minority, limited English-proficient, elderly, and chronic disease patient groups should include assessments of health literacy and patient-provider communication. Second, clinical interventions that educate, activate, and empower patients, including those that incorporate clinical decision aids tailored for low-literate patients and those that target providers and the health care system to improve patient participation in care need to be developed and tested.

A third promising area for further research is community-based participatory research to empower persons with low literacy to become more active participants in their own health care decisions. A recent study used community-based participatory research methods to design and implement an intervention that uses in-home Internet access and training for volunteers in a 57-block area on the west side of Chicago (a low-income urban community).[61] These volunteers, along with a comparison group, were interviewed prior to and one year after initiation of the program. The objective of the study was to determine whether access to health information via in-home Internet technology could positively influence empowerment among residents of a low-income urban community. Twenty-five community residents completed all phases of the technology intervention, and 35 randomly selected neighbors of these residents served as the comparison group. Members of the intervention group received Internet access via WebTV, training, technical support, and access to a community-specific, health-oriented Web page during the study. The results showed that intervention group members were similar to comparison group members in terms of empowerment at baseline and that, after receiving Internet access and training, empowerment related to health decision-making improved significantly in the intervention group, while similar changes did not occur in the comparison group. Affinity for and appreciation of information technology also increased in the intervention group but not in the comparison group. The authors concluded that Internet access to community-specific and general health information can lead to increased empowerment and appreciation of information technology when community-based participatory research methods are used.

CONCLUSION

In conclusion, PDM has documented benefits, including patient understanding and recall of information, patient satisfaction, and improved health outcomes. Studies relating health literacy to PDM are limited; however, lower levels of PDM have been linked to factors associated with low health literacy, including lower educational attainment, older age, ethnic minority status, ethnic discordance in the patient-provider relationship, and poor health status. It is unclear whether shared decision-making requires the use of sophisticated technology such as audiovisual and computer-based programs or whether the same results can be obtained with simpler methods such as written pamphlets, newsletters, or decision boards. Future studies should focus on improving measurement of the nature of communication difficulties that serve as barriers to PDM for low-literate patients and linking the specific effects of shared decision-making in this population to patient reports of care and health outcomes. These studies may help identify the most effective patient-provider, health system, and community-based strategies to increase low-literate patients' involvement in decisions about their own health care.

REFERENCES

1. Beauchamp TL, Childress JF. *Principles of Biomedical Ethics*. New York, NY: Oxford University Press; 2001.

2. Byrne P, Long B. *Doctors Talking to Patients*. London: HMSO; 1976.

3. Brody DS. The patient's role in clinical decision-making. *Ann Intern Med*. 1980;93(5):718–722.

4. Charles C, Gafni A, Whelan T. Shared decision-making in the medical encounter: what does it mean? (or it takes at least two to tango). *Soc Sci Med*. 1997;44(5):681–692.

5. Stewart M, Brown BJ, Weston WW, McWhinney I, McWilliam CL, Freeman TR, eds. *Patient-centered Medicine: Transforming the Clinical Method*. Thousand Oaks, Calif: Sage;1995:216–228.

6. Laine C, Davidoff F. Patient-centered medicine. A professional evolution. *JAMA*. 1996;275(2):152–156.

7. Mead N, Bower P. Patient-centeredness: a conceptual framework and review of the empirical literature. *Soc Sci Med*. 2000;51(7):1087–1110.

8. Kaplan SH, Gandek B, Greenfield S, Rogers W, Ware JE. Patient and visit characteristics related to physicians' participatory decision-making style: results from the Medical Outcomes Study. *Medical Care*. 1995;33:1176–1183.

9. Heisler M, Bouknight RR, Hayward RA, Smith DM, Kerr EA. The relative importance of physician communication, participatory decision making, and patient understanding in diabetes self-management. *J Gen Intern Med*. 2002;17(4):243–252.

10. Charles C, Gafni A, Whelan T. Decision-making in the physician-patient encounter: revisiting the shared treatment decision-making model. *Soc Sci Med*. 1999;49(5):651–661.

11. Greenfield S, Kaplan SH, Ware JE Jr, Yano EM, Frank HJL. Patients' participation in medical care: effects on blood sugar control and quality of life in diabetes. *J Gen Intern Med*. 1988;(3):448–457.

12. Kaplan SH, Greenfield S, Ware JE Jr. Assessing the effects of physician-patient interactions on the outcomes of chronic disease. *Medical Care*. 1989;27:S110–S127.

13. Stewart MA. Effective physician-patient communication and health outcomes: A review. *Can Med Assoc J*. 1995;152:1423–1433.

14. Kaplan SH, Greenfield S, Gandek B, Rogers WH, Ware JE. Characteristics of physicians with participatory decision-making styles. *Ann Intern Med*. 1996;124:497–504.

15. Marquis MS, Davies AR, Ware JE Jr. Patient satisfaction and change in medical care provider: a longitudinal study. *Med Care*. 1983;21(8):821–829.

16. Lerman CE, Brody DS, Caputo GC, Smith DG, Lazaro CG, Wolfson HG. Patients' Perceived Involvement in Care Scale: relationship to attitudes about illness and medical care. *J Gen Intern Med*. 1990;5(1):29–33.

17. Brody DS, Miller SM, Lerman CE, Smith DG, Caputo GC. Patient perception of involvement in medical care: relationship to illness attitudes and outcomes. *J Gen Intern Med*. 1989;4(6):506–511.

18. Cooper-Patrick L, Gallo JJ, Gonzales JJ, et al. Race, gender, and partnership in the patient-physician relationship. *JAMA*. 1999;282;583–589.

19. Pendleton DA, Bochner S. The communication of medical information in general practice consultations as a function of patients' social class. *Soc Sci Med*. 1980;14A:669–673.

20. Waitzkin H. Information giving in medical care. *J Health Soc Behav*. 1985;26:81–101.

21. Gazmararian JA, Baker DW, Williams MV, et al. Health literacy among Medicare enrollees in a managed care organization. *JAMA*. 1999;281(6):545–551.

22. Bartlett EE, Grayson M, Barker R, Levine DM, Golden A, Libber S. The effects of physician communication skills on patient satisfaction, recall, and adherence. *J Chron Dis*. 1984;37:755–764.

23. Epstein AM, Taylor WC, Seage GR III. Effects of patients' socioeconomic status and physicians' training and practice on patient-doctor communication. *Am J Med*. 1985;78:101–106.

24. Hooper EM, Comstock LM, Goodwin JM, Goodwin JS. Patient characteristics that influence physician behavior. *Med Care*. 1982;20:630–638.

25. Ross CE, Mirowsky J, Duff RS. Physician status characteristics and client satisfaction in two types of medical practice. *J Health Soc Behav*. 1982;23:317–329.

26. Wasserman RC, Inui TS, Barriatua RD, Carter WB, Lippincott P. Pediatric clinicians' support for parents makes a difference: an outcome-based analysis of clinician-parent interaction. *Pediatrics*. 1984;74:1047–1053.

27. Cooper-Patrick L, Ford DE, Vu HT, Powe NR, Steinwachs DM, Roter DL. Patient-physician race concordance and communication in primary care. *J Gen Intern Med*. 2000;15:106.

28. Baker DW, Hayes R, Fortier JP. Interpreter use and satisfaction with interpersonal aspects of care for Spanish-speaking patients. *Med Care.* 1998;36(10):1461–1470.

29. Collins KS, Hughes DL, Doty MM, Ives BL, Edwards JN, Tenney K. *Diverse Communities, Common Concerns: Assessing Health Care Quality for Minority Americans.* New York, NY: The Commonwealth Fund; 2002.

30. Report of the National Work Group on Literacy and Health. Communicating with patients who have limited literacy skills. *J Fam Pract.* 1998;46(2):168–176.

31. Williams MV, Parker RM, Baker DW, et al. Inadequate functional health literacy among patients at two public hospitals. *JAMA.* 1995;274(21):1677–1682.

32. Cooper LA, Roter DL, Johnson RL, Ford DE, Steinwachs DM, Powe NR. Patient-centered communication in race-concordant and race-discordant primary care visits. *Ann Intern Med.* 2003;139:907–915.

33. Baker DW, Parker RM, Williams MV, Clark WS, Nurss J. The relationship of patient reading ability to self-reported health and use of health services. *Am J Public Health.* 1997;87(6):1027–1030.

34. Baker DW. Reading between the lines: deciphering the connections between literacy and health. *J Gen Intern Med.* 1999;14(5):315–317.

35. Baker DW, Gazmararian JA, Sudano J, Patterson M, Parker RM, Williams MV. Health literacy and performance on the Mini-Mental State Examination. *Aging Ment Health.* 2002;6(1):22–29.

36. Gazmararian J, Baker D, Parker R, Blazer DG. A multivariate analysis of factors associated with depression: evaluating the role of health literacy as a potential contributor. *Arch Intern Med.* 2000;160(21):3307–3314.

37. Strull WM, Lo B, Charles G. Do patients want to participate in medical decision making? *JAMA.* 1984;252(21):2990–2994.

38. Arora NK, McHorney CA. Patient preferences for medical decision making: who really wants to participate? *Med Care.* 2000;38(3):335–341.

39. Adams RJ, Smith BJ, Ruffin RE. Impact of the physician's participatory style in asthma outcomes and patient satisfaction. *Ann Allergy Asthma Immunol.* 2001;86(3):263–271.

40. Pendleton L, House WC. Preferences for treatment approaches in medical care. College students versus diabetic outpatients. *Med Care.* 1984;22(7):644–646.

41. Baker DW, Parker RM, Williams MV, et al. The health care experience of patients with low literacy. *Arch Fam Med.* 1996;5(6):329–334.

42. Parikh NS, Parker RM, Nurss JR, Baker DW, Williams MV. Shame and health literacy: the unspoken connection. *Patient Educ Couns.* 1996;27(1):33–39.

43. Roter DL, Rudd RE, Comings J. Patient literacy. A barrier to quality of care. *J Gen Intern Med.* 1998;13(12):850–851.

44. Williams MV, Baker DW, Parker RM, Nurss JR. Relationship of functional health literacy to patients' knowledge of their chronic disease. A study of patients with hypertension and diabetes. *Arch Intern Med.* 1998;158(2):166–172.

45. Williams MV, Baker DW, Honig EG, Lee TM, Nowlan A. Inadequate literacy is a barrier to asthma knowledge and self-care. *Chest.* 1998;114(4):1008–1015.

46. Gazmararian JA, Parker RM, Baker DW. Reading skills and family planning knowledge and practices in a low-income managed-care population. *Obstet Gynecol.* 1999;93(2):239–244.

47. Lindau ST, Tomori C, Lyons T, Langseth L, Bennett CL, Garcia P. The association of health literacy with cervical cancer prevention knowledge and health behaviors in a multiethnic cohort of women. *Am J Obstet Gynecol.* 2002;186(5):938–943.

48. Scott TL, Gazmararian JA, Williams MV, Baker DW. Health literacy and preventive health care use among Medicare enrollees in a managed care organization. *Med Care.* 2002;40(5):395–404.

49. Schillinger D, Piette J, Grumbach K, et al. Closing the loop: physician communication with diabetic patients who have low health literacy. *Arch Intern Med.* 2003;163(1):83–90.

50. Schillinger D, Bindman A, Stewart A, Wang F, Piette J. Health literacy and the quality of physician-patient interpersonal communication. *Pat Educ Couns.* 2004;3:315–323.

51. Liao L, Jollis JG, DeLong ER, Peterson ED, Morris KG, Mark DB. Impact of an interactive video on decision making of patients with ischemic heart disease. *J Gen Intern Med.* 1996;11(6):373–376.

52. Schapira MM, Meade C, Nattinger AB. Enhanced decision-making: the use of a videotape decision-aid for patients with prostate cancer. *Patient Educ Couns.* 1997;30(2):119–127.

53. Whelan T, Gafni A, Charles C, Levine M. Lessons learned from the Decision Board: a unique and evolving decision aid. *Health Expect.* 2000;3(1):69–76.

54. Gomella LG, Albertsen PC, Benson MC, Forman JD, Soloway MS. The use of video-based patient education for shared decision-making in the treatment of prostate cancer. *Semin Urol Oncol.* 2000;18(3):182–187.

55. DePalma A. Prostate Cancer Shared Decision: a CD-ROM educational and decision-assisting tool for men with prostate cancer. *Semin Urol Oncol.* 2000;18(3):178–181.

56. O'Connor AM, Stacey D, Entwistle V, et al. Decision aids for people facing health treatment or screening decisions. *Cochrane Database Syst Rev.* 2003;(2):CD001431. Review.

57. Kim SP, Knight SJ, Tomori C, et al. Health literacy and shared decision making for prostate cancer patients with low socioeconomic status. *Cancer Invest*. 2001;19(7):684–691.

58. Cooper LA, Roter DL, Bone LR, Miller E, et al. Patient-physician partnership to improve high blood pressure adherence. *Circulation*. 2004;109:293.

59. Elwyn G, Edwards A, Mowle S, et al. Measuring the involvement of patients in shared decision-making: a systematic review of instruments. *Patient Educ Couns*. 2001;43(1):5–22.

60. Frosch DL, Kaplan RM. Shared decision making in clinical medicine: past research and future directions. *Am J Prev Med*. 1999;17(4):285–294.

61. Masi CM, Suarez-Balcazar Y, Cassey MZ, Kinney L, Piotrowski ZH. Internet access and empowerment. *J Gen Intern Med*. 2003;18(7):525–530.

chapter 8

The Challenges of Informed Consent for Low-Literate Populations

Michael K. Paasche-Orlow, MD, MA, MPH

> *The object of language is not to bemuse grammarians, but to convey ideas, and the more simply it accomplishes that object the more effectively it meets the needs of an energetic and practical people.*
> —H. L. Mencken,
> *The American Language, 1921.*[1]

Many of the activities of health care and medical research are outside the bounds of normal social interaction. Clinicians, investigators, and the institutions they work for protect themselves against claims of impropriety with the doctrine of informed consent. For example, under normal circumstances, when a surgeon suggests an operation, the surgeon cannot proceed unless the patient agrees. This agreement must be based on a fair understanding of what to expect from the surgery. The surgeon has an obligation to teach the patient about the risks, benefits, and alternatives to the proposed procedure. With this information, the patient can decide to refuse or accept the operation.

Although patient comprehension is crucial to the informed consent process, elements of the consent process have consistently been found to be highly formal and complex.[2–12] This complexity presents a major barrier to comprehension for all patients but especially for approximately one quarter of the adult population in the United States with low literacy skills.[13]

Because informed consent is a communication process, many themes that emerge in this chapter mirror those of other chapters that explore the role of health literacy in physician-patient communication. Concern for the protection of rights for low-literate adults is especially salient in

the case of informed consent, because the ethical and legal obligations
inherent in this type of communication process may not be fulfilled
by typical patterns of practice. Essentially, low-literate adults are a
vulnerable population with respect to informed consent.[14] This vulnera-
bility is also a danger for providers. When the consent process is
inadequate, health care providers not only fail in their professional
and ethical obligation but are exposed to liability.[15–18]

While many features of the traditional informed-consent process are
known to be challenging for low-literate patients, there is still much
unexplored territory. This chapter evaluates the role of health literacy
in various aspects of the informed-consent process. Specifically, the
chapter discusses formal and informal consent; barriers experienced by
low-literate patients, challenges to preserving patient rights, the reliability of informed-consent forms, and consent as a protection of human
subjects. The chapter concludes with suggestions for future research
and advocacy to promote the autonomy of low-literate adults.

INFORMAL AND FORMAL CONSENT

In extreme circumstances (eg, delirium, incompetence, or dangerous-
ness), health care providers may have a positive duty and legal
obligation to oppose a patient's stated wishes. However, generally, people do not cede their right of self-determination by becoming a patient.
Negotiating the details of what health providers may do with patients
during the course of treatment is the arena of informed consent. While
much of the consent literature has focused on written documents,
these represent only a small part of physician-patient interactions
involving informed consent.[19] Most consent is elicited informally and
sometimes nonverbally; indeed, it is the minority of instances in which
informed consent is confirmed in writing. While the issue of low
literacy tends to be raised exclusively for formal written consent documents, low-literate patients may have difficulty with comprehension in
multiple aspects of the informed-consent process.[20]

Typically, higher medical risk (including risk of physical, economic,
psychological, and social harm) is associated with a more formalized
consent procedure. For example, invasive surgery is almost always
accompanied by an executed informed-consent document, while many
simple, low-risk procedures and tests may proceed with a head nod.[21]
However, rules for what types of activities require formalized consent
are difficult to discern. HIV and genetic testing are done subsequent to
counseling and the completion of written informed-consent documents.
However, this is not typical for other tests like syphilis testing, despite
mandatory reporting laws and the implicit risk for loss of privacy.

The level of risk that will trigger the use of more formalized consent
procedures is highly variable. Myriad factors—including local convention,

legal constraints, personal preference, and training—influence the type of informed-consent process that is considered appropriate for various clinical interactions. Patients cannot assume that the absence of a formal process implies the relative safety or appropriateness of clinical decisions. For example, medication regimens with important risks and side effects are often initiated without a signed document in primary care.

BARRIERS EXPERIENCED BY LOW-LITERATE PATIENTS IN THE INFORMED-CONSENT PROCESS

Theoretical and empirical evaluations of informed consent and decision-making have established the elements needed to ensure that patients have attained substantive and meaningful informed consent.[17, 21–25] Table 8-1 exhibits these elements and notes specific ways patients with low literacy may have difficulty with the consent process.

Decision-Making Capacity

According to Table 8-1, a starting condition is assessment of decision-making capacity. Because low literacy has been shown to decrease performance on several commonly used neuropsychiatric tests, it is possible that some low-literate adults, particularly the elderly, will be wrongly classified as incompetent.[26–28] Misclassification may result in fewer attempts to obtain informed consent directly from the patient and greater reliance on family members or other proxies.

Process of Decision-Making

Next, Table 8-1 represents informed consent as a process that includes multiple levels of communication. An underlying feature of patient-physician communication involves establishing the model of relationship that will guide the informed-consent process; in paternalistic decisions the physician is dominant; the reverse is true in a consumer model, and in a collaborative decision-making relationship a balance is established.[29] While the informed consent process need not conform exactly to a theoretical model, insight into the dynamics of decision-making allows clinicians and patients to adjust their communication accordingly.

Because informed consent is an ongoing interactive process, features of the clinical encounter that interfere with physician-patient communication are also barriers to informed consent.[30] Among the typical communication barriers that may complicate physician–patient communication, several are common, particularly for low-literate patients (eg, socioeconomic differences, general physician-patient differences, and cultural differences).[31] Haste and the use of technical jargon by health care providers and investigators are common

TABLE 8-1

Areas of Concern for Low-Literate Adults in Informed Consent

Elements of Informed Consent*	Possible Concerns
Patient has decision-making capacity	Literacy may affect assessment of competence
Process of decision-making†:	
Paternalism — "You're the doctor; you tell me what to do."	May have anxiety from collaborative decision-making or choose a Paternalistic Model to not be exposed as low literate
Consumerism — "Tell me about this so I can make my decision."	
Collaboration — "Let's talk about this and decide together."	
■ Characteristics of the primary option being offered	May be overly influenced by physician's opinion or have problem with numeracy or number and order of alternatives
■ Risks of primary option	
■ Benefits of primary option `[Often presented as numerical estimate]`	
■ Degree of uncertainty	
■ Alternatives to primary option	
■ What is implied by consent	May have misconception about the legal implications of consent
■ Lack of coercion	May be reluctant to admit lack of understanding, ask questions, or contradict the physician
■ Confirm authenticity of choice	
■ Confirm understanding	
■ Confirm preferences	
■ Confirm decision	

Information Exchange

Consent (Voluntariness)

*Elements of informed consent collected from theoretical and empirical research as described in text.

pitfalls.[32] Even nontechnical health terms are often interpreted differently by physicians and patients with little education.[33]

In addition, the nature of these barriers depends on the etiology of low functional literacy. Functional literacy is predicated on having adequate vision, reading ability, and cognitive capacity. Stigma may preclude open disclosure of such deficits. Many low-literate adults experience their illiteracy as shameful and use a range of techniques to hide their deficiency.[34,35] Indeed, they are often successful; most physicians are not able to identify which of their patients are functionally illiterate.[36–38] Furthermore, people have varied levels of insight about their functional limitations.

Paternalism as a model for physician-patient communication and decision-making may be an authentic choice embraced by patients for a myriad of reasons. However, if this hierarchical model is chosen because of a stigmatizing condition, the freedom with which this choice is made is limited. Generally, people who do not feel empowered to engage in a collaborative decision-making process with their providers should be supported to do so.

Information Exchange

In Table 8-1, the next element of informed consent involves information exchange. For decisions to be substantively informed, people need to be informed of and understand five content domains: (1) the essential features of the option under consideration, (2) the potential risks, (3) the potential benefits, (4) the degree of uncertainty surrounding these items, and (5) the alternatives. Unfortunately, there is a very large gap between theory and practice. In an evaluation of 540 hospitals' informed consent for procedure forms, only 26.4% of these forms included information on all four central content areas evaluated: nature of procedure, risks, benefits, and alternatives.[39]

Numerous studies have shown that low-literate patients have a lower fund of knowledge about their medical conditions than other patients.[40–43] Because of this, low-literate patients may need to overcome a larger informational hurdle to be in a position to comprehend these content domains. Furthermore, particular aspects of these content domains are commonly presented in a manner that may be problematic for low-literate patients. For example, clinicians often depict risks, benefits, and the degree of certainty in statistical terms. Because numeracy is an integral component of functional literacy, fulfilling these domains of informed consent may be a particular challenge for low-literate adults.

A sixth content domain that is easily overlooked relates to the basic meaning and implication of consent. Consent is an authorization that allows a provider or investigator to do something he or she would not otherwise do. The significance of this authorization depends on the context, but patients and physicians may understand this aspect of informed consent differently. Patients need to understand that consent constitutes a limited authorization and should not get the impression that signing an informed-consent form involves signing away any rights they otherwise retain.[17] The meaning of the authorization put in motion by informed consent is often unarticulated and not evaluated in research. It is unclear if low-literate patients have more difficulty than other patients do in apprehending this aspect of informed consent.

Consent (Voluntariness)

The final element of informed consent in Table 8-1 deals with the consent itself. For decisions to be substantively voluntary, they must be made without coercion and must represent the patient's actual intentions; confirmation of the authenticity of a patient's decision has been recommended.[44] For example, comparison of the current decision being made to prior decisions can help make a person's values over time more explicit. While there is no requirement that a person's decisions correspond with their stated values, many people want their health care decisions to reflect their values; discordance may reflect a departure from prior ethical commitments or may simply be evidence of misunderstanding. There are subtle ways that the authenticity of a person's decision can be compromised. Cognitive research in decision-making has shown that patients' choices are sensitive to the order and number of alternatives they are given and that people often choose options that run counter to their stated desires.[45] While these findings have not yet been evaluated in patients with low literacy, such patients may have a low sense of their own decisional authority and may have more anxiety than other patients when presented with a set of alternatives.

Furthermore, patients are highly influenced by recommendations presented by physicians.[46] Low-literate patients with a lower sense of self-efficacy may have even more difficulty opposing the authority of the physician than other patients. Consequently, low-literate patients may incorrectly experience a physician's description of the primary option as a Hobson's choice—a situation in which you have to take the one poor option that is offered or get nothing at all.

Note that Table 8-1 represents informed consent as a discrete episode of decision-making and does not capture the complexity that is introduced by an ongoing process with multiple parties over time.[30, 47] Time is needed for education and to allow for synthesis of complicated ideas and the application of personal values by the patient. Time is also needed for confirmation of patient understanding, preferences, and decisions by the health care provider. The process is not over when a document is signed. Opportunity for discussion with family and other confidants may solidify a person's decision or provoke concern and introduce uncertainty. Questions and answers continue to be relevant to reinforce not only the central elements of the decision but also the physician-patient relationship itself. Asking patients to recount key information may be an effective method of confirming understanding.[48] While a form may be used at a particular time to document a decision, ongoing information exchange is crucial. The act of signing may give the impression that discussion has been closed off or irreparably sealed.

While each element of informed consent need not be the focus of explicit deliberation in every clinical decision,[49] observation studies regarding how many of the essential domains of informed consent are actually used in clinical decision-making have shown that norms clearly fail ethical standards.[19,21,50] For example, audiotape analysis of 81 ambulatory care visits revealed that in only 2% of the 262 clinical decisions evaluated was there any assessment of patient understanding.[51]

CHALLENGES TO PRESERVING PATIENT RIGHTS IN FORMALIZED INFORMED CONSENT

The act of signing a consent form is typically reserved for the most formal types of informed consent such as for invasive surgical procedures, the receipt of blood products, or the recruitment of human subjects for research. There are different ways to formally designate that a decision has been made. Physicians and patients can write and sign a contract or review and sign a preprinted contract. These documents may be cosigned, witnessed, copied, and filed.

These activities confirm that a decision was made at a specific time. Unfortunately, such formality has similar attributes to other signed legal agreements and contracts, and people may mistakenly apply attributes of other documents they sign to the informed-consent context. In the recruitment of human subjects, federal regulations preclude the use of exculpatory language in informed consent forms that would "waive or appear to waive any of the subject's rights" to pursue compensation for injury.[52] However, this is exactly the purpose of the liability waivers people sign in nonmedical contexts, and low-literate adults may associate the legal formalities of informed-consent forms with such a waiver of rights.[53]

The Federal Office for Human Research Protection (OHRP) encourages careful wording of informed-consent language to ensure that subjects do not think they give up any rights when they sign consent forms.[54] However, failure appears commonplace. As one researcher noted, "It is doubtful that many subjects understand these studied attempts to protect the institution. The researcher, who supposedly is seeking informed consent, rarely will be able to explain the statement.

Thus, the very essence of the relation of informed consent between subject and investigator is compromised."[55]

If comprehension has been compromised, the consent may be nullified. Medical malpractice case law supports functional illiteracy as a basis for overriding an executed consent form. For example, the Intermediate Court of Appeals of Hawaii, in a 1991 opinion nullifying an informed consent form due to a patient's low literacy, stated that it would "pervert the law of informed consent to allow a physician to discharge his or her affirmative duty by merely securing a signature—even that of a...confused or uneducated patient on an abstruse, jargon-ridden, and largely unintelligible preprinted consent form."[56]

The Food and Drug Administration (FDA) has also established a special obligation to protect the rights of illiterate individuals during the consent process and warns that:

> Clinical investigators should be cautious when enrolling subjects who may not truly understand what they have agreed to do. The Institutional Review Board (IRB) should consider illiterate persons as likely to be vulnerable to coercion and undue influence and should determine that appropriate additional safeguards are in place when enrollment of such persons is anticipated.[57]

Despite these concerns, the FDA offers no guidance for literacy assessment and does not elaborate criteria for assessment of "illiterate individuals." The only hint regarding their definition of illiteracy is from guidance that states: "Illiterate persons who understand English may have the consent read to them and 'make their mark,' if appropriate under applicable state law." This is neither adequate guidance for managing the barriers presented by low literacy nor an adequate operational definition of illiteracy. Most of the 40 to 44 million American adults estimated to be functionally illiterate are able to sign their names without difficulty.[13]

In most circumstances where formalized consent is used, both clinician and patient may benefit from the procedure. Where there is risk of bodily harm, possible dissatisfaction, high cost, abuse, or potential exposure to discrimination for the patient, there is also risk of potential liability for the provider. The overwhelming complexity of many formalized consent materials, however, is evidence that the central focus of formalization is not patient education but an attempt to avoid professional liability.

READABILITY OF INFORMED-CONSENT FORMS

Most adults admit to not reading consent forms.[58] This is not surprising as informed-consent forms are too long, have poor layout, use font sizes that are too small for many readers, and use unexplained medical jargon and legal patois. Despite decades of reports decrying this problem, informed-consent forms have largely remained complex and are getting longer.[59,60]

Expanding disclosure obligations have exacerbated this trend.[61,62] For example, in an attempt to protect patients' privacy rights, the recent Health Insurance Portability and Accountability Act (HIPAA) has added a considerable amount of additional text to consent forms. The current informed-consent form HIPAA section required for the recruitment of human subjects at Johns Hopkins is comparatively brief at 727 words long, or roughly 2½ pages (www.hopkinsmedicine. org/irb/jhmirb). Because marginal readers read simple text at 80 to 160 words per minute, this one mandatory section will add about 9 minutes of reading time.[63] While it is possible that a low-literate reader could make it through the text, it is unlikely that poor readers will sustain such an effort.

Research on readability analysis was initiated more than 75 years ago to evaluate grade-school textbooks.[64,65] Since then, dozens of techniques have been developed. These analysis systems operate with word lists and evaluate cognitive and organizational complexity, and/or by means of formulas based on text characteristics, such as average word length (semantics) and average sentence length (syntactics). No word-list system has been validated for decades, and shifts in word use may have made these systems obsolete. An automated and combined approach with an updated word list would maximize the benefit of traditional readability measures.

One particular readability formula is the Flesch-Kincaid formula, which is based on average sentence length and the average number of syllables per word. Because the Flesch-Kincaid formula has been incorporated into Microsoft's word readability statistics, it has become broadly available and the most frequently used in the medical literature. Unfortunately, though it has been validated in adults up to a 16th-grade level, the formula is truncated erroneously at a 12th-grade level in Microsoft Word.[63, 66–68]Consequently, many studies that have used Flesch-Kincaid analysis likely present falsely low evaluations.

Readability formulas do not ensure that text will be understandable. For example, they are not able to identify authors who know the operating parameters of the formula and purposefully write in short but arcane argot and cant. The formulas serve to highlight problem areas and should never be the only tool used to ensure that text is clearly written.[69–72]

While the appropriate readability level will vary from setting to setting, many institutions set a particular grade-level readability standard and give the impression that documents will be acceptable providing they are written at a lower readability level than the chosen standard.[73] In a survey of US medical schools, grade-level readability

TABLE 8-2

Examples of Informed-Consent Text Provided by Institutional Review Boards at US Medical Schools*

Readability Level	Voluntary Participation	New Information About Risks	No Direct Benefits	Involuntary Removal
Fourth grade†	"You don't have to be in this research study. You can agree to be in the study now and change your mind later. Your decision will not affect your regular care. Your doctor's attitude toward you will not change."	"We may learn about new things that might make you want to stop being in the study. If this happens, you will be informed. You can then decide if you want to continue to be in the study."	"There is no benefit to you from being in the study. Your taking part may help patients in the future."‡	"You may be taken out of the study if: 1. Staying in the study would be harmful. 2. You need treatment not allowed in this study. 3. You fail to follow instructions. 4. You become pregnant. 5. The study is canceled." ‡
Sixth grade†	"Taking part in this study is your choice. If you decide not to take part, this will not harm your relations with your doctors or with the University."	"We may learn new things during the study that you may need to know. We can also learn about things that might make you want to stop participating in the study. If so, you will be notified about any new information."	"You may receive no direct benefit from being in this study. However, your taking part may help patients get better care in the future."	§
Eighth grade†	"Participation in this study is entirely voluntary. You have the right to leave the study at any time. Leaving the study will not result in any penalty or loss of benefits to which you are entitled."	"We will tell you about new information that may affect your willingness to stay in this study."	"There is no direct benefit to you from being in this study. However, your participation may help others in the future as a result of knowledge gained from the research."	"The study doctors have the right to end your participation in this study for any of the following reasons: 1. It would be dangerous for you to continue. 2. You do not follow study procedures as directed by the study doctors. 3. The sponsor decides to end the study."
Tenth grade¶	"Your participation in this study is voluntary and you are free to withdraw at any time. Participation or withdrawal will not affect any rights to which you are entitled."	"We will tell you about new information that may affect your health welfare or willingness to stay in this study."	"There is no guarantee that you will receive direct benefit from your participation in this study."	"The study doctor, per the sponsor, may stop my participation in this study without my consent."

Continued

T A B L E 8-2 (Continued)

Examples of Informed-Consent Text Provided by Institutional Review Boards at US Medical Schools*

Readability Level	Voluntary Participation	New Information About Risks	No Direct Benefits	Involuntary Removal
Twelfth grade¶	"Your participation in this study is strictly voluntary. You have the right to choose not to participate or to withdraw your participation at any point in this study without prejudice to your future health care or other services to which you are otherwise entitled."	"You will be promptly notified if any new information develops during the conduct of this research study, which may cause you to change your mind about continuing to participate. If new information becomes known that will affect you or might change your decision to be in this study, you will be informed by the investigator."	"There may be no direct benefit to me; however, information from this study may benefit other patients with similar medical problems in the future."	"You may be terminated from this study without your consent if you have serious side effects, you fail to follow your doctor's instructions, your disease gets worse, or the sponsor closes the study. If this should happen, your doctor can discuss other available treatment options with you."
College¶	"You voluntarily consent to participate in this research investigation. You may refuse to participate in this investigation or withdraw your consent and discontinue participation in this study without penalty and without affecting your future care or your ability to receive alternative medical treatment at the University."	"During the course of the study, you will be informed of any significant new findings (either good or bad), such as changes in the risks or benefits resulting from participation in the research or new alternatives to participation that might cause you to change your mind about continuing in the study. If new information is provided to you, your consent to continue participating in this study will be re-obtained."	"The research physician treats all subjects under a specific protocol to obtain generalizable knowledge and on the premise that you may or may not benefit from your participation in the study."	"Your participation in this research project may be terminated by your doctor without your consent if you are not benefiting from the treatment/procedure, or if the treatment/procedure is determined to be inappropriate to your case. You may also be terminated from participation at any time, at the study physician's discretion, for any reason he/she deems appropriate."

*All the examples are taken directly from medical-school Web sites, unless otherwise noted.

† The readability level is based on the Flesch-Kincaid readability scale.

‡ The passage was modified to present key concepts at a fourth-grade reading level.

§ No passage was found at this reading level.

¶ The readability level is based on the Fry readability formula.

Source: Paasche-Orlow MK, Taylor HA, Brancati FL. Readability standards for informed-consent forms as compared with actual readability. *N Engl J Med.* 2003;348:721–726.

standards for informed consent documents ranged from a fifth-grade readability level to a 10th-grade level.[73] The most commonly cited grade level for a readability standard in this study was an eighth-grade level. However, this standard is neither based on the epidemiology of local rates of low literacy nor actually fulfilled in the template text presented by these same institutions.

Indeed, only 8% of US medical schools met their own target standards in the template language they promulgate. The template language is produced by the institution and is typically used as a boilerplate to build study-specific informed consent documents. See Table 8-2 for template text excerpts from US medical schools written at different grade levels. The mean observed Flesch-Kincaid readability level of the template text in this study was 10.6-2.8 ($P < .001$) grade levels higher than stated standards. The magnitude of this disparity was amplified by application of the Fry readability formula, which is based on the number of sentences and syllables in three 100-word passages. In a representative subsample of 24 texts, modal readability was 13th grade (range, sixth to 16th) and the mean was 13.0.[73] These examples show that institutional review boards charged with safeguarding people with limited literacy[51,52] may ironically play an inadvertent role in promulgating unreadable forms.

CONSENT AS A PROTECTION OF HUMAN SUBJECTS

The highest standards for consent are applied to the recruitment of human subjects for medical research. The OHRP has identified readability of informed-consent forms as a priority area in its review process. Informed consent for medical research is particularly sensitive because comprehension beyond the requisite of usual care is required and there are historic concerns about exploitation of vulnerable populations.[74]

A great deal has changed over the last 50 years in human subjects research. In a landmark study in 1966, Beecher reviewed the ethics of 50 studies and found that consent was mentioned in only 2 studies. He wrote: "If suitably approached, patients will accede, on the basis of trust, to about any request their physician may make."[75] Beecher supported mandating informed consent for research but also felt that such consent would be a safeguard for patient protection only in the hands of responsible investigators. Furthermore, he felt that the best informed-consent forms are meaningless if investigators do not engage the process with integrity.

A particular barrier to informed consent in research is the broad misunderstanding of the central concepts of medical research and the pivotal vocabulary commonly used to describe them. For example, more than three quarters of subjects do not understand the word "randomly."[54,76,77] To achieve systemic change in the readability of informed-consent forms for research, institutional review boards will need to improve the template and sample text offered to investigators. Federal review appears to improve readability of informed-consent text offered to investigators; in fact, US medical schools that have undergone federal compliance oversight were found to have informed-consent form templates with better readability than those that had not undergone such review. In addition, models already exist to aid interested medical schools.[73] Institutions as diverse as the National Cancer Institute and the State University of New York Downstate Medical School have presented informed-consent templates and sample forms that are below an eighth-grade readability level.[78,79] These forms can serve as models for a national informed consent form template to markedly improve much of the current text offered by institutional review boards.

A randomized controlled trial of an easy-to-read informed consent form of 226 patients at 44 institutions revealed that an informed consent form with a decreased readability level was associated with less anxiety, higher satisfaction, and higher accrual rate.[80] Other studies have suggested that improved forms may decrease medical litigation[81] and that lowering readability levels of written materials improves patient satisfaction and comprehension for patients, even if they are fully literate.[82–85]

However, while lowering the readability level of informed-consent documents is crucial, it does not ensure comprehension. Subjects commonly think they will personally have medical benefits from phase I protocols, despite enrolling with consent documents that say otherwise.[86] This type of confusion will not be completely ameliorated by improving the readability of the text. Improving methods for presenting information to potential research subjects is an ongoing challenge and is itself an enduring topic of randomized trials.[87,88] Ultimately, confirmation of comprehension is the safest approach.

CONCLUSION

Informed consent can be a technique for empowering patients and research subjects. It is also a technique for clinicians, investigators, and institutions to use to manage risk and liability. Both agendas will be advanced by improvements in the informed-consent process. The overwhelming complexity of many consent forms gives the impression that medical institutions seek to disempower their clients with obfuscatory confabulations.

With regard to informed-consent forms, it must be remembered that these educational documents are intended to facilitate the decision-making process.[39] An obvious barrier to fulfilling this purpose is the readability level of these documents. Many institutions have adopted an eighth-grade readability level as the upper limit of understandability, but in reality, this standard is too high. Furthermore, this standard is inconsistently adhered to in the template text presented by many institutions. As demonstrated in Table 8-2, the central concepts of informed consent can be written at a fourth grade level. Reasonable grade-level readability standards may remove the barrier of low literacy currently built into consent forms.

Quality control must be extended beyond the use of readability formulas. Readability formulas, such as the Flesch-Kincaid and Fry formulas, are ubiquitous, easy to use, and easy to fool. Adding a few periods and acronyms will improve a readability statistic more than actually advancing clarity or general understandability. Materials such as informed-consent documents should be developed and tested with target populations.[89–91]

Beyond shorter words and sentences, other techniques may help improve the comprehension of informed-consent materials. These techniques include modifying features such as font, layout, length, and conceptual complexity as well as using multimedia presentations, including video- and audiotape, and interactive computer programs.[7,71,92–103] There may also be a benefit to supplementing consent documents with systems, known as decision aids, that contextualize abstract risk concepts and compare the consequences of various options. These may take many forms, ranging from personalized risk profiles derived from questionnaires or computer programs that deliver tailored messages to interactive CD-ROM or Web-based instruction. Decision aids have been found to have a range of benefits in the communication of risk information, although they have not been specifically evaluated in low-literate populations. In particular, decision aids have been shown to improve knowledge, improve accuracy of risk/benefit assessment, promote shared decision-making, and improve concordance between patients' stated values and the decision to pursue cancer screening.[104–107] Future research may indicate that this approach to risk communication is useful in the informed consent process with low-literate patients.

The consent document and any ancillary materials, however, are simply tools of the communication process that must be present to ensure high-quality informed consent. The larger context of communication involves examining the assumptions and expectations that inform not only the specific decision that is being considered but also as the nature, purpose, and meaning of consent itself. Low-literate patients may be less likely to ask physicians questions to confirm their understanding. Research may confirm that a communication process in which patient questions are solicited and addressed is more likely to result in accurate patient understanding.

Unfortunately, the present culture of medical care allows routine abrogation of patient rights through a desultory and cursory approach to informed consent. Trainees are often sent to obtain a patient's consent without adequate training in the informed-consent process and without adequate knowledge of the procedure being offered.[108–113] Clinicians often view the process as "consenting a patient" rather than of helping a patient decide whether or not to pursue a particular option.[114] Part of this problem stems from the amount of time it may take to adequately perform the informed-consent process. It is possible that clinicians may be encouraged to invest the required amount of time if the consent process becomes a billable item, as has been done in Japan.[115]

A cultural shift toward a patient-centered model could significantly advance the opportunity for high-quality informed consent.[116,117] This may especially be true for low-literate patients who often know less about their medical conditions and may be less likely to question their health care providers. What are the patient's objectives for their care? What are the potential research subject's goals? If health professionals elicit responses to these core questions, they will be oriented to the patient's perspectives and level of understanding and have the opportunity to begin a dialogue that can lead to a successful informed-consent process.

Physicians and medical institutions have a responsibility and incentive to optimize the consent process. When informed-consent documents are at readability levels that exceed the reader's capacity, physicians and medical institutions fail a significant ethical precept and expose themselves to legal risk.[15,16] Beyond legal and ethical obligations, there is also a pragmatic benefit from having a fully informed constituency. Nonetheless, optimization of the informed-consent process should be driven primarily by the purpose of informed consent—namely, the education of patients—rather than fear of liability. After all, the transformation of the largely incomprehensible informed-consent process to clear, plain, and direct communication that conveys honesty and understanding is nothing less than what the "energetic and practical" people of our country deserve.

REFERENCES

1. Mencken HL. *The American Language: An Inquiry into the Development of English in the United States*. New York, NY: A.A. Knopf; 1921.

2. Fitzmaurice DA, Adams JL. A systematic review of patient information leaflets for hypertension. *J Hum Hypertens*. 2000;14:259–262.

3. Andrus MR, Roth MT. Health literacy: a review. *Pharmacother*. 2002;22:282–302.

4. Mohrmann CC, Coleman EA, Coon SK, et al. An analysis of printed breast cancer information for African American women. *J Cancer Educ.* 2000;15:23–27.

5. Gribble JN. Informed consent documents for BRCA1 and BRCA2 screening: how large is the readability gap? *Patient Educ Couns.* 1999; 38:175–183.

6. Grundner TM. On the readability of surgical consent forms. *N Engl J Med.* 1980;302:900–902.

7. Heinze-Lacey B, Saunders C, Sugar A. Improving the readability of informed consent documents. *IRB.* 1993;15:10–11.

8. Hearth-Holmes M, Murphy PW, Davis TC, et al. Literacy in patients with chronic disease: Systemic lupus erythematosus and the reading level of patient education materials. *J Rheumatol.* 1997;24:2335–2339.

9. Hopper KD, TenHave TR, Tully DA, Hall TE. The readability of currently used surgical/procedure consent forms in the United States. *Surgery.* 1998;123:496–503.

10. Meade CD, Byrd JC. Patient literacy and the readability of smoking education literature. *Am J Public Health.* 1989;79:204–206.

11. Morrow GR. How readable are subject consent forms? *JAMA.* 1980;244:56–58.

12. Wagner L, Davis S, Handelsman MM. In search of the abominable consent form: the impact of readability and personalization. *J Clin Psychol.* 1998;54:115–120.

13. Kirsch JS, Junegeblut A, Jenkins L, Kolstad A. Adult literacy in America: a first look at the results of the National Adult Literacy Survey (NALS). Washington, DC:US Department of Education; 1993.

14. Mazur D. Influence of the law on risk and informed consent. *BMJ.* 2003;327:731–734.

15. Health Literacy Project and consulting attorneys. *Literacy, Health, and the Law.* Philadelphia, Pa: Health Promotion Council of Southeastern Pennsylvania; 1996.

16. Pape T. Legal and ethical considerations of informed consent. *AORN J.* 1997;65:1122–1127.

17. Faden RR, Beauchamp TL. *A History and Theory of Informed Consent.* New York, NY: Oxford University Press; 1986.

18. Mello MM, Studdert DM, Brennan TA. The rise of litigation in human subjects research. *Ann Intern Med.* 2003;139:40–45.

19. Braddock CH, III, Fihn SD, Levinson W, Jonsen AR, Pearlman RA. How doctors and patients discuss routine clinical decisions: informed decision making in the outpatient setting. *J Gen Intern Med.* 1997;12:339–345.

20. Holmes-Rovner M, Wills CE. Improving informed consent: insights from behavioral decision research. *Med Care.* 2002;40:V30–V38.

21. Braddock CH III, Edwards KA, Hasenberg NM, Laidley TL, Levinson W. Informed decision making in outpatient practice: time to get back to basics. *JAMA*. 1999;282:2313–2320.

22. Jonsen AR. A map of informed consent. *Clin Res*.1975;23:277–279.

23. Nora LM, Benvenuti RJ III. Medicolegal aspects of informed consent. *Neurol Clin*. 1998;16:207–216.

24. Meisel A, Roth LH, Lidz CW. Toward a model of the legal doctrine of informed consent. *Am J Psychiatry*. 1977;134:285–289.

25. Meisel A, Kuczewski M. Legal and ethical myths about informed consent. *Arch Intern Med*. 1996;156:2521–2526.

26. Santacruz KS, Swagerty D. Early diagnosis of dementia. *Am Fam Physician*. 2001;63:703–708.

27. Weiss BD, Reed R, Kligman EW, Abyad A. Literacy and performance on the Mini-Mental State Examination. *J Am Geriatr Soc*. 1995;43:807–810.

28. Baker DW, Gazmararian JA, Sudano J, Patterson M, Parker RM, Williams MV. Health literacy and performance on the Mini-Mental Status Examination. *Aging Ment Health*. 2002;6:22–29.

29. Roter D, Hall JA. *Doctors Talking to Patients / Patients Talking to Doctors: Improving Communication in Medical Visits*. Westport, Conn: Auburn House; 1992.

30. Lidz CW, Meisel A, Osterweis M, Holden JL, Marx JH, Munetz MR. Barriers to informed consent. *Ann Intern Med*. 1983;99:539–543.

31. Quill TE. Recognizing and adjusting to barriers in doctor-patient communication. *Ann Intern Med*. 1989;111:51–57.

32. Bourhis RY, Roth S, MacQueen G. Communication in the hospital setting: a survey of medical and everyday language use amongst patients, nurses and doctors. *Soc Sci Med*. 1989;28:339–346.

33. Hadlow J, Pitts M. The understanding of common health terms by doctors, nurses and patients. *Soc Sci Med*. 1991;32:193–196.

34. Lazare A. Shame and humiliation in the medical encounter. *Arch Intern Med*. 1987;147:1653–1658.

35. Baker DW, Parker RM, Williams MV, et al. The health care experience of patients with low literacy. *Arch Fam Med*. 1996;5:329–334.

36. Bass PF III, Wilson JF, Griffith CH, Barnett DR. Residents' ability to identify patients with poor literacy skills. *Acad Med*. 2002; 77:1039–1041.

37. Lindau ST, Tomori C, Lyons T, Langseth L, Bennett CL, Garcia P. The association of health literacy with cervical cancer prevention knowledge and health behaviors in a multiethnic cohort of women. *Am J Obstet Gynecol*. 2002;186(5):938–943.

38. Montalto NJ, Spiegler GE. Functional health literacy in adults in a rural community health center. *WV Med J*. 2001;97:111–114.

39. Bottrell MM, Alpert H, Fischbach RL, Emanuel LL. Hospital informed consent for procedure forms: facilitating quality patient-physician interaction. *Arch Surg*. 2000;135:26–33.

40. Kalichman SC, Rompa D. Functional health literacy is associated with health status and health-related knowledge in people living with HIV-AIDS. *J Acquir Immune Defic Syndr*. 2000;25:337–344.

41. Kalichman SC, Benotsch E, Suarez T, Catz S, Miller J, Rompa D. Health literacy and health-related knowledge among persons living with HIV/AIDS. *Am J Prev Med*. 2000;18:325–331.

42. Williams MV, Baker DW, Honig EG, Lee TM, Nowlan A. Inadequate literacy is a barrier to asthma knowledge and self-care. *Chest*. 1998;114:1008–1015.

43. Williams MV, Baker DW, Parker RM, Nurss JR. Relationship of functional health literacy to patients' knowledge of their chronic disease: a study of patients with hypertension and diabetes. *Arch Intern Med*. 1998;158(2):166–172.

44. Nelson RM, Merz JF. Voluntariness of consent for research: an empirical and conceptual review. *Med Care*. 2002;40:V69–V80.

45. Ubel PA. Is information always a good thing? Helping patients make "good" decisions. *Med Care*. 2002;40:V39–V44.

46. Gurmankin AD, Baron J, Hershey JC, Ubel PA. The role of physicians' recommendations in medical treatment decisions. *Med Decis Making*. 2002;22:262–271.

47. Lidz CW, Appelbaum PS, Meisel A. Two models of implementing informed consent. *Arch Intern Med*. 1988;148:1385–1389.

48. Pizzi LT, Goldfarb NI, Nash DB. Procedures for obtaining informed consent. In: Shojania KG, Duncan BW, McDonald KM, eds. *Making Health Care Safer: A Critical Analysis of Patient Safety Practices*. Rockville, Md: Agency for Healthcare Research and Quality; 2001:546–554.

49. Sprung CL, Winick BJ. Informed consent in theory and practice: legal and medical perspectives on the informed consent doctrine and a proposed reconceptualization. *Crit Care Med*. 1989;17:1346–1354.

50. Wu WC, Pearlman RA. Consent in medical decision making: the role of communication. *J Gen Intern Med*. 1988;3:9–14.

51. Department of Health and Human Services, Office for Human Research Protection. *Institutional Review Board Guidebook*. Washington, DC: Government Printing Office; 1993.

52. National Archives and Records Administration, Office of the Federal Register. *Code of Federal Regulations*. Protection of Human Subjects. Title 45, 46.109 and 50.20. Washington, DC: Government Printing Office; 1993.

53. Cassileth BR, Zupkis RV, Sutton-Smith K, March V. Informed consent: why are its goals imperfectly realized? *N Engl J Med*. 1980;302:896–900.

54. Waggoner WC, Sherman BB. Who understands? II: A survey of 27 words, phrases, or symbols used in proposed clinical research consent forms. *IRB*. 1996;18:8–10.

55. Curran WJ. Compensation for injured research subjects. Regulation by informed consent. *N Engl J .Med*. 1979;20:648–649.

56. *Keomaka v. Zakaib*, 8 Haw. App. 533, 811P.2d 487, 6-7 (1991).

57. FDA/Office of Science Coordination and Communication. Guidance for Institutional Review Boards and Clinical Investigators. Available at: http://www.fda.gov/oc/ohrt/irbs/informedconsent.html#illiterate. Accessed August 30, 2003.

58. Lavelle-Jones C, Byrne DJ, Rice P, Cuschieri A. Factors affecting quality of informed consent. *BMJ*. 1993;306:885–890.

59. LoVerde ME, Prochazka AV, Byyny RL. Research consent forms: continued unreadability and increasing length. *J Gen Intern Med*. 1989;4:410–412.

60. Sugarman J, McCrory DC, Powell D, et al. Empirical research on informed consent: an annotated bibliography. *Hastings Cent Rep*. 1999;29:S1–S42.

61. LeBlang TR. Informed consent and disclosure in the physician-patient relationship: expanding obligations for physicians in the United States. *Med Law*. 1995;14:429–444.

62. Petrila J. The emerging debate over the shape of informed consent: can the doctrine bear the weight? *Behav Sci Law*. 2003;21:121–133.

63. Gray WB Jr. *How to Measure Readability*. Philadelphia, Pa: Dorrance & Company; 1975.

64. Klare GR. *The Measurement of Readability*. Ames, Iowa: The Iowa State University Press; 1963.

65. Chall JS, Dale E. *Readability Revisited: The New Dale-Chall Readability Formula*. Cambridge, Mass: Brookline Books;1995.

66. McLaughlin GH. SMOG Grading—New Readability Formula. *J Reading*. 1969;12:639–646.

67. Kincaid JP, Fishburne RP, Rogers RL, Chissom BS. Derivation of New Readability Formulas (Automated Readability Index, Fog Count, and Flesch Reading Ease formula) for Navy Enlisted Personnel. Research Branch Report. Chief of Naval Technical Training: Naval Air Station Memphis. 8–75. 1975.

68. Kincaid J, Gamble L. Ease of comprehension of standard and readable automobile insurance policies as a function of reading ability. *J Reading Behav*. 1977;9:85–87.

69. Hochhauser M. Some overlooked aspects of consent form readability. *IRB*. 1997;19:5–9.

70. Meade CD, Wittbrot R. Computerized readability analysis of written materials. *Comput Nurs*. 1988;6:30–36.

71. Peterson BT, Clancy SJ, Champion K, McLarty JW. Improving readability of consent forms: what the computers may not tell you. *IRB*. 1992;14:6–8.

72. Philipson SJ, Doyle MA, Gabram SG, Nightingale C, Philipson EH. Informed consent for research: a study to evaluate readability and processability to effect change. *J Investig Med*. 1995;43:459–467.

73. Paasche-Orlow MK, Taylor HA, Brancati FL. Readability standards for informed-consent forms as compared with actual readability. *N Engl J Med*. 2003;348:721–726.

74. The National Commission for the Protection of Human Subjects of Biomedical and Behavioral Research. The Belmont Report: Ethical Principles and Guidelines for the Protection of Human Subjects of Research. 4–18-1979.

75. Beecher HK. Ethics and clinical research. *N Engl J Med*.1966;274: 1354–1360.

76. Lawson SL, Adamson HM. Informed consent readability: subject understanding of 15 common consent form phrases. *IRB*. 1995;17:16–19.

77. Waggoner WC, Mayo DM. Who understands? A survey of 25 words or phrases commonly used in proposed clinical research consent forms. *IRB*. 1995;17:6–9.

78. Comprehensive Working Group on Informed Consent in Cancer Clinical Trials. Simplification of Informed Consent Documents. Available at www.cancer.gov/clinical_trials. Accessed August 30, 2003.

79. Padberg RM, Flach J. National efforts to improve the informed consent process. *Semin Oncol Nurs*. 1999;15:138–144.

80. Coyne CA, Xu R, Raich P, et al. Randomized, controlled trial of an easy-to-read informed consent statement for clinical trial participation: a study of the Eastern Cooperative Oncology Group. *J Clin Oncol*. 2003;21:836–842.

81. Faden RR, Becker C, Lewis C, Freeman J, Faden AI. Disclosure of information to patients in medical care. *Med Care*. 1981;19:718–733.

82. Meade CD, Byrd JC, Lee M. Improving patient comprehension of literature on smoking. *Am J Public Health*. 1989;79:1411–1412.

83. Davis TC, Holcombe RF, Berkel HJ, Pramanik S, Divers SG. Informed consent for clinical trials: a comparative study of standard versus simplified forms. *J Natl Cancer Inst*. 1998;90(9):668–674.

84. Jolly BT, Scott JL, Sanford SM. Simplification of emergency department discharge instructions improves patient comprehension. *Ann Emerg Med*. 1995;26:443–446.

85. Young DR, Hooker DT, Freeberg FE. Informed consent documents: increasing comprehension by reducing reading level. *IRB*. 1990;12:1–5.

86. Lidz CW, Appelbaum PS. The therapeutic misconception: problems and solutions. *Med Care*. 2002;40:V55–V63.

87. Lavori PW, Sugarman J, Hays MT, Feussner JR. Improving informed consent in clinical trials: a duty to experiment. *Control Clin Trials*. 1999;20:187–193.

88. Peduzzi P, Guarino P, Donta ST, Engel CC Jr, Clauw DJ, Feussner JR. Research on informed consent: investigator-developed versus focus group-developed consent documents, a VA cooperative study. *Control Clin Trials*. 2002;23:184–197.

89. Taub HA, Baker MT, Sturr JF. Informed consent for research. Effects of readability, patient age, and education. *J Am Geriatr Soc*. 1986;34:601–606.

90. Taylor HA. Barriers to informed consent. *Semin Oncol Nurs*. 1999;15:89–95.

91. Doak CC, Doak LG, Root JH. *Teaching Patients with Low-Literacy Skills*, 2nd ed. Philadelphia, Pa: JB Lippincott; 1996.

92. Berto D, Peroni M, Milleri S, Spagnolo AG. Evaluation of the readability of information sheets for healthy volunteers in phase-I trials. *Eur J Clin Pharmacol*. 2000;56:371–374.

93. Jimison HB, Sher PP, Appleyard R, LeVernois Y. The use of multimedia in the informed consent process. *J Am Med Inform Assoc*. 1998;5:245–256.

94. Bjorn E, Rossel P, Holm S. Can the written information to research subjects be improved?—an empirical study. *J Med Ethics*. 1999;25:263–267.

95. Doak CC, Doak LG, Friedell GH, Meade CD. Improving comprehension for cancer patients with low literacy skills: strategies for clinicians. *CA Cancer J Clin*. 1998;48:151–162.

96. Loughrey L. Improving readability of hospital forms. *J Nurs Staff Dev*. 1986;2:37–38.

97. Meade CD, Howser DM. Consent forms: how to determine and improve their readability. *Oncol Nurs Forum*. 1992;19:1523–1528.

98. Meade CD. Producing videotapes for cancer education: methods and examples. *Oncol Nurs Forum*. 1996;23:837–846.

99. Philipson SJ, Doyle MA, Nightingale C, Bow L, Mather J, Philipson EH. Effectiveness of a writing improvement intervention program on the readability of the research informed consent document. *J Investig Med*. 1999;47:468–476.

100. Barbour GL, Blumenkrantz MJ. Videotape aids informed consent decision. *JAMA*. 1978;240:2741–2742.

101. Benitez O, Devaux D, Dausset J. Audiovisual documentation of oral consent: a new method of informed consent for illiterate populations. *Lancet*. 2002;359:1406–1407.

102. Dunn LB, Lindamer LA, Palmer BW, Schneiderman LJ, Jeste DV. Enhancing comprehension of consent for research in older patients with psychosis: a randomized study of a novel consent procedure. *Am J Psychiatry*. 2001;158:1911–1913.

103. Weston J, Hannah M, Downes J. Evaluating the benefits of a patient information video during the informed consent process. *Patient Educ Couns*. 1997;30:239–245.

104. Paling J. Strategies to help patients understand risks. *BMJ*. 2003;327:745–748.

105. Gigerenzer G, Edwards A. Simple tools for understanding risks: from innumeracy to insight. *BMJ*. 2003;327:741–744.

106. O'Connor AM, Stacey D, Entwistle V, et al. Decision aids for people facing health treatment or screening decisions (Cochrane Review). In: The Cochrane Library, Issue 1. Chichester, UK: John Wiley & Sons, Ltd; 2004.

107. Holmes-Rovner M, Valade D, Orlowski C, Draus C, Nabozny-Valerio B, Keiser S. Implementing shared decision-making in routine practice: barriers and opportunities. *Health Expect*. 2000;3:182–191.

108. Yahne CE, Edwards WS. Learning and teaching the process of informed consent. *Proc Annu Conf Res Med Educ*. 1986;25:30–35.

109. Cohen DL, McCullough LB, Kessel RW, Apostolides AY, Heiderich KJ, Alden ER. A national survey concerning the ethical aspects of informed consent and role of medical students. *J Med Educ*. 1988;63:821–829.

110. Johnson SM, Kurtz ME, Tomlinson T, Fleck L. Teaching the process of obtaining informed consent to medical students. *Acad Med*. 1992;67:598–600.

111. Huntley JS, Shields DA, Stallworthy NK. Consent obtained by the junior house officer—is it informed? *JR Soc Med*. 1998;91:528–530.

112. Wear S. Enhancing clinician provision of informed consent and counseling: some pedagogical strategies. *J Med Philos*. 1999;24:34–42.

113. Srinivasan J. Observing communication skills for informed consent: an examiner's experience. *Ann R Coll Physicians Surg Can*. 1999;32:437–440.

114. Hope T. Don't 'consent' patients, help them to decide. *Health Care Anal*. 1996;4:73–76.

115. Akabayashi A, Fetters MD. Paying for informed consent. *J Med Ethics*. 2000;26:212–214.

116. Bridson J, Hammond C, Leach A, Chester MR. Making consent patient centred. *BMJ*. 2003;327:1159–1161.

117. Sullivan M. The new subjective medicine: taking the patient's point of view on health care and health. *Soc Sci Med*. 2003;56:1595–1604.

chapter 9

Using the Internet to Move Beyond the Brochure and Improve Health Literacy

Cynthia E. Baur, PhD

The Internet, it is said, has changed everything, including the way we think about reading and understanding texts. Other chapters in this book document the problems with the quality and utility of standard print health information for most everyone, and especially for low-literate persons. It is not yet clear if use of the Internet to deliver health information will exacerbate or mitigate these problems.[1,2] Will producers and distributors of health information continue to repackage standard public health brochures and patient education materials, creating a barrage of "brochureware" on demand? Or will they use the Internet to do something different to reach people in a more immediate and meaningful way than previously possible?

Not only are the quality and utility of health information important considerations, but there is also the issue of a "digital divide" that is, unequal access to and use of electronic devices and the Internet for low-literate persons. Access to the Internet cannot be taken for granted among many population groups, including low-literate and disabled populations and those 65 years and older. If low-literate persons also have limited access to the Internet, using technology to deliver enhanced health information is likely to deepen health and social disparities for vulnerable populations and leave them even further behind.[2,3] Even if they have access to the technology, inappropriate content diminishes the value of access.

This chapter considers these issues and examines the nature of informational resources available on the Internet and the accessibility of these resources to low-literate populations. Opportunities to use the Internet to enhance health literacy for vulnerable populations by increasing its utility, attractiveness, and interactivity as a health information source are also explored.

THE DEMOGRAPHICS OF INTERNET ACCESS

Before considering the types of health information on the Internet, it is important to know who has access to the Internet and is likely to use it as a health information source. Identifying who uses the Internet and for what is a burgeoning business; it seems that everyone wants to know who is on the Internet and what he or she is doing there. Estimates of the number of persons in the United States who use the Internet in general and for health-related purposes vary. There are data for many aspects of Internet use, including numbers of both households and individuals with computers and Internet connections. There are also data for the number of individuals who search the Internet for health information and estimates of the number of searches conducted by searchers for themselves and on behalf of others. The US Census Bureau fields a supplement approximately every 2 to 3 years that asks respondents about their ownership of computers and other electronic devices and if these devices are connected to the Internet. Based on this data, the Department of Commerce has issued a series of reports on the nature and scope of the digital divide. The most current data from the Census indicate that 54% of the US population had Internet access in September 2001.[4]

Because of concern that the digital divide will exacerbate health disparities for poor, minority, and low-literate populations, the US Department of Health and Human Services uses Census Bureau data to report on households with access to the Internet in the *Healthy People 2010* national objective.[5] The 2003 National Assessment of Adult Literacy (NAAL), fielded by the National Center for Education Statistics, US Department of Education, will also consider the nature of the digital divide by collecting data on the proportion of persons with different levels of literacy and health literacy skills who use the Internet as an information source. The NAAL will also provide the first-ever national population measures of print health literacy. This information will be used for the *Healthy People 2010* objective to improve health literacy.[5]

On a much more frequent basis, commercial and nonprofit polling firms ask Americans about their Internet use and habits. The Pew Internet and American Life Project, a nonprofit research group that has conducted a series of surveys on Internet use and the impact of the Internet on different sectors of society, reports that, as of spring 2002, 58% of Americans had Internet access.[6] Even though Internet use is growing among minority, elderly, and lower-income and lower-education segments of the population, the characteristics listed in Table 9-1 are important for understanding who is more or less likely to use the Internet.

TABLE 9-1

Demographic Characteristics of Internet Users

More Likely to Use Internet	Less Likely to Use Internet
Younger	Older (>65 years)
Higher income	Lower income (< $50,000/year household)
Employed	Unemployed
Caucasian	African-American and Hispanic
More education	Less education (<high school diploma)
Suburban and urban	Rural
Parents with children at home	Nonparents

Adapted from Lenart A. The ever-shifting Internet population. Washington, DC: The Pew Internet & American Life Project. Available at www.pewinternet.org. Accessed June 2, 2003.

Although many individuals who lack Internet access cite barriers of cost, lack of a computer, concerns about safety, and the difficulty and time involved in learning how to use new technology, not everyone reports lack of Internet access as a problem. More than half of the 42% of Americans without Internet access say they do not want or need the Internet.[6] This response was most frequently given by older respondents, women, rural and suburban dwellers, and Caucasians. Despite an increasing social, political, and commercial environment in which the Internet and the Web have penetrated virtually all aspects of life, resistance to Internet use on the basis of utility is worrisome and indicates that there may not yet be a compelling reason for many people to think of the Internet as a primary source of relevant information.

BARRIERS TO INTERNET USE
FOR LOW-LITERATE PERSONS

Numerous barriers to Internet use for low-literate persons have been identified. These include the technical skills needed to access and utilize the Internet, the reading skills needed to read and understand information on the Internet, and the demands of seeking health information in an electronic environment.

Technical Skills as a Barrier

When the Internet is the channel for health information, gaining access is the first hurdle for low-literate persons; knowing how to use technology is the second. Other chapters in this book describe the skills and demands involved in reading typical health materials, navigating the health care and public health systems, and understanding unfamiliar terms and practices. It is not difficult to appreciate that the same barriers are transferred to the Internet and compounded by the need to acquire additional skills to use the Internet and Internet-access devices, such as computers.[7-9] Additional barriers are created because most Web sites are inaccessible for people with visual, cognitive, or motor disabilities, including the elderly who may experience age-associated declines in function.

Unlike the print world in which the skills of reading and using print materials (eg, books, pamphlets, and handouts) are learned simultaneously, individuals bring whatever literacy skills and health knowledge they have to the new context of electronic technologies. Using the Internet for health information requires not only reading skills and familiarity with health vocabularies, practices, and systems but also multiple new skills related to the use of technology and the way that information is organized.[10] Individuals must make decisions about what kinds of technology are appropriate for gaining access to the types of information they want. They must learn how to operate different technologies by typing in queries, touching screens, moving a mouse, and opening a Web browser. There are also the conventions of Web pages—scrolling and using radio buttons, hyperlinks, and search boxes—that require users to move around a space and make multiple decisions, including where to focus their attention, the relevance of the information that appears, and the relationships among the information on a screen. Each technical demand adds layers of complexity to the health literacy challenge.[9]

One project that examined low-literate learners' ability to use Internet-based materials for literacy education found that, even when Web content had been designed to meet their literacy needs, limited prior experience with computers and the Internet presented an obstacle to use.[11] The researchers noted that sufficient practice with technology was required before learners could proceed with content training. A second finding was that, even though learners developed a basic understanding of how to use computers and the Internet, skills did not always carry over from one information-seeking session to the next. In other words, low-literate learners faced essentially a new task of sorting and organizing information each time they accessed the Web. If future research confirms this finding, it will lend strength to the theory that low-literate users may find it difficult to develop the sophisticated health-information–seeking skills that they will need to navigate the Internet successfully and adapt to changing technologies.

Reading Skills as a Barrier

Print has long been a central means for communicating health information and it remains central to the Internet world. A key barrier for low-literate persons using the Internet for health information is the continued dominance of print as the preferred way to present information and the high-literacy demands placed on information seekers. Although the history of print brochures as a public health and health education tool is not well documented, it is likely that the rise in use of print materials to transmit health information was associated with the increasing complexity of and knowledge about health conditions and treatments at the turn of the 20th century.[12] As scientific knowledge about the causes and consequences of disease advanced, complex compendiums of medical information became increasingly commonplace. Health professionals needed some way to capture large amounts of information for reference and simultaneously transmit this information to the public in general and to affected patients in particular.[12] Consequently, patient education materials tend to reflect medical and public health perspectives and burden readers with medical terms and complex formats that impair comprehension and utility.

It is clear that the first wave of the Internet has involved transferring the idiom and practices of print publishing to the Internet. Posting materials online is referred to as "electronic publishing," which links the printing press and pamphlets to electronic media and brochureware. The Internet has been referred to as the world's biggest library, implying that text and reading are currently key elements of Internet-based communication. Despite our culture's love of movies, music, and photographs and the attractiveness and excitement that these can add to communication, there are both technical and financial reasons for the Internet's current heavy dependence on text. Text is cheaper to create than multimedia content and can be more easily transmitted over slower Internet connections than images and sound. Broadband connections, which are designed to carry multimedia content, have only recently become widely available and remain far more expensive than dial-up connections for the average user.

Since quite a bit of health information on the Internet has its origins in the print world and the electronic counterpart has tended to mimic the original source, the issue of reader burden for Internet materials is of concern. Some experts have pointed out that developers of interactive health communication applications have a responsibility to consider the literacy skills of intended users.[13] Research on the readability of print materials on the Internet indicates that developers rarely meet this responsibility. One widely reported study from RAND Health (a research division of the RAND organization) reviewed Web sites with print materials for common health conditions.[14] It was found that all of the English-language and more than half of the Spanish-language materials tested at a ninth-grade readability level or higher. Based on comparisons with data from the 1992 NALS and other assessments of reading levels in populations of nonnative speakers of English, the RAND researchers concluded that "the reading level of health-related information provided on the Internet is too high for most English- and Spanish-speaking patients."[14]

Other studies on the readability of Web materials have yielded similar findings.[7,15,16] Researchers at the Children's Partnership, a research and advocacy organization for disadvantaged populations, estimate that Internet content does not meet the needs of at least 20% of Americans. For these users, the Web content is in the wrong language or at too high a readability level, based on incongruent cultural beliefs and values, not relevant to patient needs and interests; or inaccessible due to patient disabilities. Indeed, the Children's Partnership researchers conclude that only 5% of Web content of potential interest to low-literate users is in a format that could be used in a meaningful way.

Health-Information–Seeking Skills as a Barrier

The act of seeking out health information is particularly important in understanding the changing demands on literacy in an electronic environment. Although radio, television, newspapers, and magazines have typically been sources of health information for the general public, the Internet with its "on-demand" capabilities brings a new, active dimension to seeking health information.[13] The Internet invites users to take the initiative and become active seekers rather than passive recipients of information via traditional mass media.[2] Survey research indicates the public is turning to the Internet to meet a variety of health information needs. According to research from the Pew Internet and American Life Project, about two thirds of all Americans expect to find health information on the Internet.[17] Eighty percent of adult Internet users and about 50% of all adults have searched the Internet at least once for health information.[18] Even as Internet access has increased among lower-income and less-educated populations, educational attainment remains a reliable predictor of health information seeking; those with more education are more likely to look for health information online.[18] Research is needed to determine the extent to which low-literacy persons are "active" Internet health information seekers.

Much of the concern about how people search for health information on the Internet stems from two issues. The first is the quality of the information that is available on the Internet, and the second is the strategies that individuals use to find health information on the Internet. In both cases, researchers, health professionals, and policymakers are concerned that health information seekers are poorly served because the information itself and the search strategies used to locate the information are often of poor quality.[1,14,19] To help address the problem of poor quality, the US Department of Health and Human Services has set a *Healthy People 2010* national objective to improve the disclosure of information, which will allow users to assess the quality of health Web sites.[5] Another approach to quality improvement is use of quality standards and Web-site accreditation (see www.urac.org for an example). There is little research, however, on the utility of these approaches to help health information seekers assess the quality of Web sites and information. One small study found that participants did not check the "about us" disclaimers, and disclosure statements of the Web sites they found, nor could participants even recall the names of the Web sites they used.[19]

Preliminary research indicates that Internet information seekers typically do not use very sophisticated strategies to locate information. A common search strategy on the Internet is to type in one or two keywords into the search box of an Internet search engine and to receive an unmanageably long list of results in response. For health information searches, a frequently used search term is "health." Searchers typically look at 10 results per search session.[20] An ethnographic study of consumer search behavior found that searchers only looked at the first page of results and did not understand that many of the results were paid placements.[21] Even if the top search results are for reliable sources, such as government or academic Web sites, information seekers still have to work through many layers of Web pages before they arrive at some useful information in response to their initial query. The cognitive load of moving through pages of nonlinearly organized information is very high for most users, even when they have some familiarity with the subject matter, and it is far more difficult for the low-literate user.[22]

If the top results include a hodgepodge of information sources, some reliable and others not, users not only have to manage the navigational challenges but also meet the challenge of sorting out the sources that are reliable and worth their consideration. Assessing the quality of information on the Internet is difficult, especially when there are no generally accepted quality standards.[23,24] The credibility of health information on the Internet is even more difficult to assess when commercial appeals are packaged in unfamiliar ways or integrated in subtle ways with other content.[21] Sorting through commercial and noncommercial information in unfamiliar contexts may be especially difficult for low-literate users. Based on the descriptions of the analytical skills of low-level readers in the 1992 National Adult Literacy Survey (NALS),[25] it is likely that the technical and health literacy demands of formulating and analyzing the results of even a simple health information search exceed the cognitive skills of most basic readers.

OVERCOMING BARRIERS TO INTERNET USE

Despite the challenges and barriers described in the preceding sections, creative approaches to applying multiple functional literacies are emerging that take advantage of the strengths of electronic technologies to meet the needs of users at various literacy levels. Some approaches focus on improving users' access and skills with technology; others alter the design and content of Web sites to meet users' needs; and some solutions use technologies as an intervention to enhance health literacy.

Community-Based Efforts

A popular strategy for overcoming barriers to Internet access and the development of necessary technological skills is to use community settings, such as community technology centers or public places such as libraries, to provide free or low-cost Internet access and skills training (see www.ctcnet.org for examples). Within these settings, users can learn with others in similar situations and receive the encouragement, feedback, and direction that will help them learn technical skills as well as navigate Internet content. Preliminary research indicates that low literacy by itself is not an insurmountable barrier to the acquisition of technology skills, but users may need assistance to apply technology skills, such as using a mouse and scrolling, to complete online tasks.[9,26] Some research findings suggest that building users' searching capacities will not only improve the quality of their searches but also improve their capacities to perform critical evaluations of Web content.[22]

Many federal and state agencies as well as nonprofit organizations have made considerable investments of public funds to create access points and training programs in low-income and isolated communities[27] (see reference 27 for examples). These promise to be valuable resources for individuals with low literacy. In addition, adult education programs, which primarily serve a low-literate population, recognize the value and necessity of integrating computers and the Internet into remedial programs. Integration of technology into adult education provides learners the opportunity to develop technology skills while they enhance their literacy skills.[28]

User-Centered Design

A critical way to make the Internet more accessible not only to those with limited literacy and health literacy but also those with disabilities and impaired function is to apply user-centered design principles and usability engineering to create audience-appropriate Web pages and content (for specific guidelines, see www.usability.gov).[7–9,29,30] It is possible that Web-site designs that accommodate the users' needs can be considered a health literacy intervention.[8,10] Organizations that wish to use the Internet as an information and communication tool are beginning to understand that they must identify their intended audiences and develop their Web resources to meet their audiences' needs, just as they would for any other health communication activity.

Some basic elements that researchers and Web designers use to reach low-literacy audiences are the same as those used to create print materials; others are more specific to the Internet and the Web. These more specific elements include writing easy-to-read text; using simple, relevant graphics and audio and video files to enhance text as needed; supplementing basic text with Frequently Asked Questions and interactive question-and-answer features; providing users the opportunity to self-identify certain characteristics so that content can be personalized; incorporating cultural attributes into design and content; and organizing information and other content so as to minimize searching and multiple layers of pages.

Methods for assessing the users' ability to interact with technology and meet their needs include user experience design and usability testing. User experience design places users at the center of the design process.[29,30] Application designers develop user and task profiles and test prototypes with user groups before moving to usability testing. Usability research is focused on understanding and improving users' experience of a given technology or technologies. Usability research has become so authoritative that the National Institutes of Health's National Cancer Institute has invested in a usability lab and Web site (www.usability.gov). According to this Web site, "usability is the measure of the quality of a user's experience when interacting with a product or system—whether a Web site, a software application, mobile technology, or any user-operated device."

One specific example of a research-and-user–based approach to Web-site development is a site for older adults developed by the National Institute on Aging (NIA) and the National Library of Medicine (NLM), both parts of the National Institutes of Health.[8] The agencies reviewed the findings on older adults' use of computers, the Internet, and the Web and found that, in general, older adults are willing to use these technologies and can learn how to use them to meet their information and communication needs. They also reviewed existing sets of Web-site development guidelines and found them lacking in applicability to older adults. The agencies applied the research findings and existing guidelines and conducted multiple rounds of user testing on the agencies' Web-site (www.seniorhealth.gov) to develop guidelines for Web-site development and Web pages appropriate for the technical and cognitive levels of the intended audience.[8] In contrast to text-heavy sites, the Web site incorporates illustrations, animation, and video and audio features that older adults like and use.

Many recommendations for Web-site design for older adults correspond with the findings from research on the use of computers and the Internet by low-literate adults. This suggests that there may be a great deal of overlap in the nature of existing problems and the development of shared solutions.[9,11,28] This is not surprising since the elderly represent a disproportionately large segment of the low-literate population. Disability considerations for the senior population as well as the general population may also be an important factor and suggest common solutions. NIA is continuing to investigate the connections among health literacy, technology, and older adults and the ways that electronic communication and information can improve low health literacy.[10]

Beyond improving Web-site design and content to facilitate and enhance users' experience, interactive design and customization is an exciting enhancement of the Internet for all segments of the population.[2,13] There are many examples of taking "dumb" text and making it "smart" in ways that respond to users' interests and needs. Based on the way a user navigates, searches, or answers questions or based on personal information that a user may volunteer, electronic technologies can respond with tailored information and choices.[12,31] For example, a recipe search may generate ideas based on indicated food preferences, purchasing history, or previous diet and cookbook searches.

Such computer-tailored information and messages have been shown to be more effective in effecting change across a variety of prevention behaviors.[12] Although health literacy may not be specifically used to tailor messages and information, the basic premise of tailoring means that messages and materials will be appropriate for each user's functional abilities. Some research indicates that traditionally underserved populations may benefit the most from use of online information and support services.[32,33] Applications that provide users structured and preselected information designed to meet their specific information needs have been shown to be more beneficial than open searching on the Internet for similar information.[32] Moreover, even if the information is not specifically tailored to reading and health literacy levels, motivated users who typically do not have good alternatives to the information provided on a Web site may tackle more difficult material if it helps them handle their health concerns.[33]

THE POTENTIAL OF ELECTRONIC TECHNOLOGIES TO IMPROVE HEALTH LITERACY

In their current forms, the Internet and the Web are far from ideal health information sources for low-literate persons. Preliminary research suggests that low-literate persons are likely to have less access to Internet technologies, are less likely to be able to use the technologies to accomplish tasks, and are less likely to find content appropriate for their interests and information needs. At the same time, other research suggests that these problems could be mitigated with a sustained focus on providing access to and training for technology use, using audience-centered content design principles and methods, streamlining information search processes, and maximizing the possibilities of interactive technologies.

If we believe that the current state of the Internet and the Web is the most that can be accomplished with electronic technologies, we will miss a tremendous opportunity that goes far beyond disseminating text. The opportunity lies with the customization and interaction that electronic technologies can provide. Digital technologies create simultaneous multimodal and multiformat communication that can "learn" from users' behaviors and adapt to users' needs much more readily than other forms of communication, such as print or video. New presentation formats enable low-literate users to benefit from the Internet by having to read *less*, not *more*, than in print-dominated environments. However, innovative ways to present information that fits users' skills will be required. The future challenge is to develop the next generation of informational and communication resources on the Web with the creativity and innovation that has not yet been evident.

Clearly, much more work needs to be done in tracking what users are already doing on the Internet, what they would like to do more of, and what might enhance access, attractiveness, and utility of the Internet and the Web for all population groups. Even with its rapid rate of diffusion, the Internet is still at a very early stage of development. The challenge is to ensure that the current features of the Internet— unstructured searches on the open Internet, tendency to post brochureware, often confusing interfaces, extraneous graphics, and difficult text—do not become permanent. Health professionals, health communicators, health education specialists, and application designers need to join forces to discover the possibilities of new technologies for all types of audiences, including those with low health literacy.

REFERENCES

1. Cline RJW, Haynes KM. Consumer health information seeking on the Internet: the state of the art. *Health Educ Res.* 2001;16(6):671–692.

2. Neuhauser L, Kreps G. Rethinking communication in the e-health era. *J Health Psychol.* 2003;8(1):7–23.

3. Institute of Medicine. Committee on Communication for Behavior Change in the 21st Century: Improving the Health of Diverse Populations. *Speaking of Health: Assessing Health Communication Strategies for Diverse Populations.* Washington, DC: National Academy Press; 2002.

4. US Department of Commerce. *A Nation Online: How Americans are Expanding Their Use of the Internet.* Washington, DC: US Department of Commerce. Available at www.ntia.doc.gov/ntiahome/dn/index.html. Accessed June 9, 2003.

5. US Department of Health and Human Services. Health Communication (Chapter 11). *Healthy People 2010.* 2nd ed. *With Understanding and Improving Health and Objectives for Improving Health.* 2 vols. Washington, DC: US Government Printing Office, November 2000. Available at www.healthypeople.gov. Accessed June 12, 2003.

6. Lenhart A. The ever-shifting Internet population. Washington, DC: The Pew Internet & American Life Project. Available at www.pewinternet.org. Accessed June 2, 2003.

7. The Children's Partnership. 2002. Online content for low-income and underserved Americans: an issue brief by The Children's Partnership. Available at www.childrenspartnership.org. Accessed June 9, 2003.

8. Morrell RW, Dailey SR, Feldman C, et al. *Older Adults and Information Technology: A Compendium of Scientific Research and Web Site Accessibility Guidelines.* Bethesda, Md: National Institute on Aging, National Institutes of Health, US Department of Health and Human Services; 2003.

9. Zarcadoolas C, Blanco M, Boyer JF. Unweaving the Web: an exploratory study of low-literate adults' navigation skills on the World Wide Web. *J Health Commun.* 2002;7:309–324.

10. Echt KV, Morrell RW. *Promoting Health Literacy in Older Adults: An Overview of the Promise of Interactive Technology.* Bethesda, Md: National Institute on Aging, National Institutes of Health, US Department of Health and Human Services; 2003.

11. Askov EN, Johnston J, Petty LI, Young SJ. Expanding access to adult literacy with online distance education. Cambridge, Mass: NCSALL. Available at http://www.ncsall.gse.harvard.edu/research/op_askov.pdf. Accessed June 10, 2003.

12. Kreuter M, Farrell D, Olevitch L, Brennan L. *Tailoring Health Messages: Customizing Communication with Computer Technology.* Mahwah, NJ: Lawrence Erlbaum; 2000.

13. Science Panel on Interactive Communication and Health. *Wired for Health and Well-Being: The Emergence of Interactive Health Communication.* Eng TR, Gustafson DH, eds. Washington, DC: US Department of Health and Human Services, US Government Printing Office; 1999.

14. RAND Health. *Proceed with Caution: A Report on the Quality of Health Information on the Internet.* Oakland, Calif: California HealthCare Foundation; 2001.

15. D'Alessandro DM, Kingsley P, Johnson-West J. The readability of pediatric patient education materials on the World Wide Web. *Arch Pediatr Adolesc Med.* 2001;155(7):807–812.

16. Graber MA, Roller CM, Kaeble B. Readability levels of patient education materials on the World Wide Web. *J Fam Prac*. 1999;48(1):58–61.

17. Horrigan J, Rainie L. Counting on the Internet. Washington, DC: The Pew Internet & American Life Project. Available at www.pewinternet. org. Accessed June 9, 2003.

18. Fox S, Fallows D. Internet health resources: health searches and email have become more commonplace, but there is room for improvement in searches and overall Internet access. Washington, DC: The Pew Internet and American Life Project. Available at www.pewinternet.org. Accessed August 18, 2003.

19. Eysenbach G, Kohler C. How do consumers search for and appraise health information on the World Wide Web? Qualitative study using focus groups, usability tests, and in-depth interviews. *BMJ*. 2002;324(7337):573–577.

20. Jansen BJ, Pooch U. A review of Web searching studies and a framework for future research. *J Am Soc Infor Sci Technol*. 2001;52(3):235–246.

21. Marable L. False oracles: Consumer reaction to learning the truth about how search engines work. Yonkers, NY: consumer WebWatch. Available at www.consumerwebwatch.org/news/searchengines/index.html. Accessed August 18, 2003.

22. Jenkins C, Corritore CL, Wiedenbeck S. Patterns of information seeking on the Web: a qualitative study of domain expertise and Web expertise. *IT & Society*, 1(3):64–89. Available at: www.ITandSociety.org. Accessed June 2, 2003.

23. Baur C, Deering MJ. Proposed frameworks to improve the quality of health Web sites: Review. *MedGenMed*. 2(3). Available at www.medscape.com/viewpublication/122_toc?vol=2&iss=3. Accessed June 12, 2003.

24. Eysenbach G, Powell J, Kuss O, Sa ER. Empirical studies assessing the quality of health information for consumers on the World Wide Web. *JAMA*. 2002;287(20):2691–2700.

25. Kirsch JS, Junegeblut A, Jenkins L, Kolstad A. Adult literacy in America: a first look at the results of the National Adult Literacy Survey (NALS). Washington, DC: US Department of Education; 1993.

26. Wofford JL, Currin D, Michielutte R, Wofford MM. The multimedia computer for low-literacy patient education: a pilot project of cancer risk perceptions. *MedGenMed* Apr 20;3(2). Available at www.medscape. com/viewpublication/122_toc?vol=3&iss=2&templateid=2. Accessed August 18, 2003.

27. US Department of Health and Human Services. Internet access in the home. In: *Communicating Health: Priorities and Strategies for Progress*. Washington, DC: US Department of Health and Human Services; 2003;9–34.

28. Rosen DJ. 1998. Using electronic technology in adult literacy education. In: *The Annual Review of Adult Learning and Literacy*. Cambridge, Mass: NCSALL. Available at: http://ncsall.gse.harvard.edu/ann_rev/vol1_8.html. Accessed June 10, 2003.

29. Office of Disease Prevention and Health Promotion. *Understanding Our Users: How to Better Deliver Online Health Information to Asian Americans, Native Hawaiians and other Pacific Islanders.* Internal evaluation report, L. Hsu, ed. US Department of Health and Human Services. Available at: http://odphp.osophs.dhhs.gov/projects/. Accessed August 19, 2003.

30. Office of Disease Prevention and Health Promotion. *Understanding Our Users: How to Better Deliver Online Health Information to American Indians and Alaska Natives.* Internal evaluation report, L. Hsu, ed. US Department of Health and Human Services. Available at: http://odphp.osophs.dhhs.gov/projects/. Accessed August 19, 2003.

31. Kreuter MW, Strecher VJ, Glassman B. One size does not fit all: the case for tailoring print materials. *Ann Behav Med*. Fall 1999;21(4):276–283.

32. Gustafson DH, Hawkins RP, Boberg EW, et al. CHESS: 10 years of research and development in consumer health informatics for broad populations, including the underserved. *Int J Med Inf*. 2002;65:169–177.

33. Gustafson DH, Hawkins R, Pingree S, et al. Effect of computer support on younger women with breast cancer. *J Gen Intern Med*. 2001; 16(7):435–445.

Health Literacy and the Delivery of Health Care

Editor: Dean Schillinger, MD, MPH

INTRODUCTION

As seen in the previous sections, health literacy plays a role in patients' health care experiences and the communication of health information. This, in turn, suggests that health literacy impacts health outcomes and the delivery of health care.

In order to examine the relationship between health literacy and health outcomes, researchers must be able to measure health literacy. Accordingly, this section begins with a discussion of literacy testing in health care research. In Chapter 10, Davis and associates describe various methods and instruments used to measure health literacy, noting that even the best tools can only approximate "the degree to which individuals have the capacity to obtain, process, and understand basic health information and services needed to make appropriate health decisions." They conclude by discussing limitations of literacy testing in research and barriers to clinical application.

While the mechanisms by which limited health literacy affects the delivery of health care have yet to be defined and validated, current research informs our understanding of this relationship. In Chapter 11, Schillinger and Davis present a conceptual framework for understanding how limited health literacy might influence health outcomes, using chronic disease care as an example. As explained by the authors, this framework is intended to highlight potential points of intervention, inform research priorities, and illuminate the broader social context that affects the quality of health care for individuals with low levels of health literacy.

155

This section concludes with an overview of the literature on health literacy and health outcomes, upon which the previous chapter's framework is based. As presented by DeWalt and Pignone in Chapter 12, research indicates that health literacy is associated with various health outcomes, including knowledge and comprehension of health information; health behaviors; screening and prevention; adherence to medical instructions; biochemical and biometric outcomes; disease prevalence, incidence, or morbidity; and use of hospital resources. Although these data suggest that a relationship exists between literacy and certain health outcomes, future research is needed to establish the extent of this relationship and elucidate the pathways from low literacy to poor quality of health.

chapter 10

Literacy Testing in Health Care Research

Terry Davis, PhD; Estela M. Kennen, MA;
Julie A. Gazmararian, MPH, PhD; and Mark V. Williams, MD, FACP

Health care providers and researchers are increasingly aware of the potential impact of patients' health literacy skills on health care utilization, communication, self-care management, and ultimately health outcomes.[1–9] In examining these relationships, however, providers and researchers have learned that it is not easy to recognize patients with limited literacy.[4–5,10–11] Information obtained from the medical interview (eg, age or level of education completed) and direct questioning regarding a patient's literacy skills may provide some guidance, but these steps do not accurately measure literacy.[10,12–15] Complicating attempts to determine patients' literacy skills is the influence of shame. Most people with limited literacy skills are ashamed of this and often attempt to hide it.[16]

In this chapter, we review adult literacy testing in health care and adult education settings. It is important to note, however, that we do not discuss methods of assessing an individual patient's actual health literacy. To accurately measure an individual's health literacy, we need to assess "the degree to which individuals have the capacity to obtain, process, and understand basic health information and services needed to make appropriate health decisions."[17] To date, there are no formal standardized assessments designed to comprehensively accomplish this task. However, multiple methods and instruments that provide a proxy measure of this have been developed and studied. These measurements have been used in the increasing body of health literacy research.

First, we discuss the discrepancy between patients' level of education and direct assessments of their reading comprehension and recognition skills. Next, we describe specific methods and instruments that have been used to screen individuals' literacy skills in health care and adult education settings in the United States and provide information on how to order the tests. Finally, we discuss limitations of the tests and the process of testing patients in general, highlighting critical issues that the researchers and providers need to consider before assessing an individual's literacy level.

EDUCATION COMPLETED
COMPARED TO LITERACY SKILLS

Until recently, researchers and clinicians used patients' education level as the primary marker for their literacy skills.[5,10,11,13,18] However, education level, although highly correlated with reading grade level and level of functional literacy, cannot accurately predict a person's reading level or functional health literacy.[10,18,19] Individuals may have graduated from high school or even taken some college classes and still have inadequate literacy skills.[10,18,20] Conversely, someone with adequate literacy skills might not have completed high school. This discrepancy probably exists because "education level measures only the number of years an individual attended school, not how much the individual learned in school."[19]

Reading tests that assess comprehension and reading recognition are more specific markers for literacy than years of education completed. Previous studies have found adult patients' reading comprehension to be two to five grade levels below their reported number of years of education completed.[5,10,13,14] Patients' socioeconomic status (SES), race, and age may all influence the magnitude of the discrepancy between years of education completed and reading ability. In a study completed in seven community clinics, the gap between education and reading comprehension was most pronounced (4.8 grade levels) in the clinic that served low-income minority patients, the majority of whom were unemployed.[10] The gap between reported education level and reading skills was least pronounced (2.6 grade levels) in a private family practice clinic that served predominantly middle-income white patients, almost all of whom were employed.[10]

The gap between patients' education level and reading grade level is usually less pronounced when literacy is assessed with standardized reading recognition tests rather than standardized reading comprehension tests.[21] Reading recognition tests assess an individual's ability to pronounce a list of words.[5,11] They are a standard method of screening reading ability in English. Reading recognition tests will likely score a patient's reading level two grades above their reading comprehension score.[11,21] Yet, the score will probably still be lower than a patient's self-reported grade level. In a study of 396 university pediatric clinics, parents' education level poorly predicted reading recognition scores.[22] The discrepancy between reading recognition level and education was most pronounced among parents who read in the lowest reading ranges. For example, parents whose reading recognition was at or below a third-grade level ($n = 44$) had an average education level of tenth grade.[22] Of note, students in most states cannot drop out of school until they have turned 16 or 17, usually necessitating completion of 9 or 10 years of school.

High school graduation is sometimes used as a marker for adequate literacy. However, the National Adult Literacy Survey (NALS) and other studies revealed a significant minority of adults who graduated from high school scored in the lowest literacy and reading levels.[10,13,15,18] The NALS reported that 24% of adults scoring in the lowest literacy level stated they graduated from high school, yet they had trouble reading a brief newspaper article and stating the main points of the article or filling out Social Security applications.[18] Thus, other methods are needed to assess patients' literacy skills in the health care setting.

LITERACY SCREENING IN HEALTH CARE SETTINGS

Clinicians and researchers often feel they need to know how to identify a patient's literacy level. Testing is the only way to quantify a patient's reading skills. Several informal methods and standardized tests have been used to assess reading ability, and we review the different options in this section.

Informal Methods

Patient behavior may indicate that patients have inadequate literacy skills. One practical suggestion is to observe how patients handle literacy tasks in the clinical setting. Common cues include patients filling out intake forms incompletely, misspelling many words, leaving the clinic before completing the form, becoming angry with having to fill out a form, or asking for help.[19] During the clinical encounter, physicians can ask patients to bring their medications and then review these with the patient. A patient who identifies a medication by opening the bottle and looking at the pill rather than reading the label may lack the needed skills to read and understand prescription labels. Also, patients who do not know why they are taking a medication or are confused about how to take the medication are likely to possess inadequate health literacy. Unfortunately, in our experience, physicians and clinic staff rarely recognize these behaviors as markers for low literacy. Health providers often assume patients do not want to actively participate in their health care when they complete forms poorly, do not respond to mailed information from the physician, or do not take medicine as prescribed.

Instruments Used to Assess Literacy

In this section, we review and compare currently available literacy measurements. MEDLINE and Cumulative Index to Nursing and Allied Health (CINAHL) database entries from January 1980 to February 2003 were searched for articles in which adult patient literacy was assessed in health care settings in the United States. A review of the literature revealed 69 studies; all but one of these have appeared since 1991. Eight different instruments were used to measure reading ability. Literacy was most commonly assessed using the Rapid Estimate of Adult Literacy in Medicine (REALM; 28 articles), followed by the Wide Range Achievement Test-Revised 3 (WRAT-R3; 17 articles) and different versions of the Test of Functional Health Literacy in Adults (TOFHLA; 12 articles) (see Table 10-1). The remaining 12 studies used other reading recognition and Cloze-type (ie, test taker is asked to supply words that have been systematically deleted from the text) comprehension assessments.

Two types of standardized reading tests—reading recognition tests and reading comprehension tests—have been used in health care settings. These tests are described in greater detail below and summarized in Table 10-1. Information about how to obtain these and other tests discussed in this chapter is available in Appendix B at the end of this book.

Reading Recognition Tests
Reading recognition tests are a useful predictor of general reading ability in English and are appropriate for individuals with some degree of fluency in the English language. They are the easiest and quickest type of instrument to administer and score, making them the most commonly used tests to identify low-level readers in health care settings.[11]

In reading recognition tests, the patient reads aloud from a list of words. Reading recognition tests do not measure reading comprehension or an individual's ability to act on written information. These tests only measure an individual's ability to read and pronounce individual words.[5,11] The rationale behind word recognition tests is that, if patients have trouble pronouncing words (a beginning-level reading skill) they are likely to have difficulty with the higher-order skill of comprehension. If the patient struggles to read simple words from the list, comprehension is likely to be limited. These tests can alert clinicians to the possibility that their patient may have difficulty with printed educational materials and oral provider-patient communication.

TABLE 10-1

Literacy Tests Used in Healthcare and in Adult Literacy and Education Settings*

	WRAT-R3	SORT-R	REALM	LAD	MART	PIAT-R	TOFHLA	IDL	TABE
Description	Word recognition test	Word recognition test	Health word recognition test	Diabetes word recognition test	Medical word recognition test printed to resemble prescription label	Reading recognition and comprehension test	Cloze-style reading comprehension of health care material	Reading comprehension test	7-section literacy test that assesses skills found in basic education curricula
Administration time	3–5 minutes	5–10 minutes	2–3 minutes	3–5 minutes	3–5 minutes	60 minutes	18–22 minutes (7 minutes for short version)	22 minutes (7 minutes for short version)	1.5–2.75 hours
Training required	Minimal	Minimal	Minimal	Minimal	Minimal	Moderate	Minimal	Moderate to extensive	Moderate to extensive
Scoring	Several score types are available that can be reconverted to specific grades or normed to specific age groups	(0–200) raw score can be converted to 10 grades ranging from pre-1, 9–12	(0–66) raw score can be converted to four grade range categories: ≤ 3rd, 4th–6th, 7th–8th, ≥ 9th	0–60 raw score can be converted to three grade range categories: ≤ 4th, 5th–8th, ≥9	Raw score can be converted to grade equivalent	Comprehension subtest score determines grade level	Inadequate, marginal, or functional health literacy	Inadequate, marginal, or functional health literacy	Electronic profile identifies specific areas in need of further study; gives grade and percentile scores for each section and the total

Continued

T A B L E 10-1

Literacy Tests Used in Healthcare and in Adult Literacy and Education Settings, cont'd

	WRAT-R3	SORT-R	REALM	LAD	MART	PIAT-R	TOHFLA	IDL	TABE
Testee age	5–74 years	≥ 4years	Adults only	Adults only	High school	All ages	Adults only	All ages	≥ 16years
Correlation with other tests	PIAT-R 0.62–0.91	PIAT-R 0.83–0.90	WRAT-R3, 0.88; SORT-R, 0.96; PIAT-R, 0.97; TOHFLA, 0.84	REALM, 0.90; WRAT-R3, 0.81	WRAT-R3 0.98	Kaufman, 0.84; Wechsler, 0.50	WRAT-R3, 0.74; REALM, 0.84	WRAT-R3, 0.74; REALM, 0.84	GED, 0.55–0.64
Primary advantages	Two equivalent forms allow pre- and post-testing; can test children	Commonly used in school and work settings	Quick, nonthreatening; large font size available	Quick; may be helpful in diabetes education	Quick; nonthreatening	Assesses comprehension and recognition; can give total reading score	Measures functional health literacy; available in short and very short forms, and in Spanish	Available in Spanish	Available in Spanish; short form available; electronic scoring available
Primary limitations	Words are difficult for patients and test administrators	Small font size; does not discriminate above a 9th grade	Does not discriminate above a 9th grade; gives grade range estimates, not specific grades	No clinical experience with diabetic patients published	No clinical experience published; words are difficult	Time and material required	Long versions are time-consuming	Long version is time-consuming; timed test can be frustrating for subjects	Manual scoring moderately complex and time-consuming; no published studies in health communication

* WRAT-R3 indicates Wide Range Achievement Test-Revised 3; Sort-R, Slosson Oral Reading Test-Revised; REALM, Rapid Estimate of Adult Literacy in Medicine; LAD, Literacy Assessment for Diabetes; MART, Medical Achievement Reading Test; PIAT-R, Peabody Individual Achievement Test-Revised; TOHFLA, Test of Functional Health Literacy in Adults; IDL, Instrumento Para Diagnosticar Lecturas (Instrument for Diagnosis of Reading); TABE, Tests of Adult Basic Education and GED, General Educational Development.

The WRAT-R3[23] and the Slosson Oral Reading Test-Revised (SORT-R)[24] are examples of word recognition tests imported from nonhealth care settings and used in medical studies. The Peabody Individual Achievement Test-Revised (PIAT-R)[21] has both word recognition and reading comprehension sections. The SORT-R is often used with youth in educational settings but can also be used in health care settings with children, adolescents, and adult patients. In educational and employment settings, the WRAT, SORT, and PIAT and their revised editions are widely used. REALM[25] is a word recognition test that was developed specifically for use in the health care setting. A shortened version, REALM-Revised,[26] has recently been developed. The Literacy Assessment for Diabetes (LAD)[27] and Medical Achievement Reading Test (MART)[28] are newer word recognition tests also developed in the health care setting.

Wide Range Achievement Test-Revised 3   The WRAT-R3 is a nationally standardized achievement test that assesses reading, spelling, and arithmetic.[21] The test was divided and restandardized in 1993 to develop two equivalent forms (Tan and Blue), thus allowing for pre- and post-testing. WRAT-R3 has been normed on individuals ages 5 to 75. Each of the two forms contains three subtests—reading recognition, spelling, and arithmetic. We will only discuss the reading subtest of WRAT-R3. Both the Tan and Blue forms of the reading subtest consist of letter reading (naming 15 letters of the alphabet) and word reading (pronouncing 42 words).[23] Figure 10-1 contains a sample of 11 words from the word reading portion of the reading subtest.

The WRAT-R3 generates several types of scores. Raw scores, which range from 1 to 57, can be converted to grade-equivalent reading levels ranging from preschool to post–high school. Absolute scores can be used for statistical analyses. Standard scores, percentile scores, and normal-curve equivalents are measures normalized to specific age groups.[23] For use in clinical settings, the raw score (converted to a grade level) is often the most useful. The WRAT-R3 is recommended for health care studies that need to discriminate patients reading above a ninth grade level.[11]

FIGURE 10-1

Sample Words from the Word Reading Portion of the WRAT-R3 Reading Subtest

book	bulk	discretionary	omniscient
even	contagious	itinerary	terpsichorean
felt	horizon	oligarchy	

WRAT-R3 has been extensively tested for its validity and reliability. Correlation between the reading subtest of the WRAT-R3 and the Total Reading score of the California Test of Basic Skills (4th ed.) is 0.72; the correlation is 0.87 with the total reading score of the Stanford Achievement Test. Test-retest alpha scores range from 0.91 to 0.98.[23]

The WRAT-R3 takes 3 to 5 minutes to administer and score, although an inexperienced examiner may take somewhat longer. The major limitation of the WRAT-R3 is its difficulty level for populations of poor readers, such as those who seek care in publicly funded health clinics.[11] The words on the WRAT-R3 rapidly become difficult for low-level readers, and many patients give up quickly. The test may cause anxiety, because it requires subjects to continue saying words aloud until they have missed 10 consecutive items. Almost one third of the words are above a ninth-grade reading level, and even health care providers struggle with words such as "assuage," "terpsichorean," and "epithalamion."[11,23]

Correct pronunciations are noted phonetically on the back of the test, but some examiners need an audiotape of the words to aid in memorizing correct pronunciations. It is possible to reduce the test's complexity by using a modified scoring method, which allows patients to quit after three consecutive words are missed. When using this method, however, the test may lose accuracy for assigning grade equivalents, and it should then only be used as an estimate of higher or lower reading ability.

Slosson Oral Reading Test-Revised 3 The Slosson Oral Reading Test-Revised (SORT-R3) is a widely used test in education settings that was restandardized in 2000.[24] It is designed for use with individuals aged 5 and above and takes about 5 to 10 minutes to administer. The SORT-R3 is composed of 10 lists of 20 core words for each grade level from kindergarten to high school. The examiner selects the list on which to start. With adults, the starting list may be three to four grade levels behind the highest grade completed in school. The individual must be able to pronounce all words on the starting list. If they miss even one word, they must move back to the previous list. Words are counted as incorrect if they are mispronounced or omitted or if the participant takes longer than 5 seconds to pronounce the word, if more than one pronunciation is given.[24]

The SORT-R3 offers grade and age equivalents, standard scores, and national percentages. The SORT-R3 has high test-retest reliability (0.99) and high criterion validity with more complex reading assessments (0.90 with the Woodcock-Johnson Tests of Achievement Letter/Word Identification subtest, 0.90 with the PIAT reading recognition subtest, and 0.83 with the PIAT-R reading comprehension subtest).[24]

The SORT-R3 is used in school settings to monitor students' progress with reading and in adult literacy programs to get a quick estimate of an adult's reading level. The major limitation of the SORT-R3 is that the 200 words are typeset in small 10-point font, making the test intimidating for poor readers and unusable for individuals with impaired visual acuity.[11, 24]

Rapid Estimate of Adult Literacy in Medicine   The REALM, a health word recognition test first developed in 1991 and revised in 1993, was specifically designed to screen for low literacy in health care settings.[25] It is now the most commonly used word recognition test in medical settings.[5,11] Composed of common medical words and layman's terms for body parts and illness, all words in the REALM were chosen from written materials commonly given to patients in primary care settings.[25] This high face validity may explain why the REALM has been well received by providers, researchers, and patients in health care settings across the country.

The REALM is highly correlated with other general reading tests and the TOFHLA.[29] The REALM has high criterion validity, correlating 0.88 with the revised WRAT-R, 0.96 with the SORT-R, and 0.97 with the PIAT-R. The correlation with the TOFHLA is 0.84. Most of the discrepancy between the TOFHLA and REALM is explained by variance among subjects scoring in the middle (seventh to eighth grade) ranges. The REALM also has high test–retest reliability, 0.97 $(P < .001)$.[25]

The REALM can be administered and scored in less than 3 minutes by personnel who can easily read and pronounce the words with minimal training.[11,25] The testing procedure involves presenting patients with a laminated sheet, available in regular and large print versions, containing three lists of 22 words each arranged according to the number of syllables and pronunciation difficulty. Patients are asked to read aloud as many words as they can, beginning with the first word. If patients are unable to pronounce several consecutive words, they are asked to look down the list and pronounce as many of the remaining words as they can. Dictionary pronunciation is the scoring standard.[25] Figure 10-2 displays the REALM's three word lists.

A primary limitation of the REALM is that it does not discriminate above a ninth-grade reading level. Also, in contrast to other instruments that assign individuals a specific grade equivalent reading level, the REALM only assigns grade-range estimates. Raw REALM scores (0–66) are converted into one of four reading grade levels: third grade or less (0–18), fourth to sixth grade (19–44), seventh to eighth grade (45–60), and ninth grade and above (61–66). In health care settings and studies in which patients need only be categorized as poor

FIGURE 10-2
REALM Word Lists

1	2	3
fat	fatigue	allergic
flu	pelvic	menstrual
pill	jaundice	testicle
dose	infection	colitis
eye	exercise	emergency
stress	behavior	medication
smear	prescription	occupation
nerves	notify	sexually
germs	gallbladder	alcoholism
meals	calories	irritation
disease	depression	constipation
cancer	miscarriage	gonorrhea
caffeine	pregnancy	inflammatory
attack	arthritis	diabetes
kidney	nutrition	hepatitis
hormones	menopause	antibiotics
herpes	appendix	diagnosis
seizure	abnormal	potassium
bowel	syphilis	anemia
asthma	hemorrhoids	obesity
rectal	nausea	osteoporosis
incest	directed	impetigo

Note: Figure 10-2 is not reproduced in actual scale. Use of this figure for literacy testing is not recommended.

(scores 0–44), marginal (scores 45–60), or adequate (scores 61–66) readers, the information provided by the REALM is generally sufficient.[25]

Rapid Estimate of Adult Literacy in Medicine-Revised   The REALM-R, a shortened version of the REALM, was designed in 2002 as a rapid screening instrument to identify patients at risk for poor literacy in a health care setting.[12] Like the REALM, the REALM-R assesses how well primary care patients read words that they commonly encounter and are expected to understand in the course of interacting with their physician.

The REALM-R is composed of 10 words derived from the original REALM. The first three are included to invite a patient's confidence and cooperation and they are not scored. A correct response is given if the word is pronounced correctly. A score of 6 or less has been used to identify patients at risk for poor literacy.[12,26]

The REALM-R correlates with the REALM (0.72) and the WRAT-R3 (0.64), but not nearly as well as the full REALM does with the

WRAT-R3 (0.88).[25,26] The time required for the REALM-R, including explanation and delivery, is less than 2 minutes.[26]

Literacy Assessment for Diabetes   The LAD, developed in 2001, is a 60-word recognition test modeled after the REALM.[27] One purpose of the test is to make literacy assessment "less embarrassing for persons with diabetes, since most people are not expected to know diabetes terms."[27] The LAD is comprised of words such as "eye," "exchange," "snack," and "retinopathy" that are commonly encountered when dealing with diabetes. Half of the words are at a fourth-grade level, the rest range from sixth- to a 16th-grade level. All words were chosen to reflect diabetes education needs.[27] Like the REALM, the LAD can be administered in 3 to 5 minutes. Raw scores can be converted into three grade equivalent ranges: fourth grade and below, fifth through eighth grade, and ninth grade and above. The LAD has significant correlation with the REALM (0.90) and the WRAT-R3 (0.81) and has a test-retest correlation of 0.86.[27]

Medical Achievement Reading Test   The MART, developed in 1997, is a 42-word reading recognition test modeled after the WRAT-R3. It was designed to measure medical literacy in a nonthreatening manner.[28] The print resembles a prescription label with its use of small print size, glossy cover, and medical terminology prescription labels.[28] The authors believed these alterations would put patients with low literacy at ease with the test.

The MART words, such as "twice," "sublingual," "pneumonia," and "anticoagulant," were chosen from 500 words found on 119 prescription labels and from a medical dictionary. Word difficulty was determined by the number of letters and number of syllables in each word. The length of the words on the MART parallels those on the WRAT-R3. Cronbach's α reliability test indicates a high level of likelihood ($\alpha = 0.9762$) that the MART raw score is a good estimate of the WRAT-R3 raw score. Cronbach's α was also conducted on the grade level estimates of the two tests, with results indicating the MART grade levels are a good estimate ($\alpha = 0.971$) of WRAT-R3 grade levels.[28]

Reading Comprehension Tests

Reading comprehension tests assess a patient's ability to read and understand text written at different levels of difficulty.[5,11] Comprehension tests require more time and skill to administer than word recognition tests. Such assessments can be useful in both clinical research and in developing and testing written health education materials. Examples of comprehension tests include use of the Cloze technique in the TOFHLA[29] and the comprehension subtest of the PIAT-R.[21]

The Cloze procedure requires readers to fill in words that have been systematically deleted from a sample of text. The assessment is based on the assumption that better readers will understand the context of the text and be able to fill in the missing words. Other types of comprehension tests require subjects to interpret and apply information gleaned from reading a passage.[5,29]

Peabody Individual Achievement Test-Revised   The PIAT-R includes components on mathematics, reading recognition, reading comprehension, spelling, and general information.[21] In the reading comprehension section of the PIAT-R, the subject reads a sentence and then identifies which one of four illustrations best matches the sentence. There are a total of 82 sentences, which increase in length and complexity. Subjects are given the reading recognition subtest first; if the subject scores below the first-grade reading level, the reading comprehension subtest is not given. The suggested starting point on the reading comprehension section is determined by the subject's score on the reading recognition test.[21] Three reading scores are possible when using the PIAT-R: a reading recognition score, a reading comprehension score, and a total reading score.[21]

Test of Functional Health Literacy in Adults   The TOFHLA has been used for health literacy research in medical and community settings.[11,20,29,30] The TOFHLA consists of a reading comprehension section that uses a modified Cloze-type procedure and a numeracy section, both composed of actual materials that patients might encounter in health care settings. The reading comprehension section measures a patient's ability to read and fill in missing words from 50 items on three selected passages: patient instructions for an upper GI (gastrointestinal) series—written at a fourth-grade reading level, the "Rights and Responsibilities" section of a Medicaid application—written at a tenth-grade reading level, and a form used to obtain informed consent for a procedure—written at a 19th grade reading level. Every fifth to seventh word in a passage is omitted and four multiple choice options are provided. The 17-item numeracy section of the TOFHLA assesses a patient's ability to use numerical skills necessary to accurately interpret instructions on a prescription bottle, understand blood glucose results, and understand appointment slips.[29] Four items from this section are reproduced in Figure 10-3.

The sum of the two sections yields the TOFHLA score, which ranges from 0 to 100. Scores from 0 to 59 indicate inadequate health literacy (patients will often misread the simplest materials, including prescription bottles and appointment slips). Scores between 60 and 74 indicate marginal health literacy, and scores from 75 to 100 indicate

FIGURE 10-3

Sample Questions from the Numeracy Section of the TOFHLA and Short TOFHLA

The questions below correspond to instructions on a prescription bottle, blood glucose results, and information on an appointment slip that are provided to the subject.

1. Have a look at this one .... If you take your first tablet at 7:00 AM, when should you take the next one?
2. Here is another direction you might be given .... If this were your score, would your blood sugar be normal today?
3. Now, take a look at this one .... When is your appointment?
4. Here is another instruction you might be given .... If you eat lunch at 12:00 noon, and you want to take this medicine before lunch, what time should you take it?

---

adequate health literacy (patients will successfully complete most of the reading tasks required to function in the health care setting, although they may still misread informed consent forms).[29]

The TOFHLA takes up to 22 minutes to administer. The exam is timed and subjects must stop after a set time period for the separate reading and numeracy sections. Content validity is robust, given that it includes actual material used in real health care settings. TOFHLA also has good criterion validity with correlation coefficients of 0.74 with the reading section of the WRAT-R3 and 0.84 with the REALM. Internal reliability using Cronbach's α is 0.98.[29]

Short TOFHLA and Very Short TOFHLA   The short TOFHLA is an abbreviated version of the TOFHLA. The reading comprehension section is a 36-item test using the initial two passages in the reading comprehension section of the full TOFHLA—instructions for preparing for an upper GI tract radiograph series and the patient "Rights and Responsibilities" section of a Medicaid application. The numeracy section of the short TOFHLA is a shortened four-item measure adapted from the full TOFHLA.[30] These four items are reproduced in Figure 10.3.

The short TOFHLA takes 12 minutes or less to administer and yields the same three levels of literacy as the TOFHLA. It has been shown to have good internal reliability (Cronbach's α 0.98 for all items combined) and validity compared to the long version of the TOFHLA (0.91) and the REALM (0.80).[30]

The large-print versions (14-point font) of both the full and short TOFHLA are available for patients with poor vision.[30] A very short version of the TOFHLA uses only the second passage from the reading comprehension section—Medicaid application—and appears to perform comparably to the short TOFHLA.[31]

ASSESSMENT OF LITERACY
FOR SPANISH SPEAKERS

Health practitioners in the United States working with Spanish-speaking patients have expressed a need for a Spanish language word recognition test for quick literacy assessment. Currently there is no Spanish version of the WRAT-R3, REALM, or similar instruments because assessment of Spanish literacy is affected by the nature of the Spanish language. Spanish has regular phoneme-grapheme correspondence, meaning that one sound is usually represented by one letter and vice versa. Therefore, compared to English, it is relatively easy to sound out and pronounce words in Spanish if one can recognize letters, making it relatively easy for low-level readers to score high on word recognition tests.[32] Conversion of the REALM into Spanish demonstrated it could not be used among Spanish-speaking patients. Therefore, valid assessments of literacy in Spanish usually require Cloze tests or other standardized comprehension tests.[9,32]

Quick, valid ways to screen Spanish-speaking patients for literacy have yet to be developed. At present, the following two tests are used in health care research, but they are limited by the amount of time needed for administration.

Spanish Test of Functional
Health Literacy in Adults

The TOFHLA, described earlier, was adapted into a Spanish version by translating the reading comprehension passages and numeracy questions into Spanish and back-translating them into English, with discrepancies corrected. The Spanish TOFLHA has good internal consistency, reliability, and content validity; as with the full English version, internal reliability using Cronbach's α is 0.98. (Note that correlations with the REALM and WRAT-R3 are not possible because the REALM is not valid in Spanish and the WRAT-R3 is not available in Spanish.) Like the full English version, it takes 22 minutes or more to administer,[29] but a short and very short version of the Spanish TOFHLA are also available.[31]

Instrument for Diagnosis of Reading

The Instrument for Diagnosis of Reading, also known as the Instrumento Para Diagnosticar Lecturas (IDL), is a comprehensive Spanish reading-assessment instrument that tests comprehension of written text.[33] As with the Spanish TOFHLA, administration of the IDL requires 20 to 30 minutes or longer. Reading levels measured by the IDL correlate well with reading levels determined with other standard

English-only reading assessment instruments (correlation coefficients varying from 0.65 to 0.70). Interrater reliability of IDL for determining reading level averages 0.78 for the English version and 0.67 for the Spanish version across all grade levels.[33]

ASSESSMENTS USED IN ADULT EDUCATION

There is no report citing the use of the following two literacy tests in the medical literature. Brief descriptions of these tests are included because they are commonly used in adult basic education and literacy settings and provide a comprehensive literacy assessment for individuals entering adult basic education programs.

Tests of Adult Basic Education Forms 7 & 8

The Tests of Adult Basic Education (TABE) Forms 7 & 8,[34] developed in 1994, are designed to measure achievement of basic skills commonly found in adult basic education curricula and taught in instructional programs. The TABE, available in English and Spanish, assesses basic reading, mathematics, and language skills. It also deals with skills such as generating ideas, synthesizing elements, and evaluating outcomes. The TABE has seven sections: reading vocabulary, reading comprehension, mathematics computation, mathematics concepts and applications, language mechanics, language expression, and spelling. The Spanish version, TABE Español, is appropriate for adults with various dialects. There are four overlapping levels, which range from easy (2.6–4.9 grade) to advanced (8.6–12.9 grade). The reading subtest of the TABE measures basic reading skills in life-skill and academic contexts in a manner appropriate for adults.[34]

There are no set time limits for the TABE, but suggested guidelines recommend 1.5 hours for the survey form and 2.75 hours to administer the complete battery. Scoring can be done by hand or with TestMate TABE software (McGraw-Hill/Contemporary, Chicago, Illinois). It has been noted that manual scoring is moderately complex and time consuming. The TABE provides percentile, scale scores, and grade equivalent scores. Scores on the TABE have correlated moderately (0.55 to 0.64) with scores on the GED (general educational development).[34]

Adult Basic Learning Examination

The Adult Basic Learning Examination (ABLE),[35] developed in 1986, was designed to measure the educational achievement of adults who have not completed 12 years of schooling and to evaluate efforts to raise the educational level of these adults. The ABLE contains six subtests (vocabulary, reading comprehension, spelling, language, number operations, and quantitative problem solving) and three levels, which correspond to skills commonly taught in grades 1–4, 5–8, and 9–12. Two equivalent forms allow for pre- and posttesting. A brief (15 minutes) locator test may be used to match the learner's skill level to the appropriate level of the test. The reading subtest of both forms uses the Cloze technique to assess reading comprehension.[35]

Suggested guidelines indicate that the test takes 3.5 hours to administer; however, there are no time limits for any of the subtests. Scores can be reported as scale scores, percentiles, stanines (S9 Formula), and grade equivalents. The ABLE has moderately high correlation with the Stanford Achievement Test: 0.69 or less for level 1, 0.68–0.81 for level 2, and 0.8 for level 3.[35]

NUMERACY

Numeracy, although an essential component of health literacy, is a far less studied aspect of patient literacy. The few studies that have explored patients' ability to apply mathematical concepts in the context of health care information did not use a standard definition or assessment of numeracy. At present, the only standard health literacy tool that assesses numeracy is the TOFHLA.

In the health literacy literature, some studies focused on numeracy in clinical medicine using the TOFHLA, which assesses a patient's ability to use numerical skills to accurately interpret instructions on prescription bottles, understand blood glucose results, and understand appointment slips.[29] Other studies had an epidemiological focus and measured a patient's ability to understand basic probability and mathematical concepts associated with perceived health risks and benefits of screening or potential treatments.[36–40] These studies, most commonly cancer related, used one to seven questions developed by the authors to assess an individual's basic familiarity with percentages and probability. Some questions were framed in the context of the study (eg, "Estimate your 10-year risk of dying from breast cancer as a number out of 1000; indicate if this risk is higher than, the same, or lower than that of an average woman your age; compare your risk of dying from breast cancer with risk of dying from heart disease."). However, most studies used generic questions, such as those developed by Schwartz and associates.* [37] Another group of epidemiological

---

*(1) "Imagine that we flip a fair coin 1,000 times. What is your best guess about how many times the coin would come up heads in 1,000 flips?" (2) "In the BIG BUCKS LOTTERY, the chance of winning a $10 prize is 1%. What is your best guess about how many people would win a $10 prize if 1,000 people each bought a ticket to BIG BUCKS?" and (3) "In ACME PUBLISHING SWEEPSTAKES, the chance of winning a car is 1 in 1,000. What percent of tickets to ACME PUBLISHING SWEEPSTAKES win a car?"

numeracy studies explored patients' understanding of risk for an illness or the benefits of a potential treatment based on different methods of mathematically or graphically presenting the data.[40-44]

In these studies, different forms of numeracy assessment were used to examine specific patient skills. Their findings indicate that numeracy is indeed a barrier to patient comprehension of health care information and that the method of expressing quantitative data may influence patient understanding. More research is needed to determine whether numeracy questions asked in addition to reading recognition or reading comprehension questions yield a more complete picture of patient literacy and, if so, which questions would be most appropriate.

SELECTING AND ADMINISTERING LITERACY TESTS

With so many assessment instruments available, deciding which to choose—or whether to screen at all—can be a difficult decision. Table 10-2 lists issues to consider when selecting and administering literacy tests. Researchers and providers must consider the cost of the test, the training required to administer and score the test, and whether the test is appropriate for the target population's age, primary language, and visual acuity.

When administering literacy tests, patient perspective should always be considered. Being a patient is stressful for many people, and patients with low literacy may experience additional anxiety, fearing that they will be required to read forms, signs, or other written materials during the visit. For many patients, particularly those with low literacy, test-taking may have been an unpleasant experience in school. Individuals enrolled in adult literacy classes have indicated that literacy testing in a health care setting, no matter how it is presented to them, can be a stressful and sometimes shameful experience. Researchers and providers who decide to test patients must ensure that testing is conducted in private. They also need to consider the rationale patients will be given about the testing. Another important consideration is that research assistants be trained to be sensitive to patients' potential embarrassment or shame regarding testing. Personnel conducting the test should not insist on testing if the patient is unwilling to participate or wishes to stop the process.

Before deciding to test, investigators need to consider what the patient will be told about the results, how results will be kept, and how results will affect care. We recommend patients be asked, "Will you be willing to say these words/answer these questions? This will help us better understand what education would be most helpful to you, how

TABLE 10-2

**Issues to be Considered Before Selecting and Administering
Literacy Tests in Health Care Settings**

General

- Purpose
- Time available
- Test location
- How will provider use the results? Will results be available to other health providers such as nurses, pharmacists, patient educators, or nutritionists in the system?
- Training required to administer and score
- Confidentiality

Patient characteristics

- Age (Is the test appropriate for pediatric, adolescent, or geriatric populations?)
- Language
- Vision
- Hearing
- Cognitive function
- Presence/absence of acute illness
- Timing (Is the patient seriously ill? Has the patient just been given bad news?)

Test characteristics

- Cost
- Validity and reliability
- Ease of administration and scoring
- Acceptability to patients
- Acceptability to providers
- Reports in the literature

to better serve you, etc." Whatever the message, it must be honest and straightforward.

LIMITATIONS OF LITERACY TESTING IN HEALTH CARE SETTINGS

In health care settings, literacy skills are best assessed using brief, simple tests. Although simple instruments make literacy assessments practical, such instruments have limitations. For example, these tests cannot determine the cause or type of reading or learning difficulty or the probability of whether a patient can or will adhere to medical instructions. Literacy tests in medical settings are thus used only to detect low literacy, not to diagnose specific reading, learning, or health literacy problems.

Limitations of Literacy Testing for Research

Many of the general considerations for selecting and administering literacy tests—eg, time needed for testing, training for administration, and scoring—can also be limitations to literacy testing for research. In addition, researchers should be aware of potential confounders. Cognitive deficits secondary to disease or medications,[45] visual deficits, distress due to personal illness or to a child's illness, crying, or hospitalization may influence research results. Regional accents and differences in pronunciation may lead to scoring difficulties when literacy is assessed with reading recognition tests. Although no research has been conducted to specifically examine the effects of these factors, researchers should be aware of these potential confounders when designing studies and examining research findings.

Another limitation of literacy testing for research is the fact that literacy tests appropriate for the health care setting are currently available only in English and Spanish. Despite the diverse population in the United States, literacy testing is possible in only two languages, which may or may not be a subject's first or preferred language. To obtain health literacy data for non-English–and non-Spanish–speaking populations, research may be needed to develop tools to measure literacy in the native language or to determine whether existing English-based tools yield meaningful results.

Limitations of Literacy Testing for Clinical Applications

Although awareness of the effects of health literacy is increasing, it is not known how common health literacy screening is in clinical settings. Several issues must be considered before patients' literacy skills are identified. Creators of the most commonly used reading tests in health care settings recommend only aggregate testing to provide profiles of the reading abilities of groups of patients in clinics or health systems.[4,11] They do not recommend testing individual patients unless specific health education interventions are being tailored for the patient.[4,9] In addition, these experts recommend not recording reading grade levels in medical records because of the potential ramifications for employment, job security, and privacy. If providers test a patient's literacy skills, they need to be sensitive to the patient's concerns and potential embarrassment, and ensure that testing results will be confidential.[5,11]

Perhaps more important, there is no evidence that literacy testing results in improved delivery of health care or improved health outcomes. A person's score on a literacy test or measured reading level is only an indication that they may struggle to understand and follow through with oral or written health care instructions. It may predict a patient's ability to acquire knowledge and understanding but not necessarily a patient's ability or willingness to learn to manage their health and health care and their health outcomes. Furthermore, if support for patients with limited literacy skills is not available, screening for limited literacy may not be useful. Data from a preliminary trial indicate that feedback to clinicians regarding their diabetic patients' health literacy screening results in lower clinician satisfaction with the visit and lower self-rated effectiveness with regard to the diabetes care they provide.[46] Clearly, additional research is needed to examine the impact and usefulness of literacy feedback to clinicians.

CONCLUSION

Numerous research studies have identified the importance of literacy skills for patients in obtaining high-quality health care and effectively managing their own and their families' health. However, the assessment of patient literacy skills in health care settings is an emerging field. As the "first steps" in this field, the instruments currently used have made it possible to measure the overall prevalence of limited literacy among many patient populations and to advance the study of literacy in health and health care.

As the field of health literacy evolves, increased investigation is needed to advance from literacy assessment for research to literacy assessment for clinical applications. The prevalence of low literacy in health care settings has already been recognized. In developing interventions, more research is needed to determine whether—and how—identifying patients with low health literacy can improve patient-provider relationships and health outcomes.

ACKNOWLEDGMENTS

The authors thank Michael Wolf, PhD, Northwestern University, and Elizabeth Quillin, medical student at Louisiana State University Health Sciences Center in Shreveport (LSUHSC-S) for careful reading of the manuscript, and Stephanie Savory, research assistant at LSUHSC-S, for research and development of Table 10-1.

REFERENCES

1. Ad Hoc Committee on Health Literacy for the Council on Scientific Affairs, American Medical Associaton. Health literacy: report of the Council on Scientific Affairs. *JAMA*. 1999;281:552–557.

2. Baker DW, Parker RM, Williams MV, Clark S, Nurss J. Functional health literacy, self-reported health status, and use of health services. *Am J Public Health*. 1997;87:1027–1030.

3. Baker DW, Parker RM, Williams MV, Clark WS. Health literacy and the risk of hospital admission. *J Gen Intern Med*. 1998;13:791–798.

4. Davis TC, Williams MV, Marin E, Parker RM, Glass J. Health literacy and cancer communication. *CA Cancer J Clin*. 2002;52:134–149.

5. Doak CC, Doak LG, Root JH. *Teaching Patients with Low-Literacy Skills*, 2nd ed. Philadelphia, Pa: JB Lippincott; 1996.

6. Weiss BD, Blanchard JS, McGee DL, et al. Illiteracy among Medicaid recipients and its relationship to health care costs. *J Health Care Poor Underserved*. 1994; 99–111.

7. Williams MV, Davis TC, Parker RM, Weiss BD. The role of health literacy in patient-physician communication. *Fam Med*. 2002:34:383–389.

8. Schillinger D, Grumbach K, Piette J, et al. Association of health literacy with diabetes outcomes. *JAMA*. 2002;288(4):475–482.

9. Parker RM, Ratzan SC, Lurie N. Health literacy: a policy challenge for advancing high-quality health care. *Health Aff (Millwood)*. 2003,Jul–Aug;22(4):147–153.

10. Davis T, Crouch M, Wills G, Miller S, Adebhou D. The gap between patient reading comprehension and the readability of patient education materials. *J Fam Pract*. 1990;31:533–538.

11. Davis TC, Michielutte R, Askov EN, et al. Practical assessment of adult literacy in healthcare. *Health Educ Behav*. 1998;25:613–624.

12. Bass PF III, Wilson JF, Griffith CH, Barnett DR. Residents' ability to identify patients with poor literacy skills. *Acad. Med*, 2002; 77:1039–1041.

13. Davis T, Mayeaux E, Fredrickson S, Bocchini J, Jackson R, Murphy P. Reading ability of parents compared with reading level of pediatric patient education materials. *Pediatrics*. 1994;93:460–468.

14. Jackson RF, Davis TC, Bairnsfather LE, Gault H. Patient reading ability: An overlooked problem in health care. *South Med J*. 1991;84(10): 1172–1175.

15. Williams MV, Parker RM, Baker DW, et al. Inadequate functional health literacy among patients at two public hospitals. *JAMA*. 1995;274: 1677–1682.

16. Parikh NS, Parker RM, Nurss JR, Baker DW, Williams MV. Shame and health literacy: The unspoken connection. *Patient Educ Counsel*. 1996;27:33–39.

17. Selden CR, Zorn M, Ratzan SC, Parker RM. *Current Bibliographies in Medicine 2000–1: Health Literacy*. Available at www.nlm.nih.gov/pubs/cbm/hliteracy.html. Accessed July 10, 2003.

18. Kirsch I, Jungeblut A, Jenkins L, Kolstad A. *Adult Literacy in America: A First Look at the Results of the National Adult Literacy Survey*. Washington, DC: National Center for Education Statistics, US Department of Education; 1993.

19. Weiss BD. *Health Literacy: A Manual for Clinicians*. Chicago, Ill: AMA Foundation; 2003.

20. Gazmararian JA, Baker DW, Williams MV, et al. Health literacy among Medicare enrollees in a managed care organization. *JAMA*. 1999; 281:545–551.

21. Markwardt FS. *Peabody Individual Achievement Test-Revised*. Circle Pines, Minn: American Guidance Service; 1989.

22. Davis T, Fredrickson D, Arnold C, Murphy P, Herbst M, Bocchini J. A polio immunization pamphlet with increased appeal and simplified language does not improve comprehension to an acceptable level. *Patient Educ Counsel*. 1998;33:25–27.

23. Wilkinson GS. *Wide Range Achievement Test – Revised 3*. Wilmington, Del: Jastak Associates; 1993.

24. Slosson RJL. *Slosson Oral Reading Tests—Revised*. East Aurora, NY: Slosson Educational Publishers; 1990.

25. Davis TC, Long SW, Jackson RH, et al. Rapid estimate of adult literacy in medicine: a shortened screening instrument. *Fam Med*. 1993;25:391–395.

26. Bass PF III, Wilson JF, Griffith CH. A shortened instrument for literacy screening. *J Gen Intern Med*. 2003;18:1036–1038.

27. Nath CR, Sylvester ST, Yasek V, Gundel E. Development and validation of a literacy assessment tool for persons with diabetes. *Diabetes Educ*. 2001;27:857–864

28. Hanson-Divers EC. Developing a medical achievement reading test to evaluate patient literacy skills: a preliminary study. *J Health Care Poor Underserved*. 1997;8:56–69.

29. Parker R, Baker D, Williams M, Nurss J. The test of functional health literacy in adults (TOFHLA): a new instrument for measuring patients' literacy skills. *J Gen Intern Med*. 1995;10:537–545. Reprinted with permission of Peppercorn Books and Press (www.peppercornbooks.com)

30. Baker DW, Williams MW, Parker RM, Gazmararian JA. Development of a brief test to measure functional health literacy. *Patient Educ Counsel*. 1999;38:33–42.

31. Nurss JR, Parker RM, Williams MV, Baker DW. *Test of Functional Health Literacy in Adults*. Snow Camp, NC: Peppercorn Books & Press; 2001.

32. Nurss JR, Baker D, Davis T, Parker R, Williams M. Difficulties in functional health literacy screening in Spanish-speaking adults. *J Reading*. 1995;38:632–637.

33. Blanchard JS, Garcia HS, Carter RM. *Instrumento Para Diagnosticar Lecturas (Español-English): Instrument for the diagnosis of reading*. Dubuque, Iowa: Kendall-Hunt; 1989.

34. Rogers BG. Review of the tests of adult basic education, forms 7 & 8. Impara JC, Plake BS, eds. *The Thirteenth Mental Measurements Yearbook*. Lincoln, Neb: Buros Institute of Mental Measurements; 1998.

35. Williams RT. Review of the Adult Basic Learning Examination, 2nd ed. Kramer JJ, Conoley JC, eds. *The Eleventh Mental Measurements Yearbook*. Lincoln, Neb: Buros Institute of Mental Measurements; 1992.

36. Lipkus IM, Samsa G, Rimer BK. General performance on a numeracy scale among highly educated samples. *Med Decis Making*. 2001;21(1):37–44.

37. Schwartz LM, Woloshin S, Black WC, Welch HG. The role of numeracy in understanding the benefit of screening mammography. *Ann Intern Med*. 1997;127(11):966–972.

38. Woloshin S, Schwartz LM, Black WC, Welch HG. Women's perceptions of breast cancer risk: how you ask matters. *Med Decis Making*. 1999;19(3):211–219.

39. Woloshin S, Schwartz LM, Moncur M, Gabriel S, Tosteson AN. Assessing values for health: numeracy matters. *Med Decis Making*. 2001;21(5):382–390.

40. Weinfurt KP, Castel LD, Li Y, et al. The correlation between patient characteristics and expectations of benefit from Phase I clinical trials. *Cancer*. 2003;98(1):166–175.

41. Adeksward V, Sachs L. The meaning of 6.8: numeracy and normality in health information talks. *Soc Sci Med*. 1996;43(8):1179–1187.

42. Hux JE, Naylor CD. Communicating the benefits of chronic preventive therapy: does the format of efficacy data determine patients' acceptance of treatment? *Med Decis Making*. 1995;15(2):152–157.

43. Mazur DJ, Hickman DH. Patients' and physicians' interpretations of graphic data displays. *Med Decis Making*. 1993;13(1):59–63.

44. Taylor KL, Shelby RA, Schwartz MD, et al. The impact of item order on ratings of cancer risk perception. *Cancer Epidemiol Biomakers Prev*. 2002;11(7):645–649.

45. Baker DW, Gazmararian JA, Sudano J, Patterson M, Parker RM, Williams MV. Health literacy and performance on the Mini-Mental Status Examination. *Aging Ment Health*. 2002;6:22–29.

46. Schillinger D, Piette J, Daher C, Liu H, Bindman AB. Should we be screening for functional health literacy problems among patients with diabetes? *J Gen Intern Med*. 2001;16(s1):172.

A Conceptual Framework for the Relationship Between Health Literacy and Health Care Outcomes: The Chronic Disease Exemplar

Dean Schillinger, MD, MPH, and Terry Davis, PhD

Note: This work was supported, in part, through the National Center for Research Resources (K-23 RR16539), the Commonwealth Fund, and the Soros Open Society Institute and has been adapted from a manuscript written for *Health Literacy: A Prescription to End Confusion* (Institute of Medicine, Washington, DC, 2004).

This chapter presents a conceptual framework that introduces the ways in which limited health literacy might influence health care outcomes. This type of framework can inform research priorities, identify points of intervention, and illuminate the broader social context that affects the quality of health care for the 40 million Americans with limited literacy and the even greater number of individuals with limited health literacy.

Currently there is a lack of precision and uniformity regarding the meaning of the term *health literacy*.[1] For that reason and for the purposes of this chapter, certain definitional issues must be addressed. Health literacy has been variably defined as (1) the degree to which individuals have the capacity to obtain, process, and understand basic health information and services needed to make appropriate health decisions[2]; (2) a constellation of skills, including the ability to perform basic reading and numerical tasks required to function in the health care environment[3]; and (3) an individual's ability to read health-related materials, as measured by the Rapid Estimate of Adult Literacy in Medicine (REALM),[4] Test of Functional Health Literacy in Adults (TOFHLA),[5] and other screening tools.[6]

It is apparent from these three definitions that, although literacy and numeracy skills are deeply embedded in the construct of health literacy, there is little consensus as to the extent to which "literacy" equates with "health literacy." In this chapter, our approach to this problem is to acknowledge that such a lack of consensus exists and to simply use the term *health literacy*. In so doing, however, it is important to point out that much of the literature we have drawn from relies on measures that predominantly capture an individual's reading skills, either in the health care or non–health care context. As described in Chapter 1, literacy skills may be necessary but not entirely sufficient to achieve health literacy. Regardless of how the meaning of the term *health literacy* evolves, it is apparent to most investigators in the field that the problems associated with having limited health literacy will remain most intense for those with limited literacy skills. In addition, since our society places high literacy demands on its members despite wide variation in literacy levels, it is apparent that attempts to reduce disparities related to health literacy must revolve around directly addressing the problem of basic literacy and/or creating a health care system in which the gap between the literacy demands of the system and the literacy skills of the patients it serves is significantly narrowed.

In developing a framework for the relationship between limited health literacy and health outcomes, we have selected the exemplar of chronic disease care. Not only are chronic diseases common, but much of the burden of chronic disease falls on the elderly and those of low socioeconomic status—populations that have also been shown to have disproportionately high rates of health literacy problems.[7,8] Since a significant proportion of health literacy research has involved chronic diseases, chronic disease care provides the greatest evidence base with which to draw our preliminary conclusions. In addition, given the ever-increasing self-management demands placed on patients with chronic conditions, chronic disease care provides an example of the growing mismatch between the demands of the health care system and the capacities of the patients and communities it serves. An analysis of chronic disease care serves both as a harbinger of the increasing complexity of the health care system and an opportunity to understand the systemic problems that patients experience, with the goal of developing a framework for reengineering.

In this chapter, we briefly review the elements of the best-accepted model for restructuring chronic disease care delivery, the Chronic Care Model of Wagner[9]; describe how limited health literacy may be associated with worse chronic disease care; apply a new framework to broaden our understanding of the Chronic Care Model and highlight opportunities to reduce health literacy–related disparities; and reflect on strategies to promote improvement in chronic disease care for patients with limited health literacy.

CHRONIC DISEASE CARE AND THE CHRONIC CARE MODEL

Chronic disease management is a major challenge facing patients and health care systems in industrialized nations. Nearly half of the US population has one or more chronic medical conditions, and nearly three quarters of all health care resources are devoted to the treatment of chronic diseases.[10] Effective disease management is predicated on systematic, interactive communication between a population of patients with the disease and the providers and health system with whom they interact,[11,12] all occurring in the context of a supportive community with resources that are aligned with patients' needs.[13] The collaboration between patients, providers, the system of care, and the community that is required to optimize health outcomes adds a significant layer of complexity to the delivery of health care to individuals with chronic disease.

The last few decades have seen tremendous advances in the care of chronic conditions, including an array of therapeutic options, risk factor modification for secondary prevention of comorbid conditions, the availability of home monitoring tools, and the growth of disease management programs.[14–18] Despite these advances, health quality for patients with chronic disease remains less than optimal and varies across sociodemographic lines.[19–23] In particular, rushed practitioners find it difficult to follow established practice guidelines, limited coordination hampers multidisciplinary care, inadequate training leaves many patients poorly equipped to manage their illnesses, and lack of active follow-up leads to preventable deterioration in function.

Some managed care organizations and integrated delivery systems have sought to correct the many deficiencies in current management of chronic diseases. To guide the reorganization of chronic disease care, Dr Ed Wagner and others developed the Chronic Care Model (Figure 11-1), which summarizes the basic elements for improving care in health systems at multiple levels.[9,24] The elements of self-management support, decision support, delivery system design, and clinical information systems exist within the level of the community and the health system. These elements feed into productive interactions between a prepared, proactive practice team and an informed, activated patient to produce improved functional and clinical outcomes.

For example, a community may have the infrastructure and resources to facilitate patients' self-management (eg, by providing transportation to appointments, safe recreational spaces for physical activity, adequate produce for healthy food choices, and opportunities for educational or communal engagement). In addition, a health system may organize its delivery of care to provide patients with self-management activities (eg, group medical visits or other organized, skill-building activities), and decision support (eg, counseling and informational materials). It may structure its delivery system design to include multidisciplinary teams, planned visits, or home visits and to use clinical information systems such as disease registries to track patients' progress, stratify intensity of care, promote outreach, and maintain continuity.

The Chronic Care Model represents an evidence-based distillation of literature that supports the importance of community-oriented care; executive leadership and incentives to promote quality;

FIGURE 11-1

Model for Improvement of Chronic Illness Care

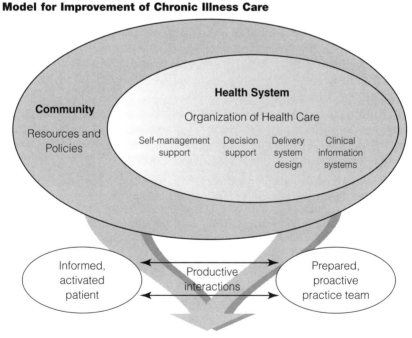

Functional and Clinical Outcomes

Source: Wagner EH. Chronic disease management: What will it take to improve care for chronic illness? *Eff Clin Pract*. 1998; 1: 2–4.

self-management training[11,25]; and systems that track and monitor patients' progress, promote outreach, and support timely provider decision-making.[26] Patients and providers who are prepared in these ways arguably can engage in more productive interactions that promote patient well-being and system efficiency.[12] Focusing on these components, in principle, will foster interactions between patients who take an active part in their care and providers who are backed up by resources and expertise. However, if the Chronic Care Model is applied without attention to the unique challenges posed by limited health literacy, there is the risk of perpetuating disparities in outcomes for those with limited health literacy.

It is increasingly apparent that the health care system has not evolved to serve those with limited health literacy. However, because self-management practices and clinical outcomes in chronic disease care appear to vary by patients' level of health literacy,[27–29] the Chronic Care Model, and similar comprehensive, population-based disease management approaches, may offer insights into the ways in which limited health literacy affects chronic disease care and highlight points of intervention. Evidence from a small randomized trial suggests that disease management strategies can reduce health literacy–related disparities in diabetes care[30] and that tailoring communication to those with limited health literacy can affect outcomes in chronic anticoagulation[31] and diabetes care.[32,33] However, we are unaware of any comprehensive disease management system that has been specifically designed to improve chronic disease care for individuals with limited health literacy. Developing such a system would most likely benefit not only those with limited health literacy but all chronic disease patients, because many of the barriers faced by those with limited health literacy are also experienced, albeit to a lesser extent, by those with adequate health literacy.

HOW LIMITED HEALTH LITERACY AFFECTS CHRONIC DISEASE OUTCOMES

Whether limited health literacy is a marker for other determinants of health, such as socioeconomic status, or is in the causal pathway to poor health is currently a matter of debate. While there is evidence that raising literacy levels in the developing world can lead to marked improvements in infant mortality and the health status of a population,[34, 35] it is not known whether the same would apply in so-called developed nations, such as the United States. The conceptual framework presented here is to be interpreted less as a causal model and more as an "ecological model," one that characterizes the complex web of factors that can influence the quality of health care, with health literacy placed at the center of this web.

While scientific advances and market forces place greater technical and self-management demands on patients, the health care system poorly prepares patients and their families to master these skills and remains resistant to the mounting need for system redesign.[36] This constellation of forces appears to engender unequal outcomes, despite equal access.[37] This dynamic is not unique to health care and has been previously characterized by adult literacy experts as being generalizable to other functional domains.[38] Despite the growing recognition that a significant proportion of US residents have limited literacy, literacy remains a value intrinsic to our society and a "demand" that our society places on its citizens. With regard to the quality of chronic disease care, which is a function of self-management, self-advocacy, ongoing monitoring, and interactive communication, the results of a number of studies suggest that health literacy may actually be in the causal pathway.

Limited health literacy may affect chronic disease care across the provider-patient interface and health system–patient interface and at the community level. A growing body of research demonstrates that limited literacy is independently associated with worse health status,[39] higher utilization of services,[40,41] and worse clinical outcomes.[28,29] In response, Figure 11-2 presents a conceptual framework for improving chronic disease care that is based on health literacy and related research. As depicted in this framework, enhanced provider-patient communication, community factors, and home-based monitoring and clinical support can lead to improved clinical outcomes and better quality of life. However, there are health literacy barriers that must first be overcome. These barriers are discussed in the following paragraphs.

Barriers in Office-Based Clinician-Patient Communication

Much of chronic disease care takes place in the context of an office visit. Communication about chronic diseases during outpatient visits may be hampered by several factors. These include the relative infrequency and brevity of visits, language barriers and limited health literacy, differences between providers' and patients' agendas and communication styles, lack of trust between the patient and provider, overriding or competing clinical problems, lack of timeliness of visits in relation to disease-specific problems, and the complexity and variability of patients' reporting of symptoms and trends in their health status. A recent study found one in three US patients leave the physician's office with important questions unanswered, two in five do not follow physician advice because it is too difficult or because they disagree with it, and two in three report that the physician did not elicit their ideas or opinions about treatment or care.[42]

Patients with chronic diseases and limited health literacy have been shown to have poor knowledge of their condition and of its management,[27,43] often despite having received standard self-management education. Patients with limited health literacy have greater difficulties accurately reporting their medication regimens and describing the reasons for which their medications were prescribed[31,44,45] and more frequently have explanatory models that may conflict with those of health care providers.[46] A recent study among patients with diabetes demonstrates that patients with limited health literacy also experience difficulties with oral communication with their physicians.[33] Patients appear to have particular problems with both the decision-making and the explanatory, technical components of clinical dialogue. Clinicians' frequent use of jargon in clinical encounters may be particularly problematic for patients with limited health literacy (Table 11-1). This jargon can range from technical jargon (words that have meaning only in the clinical context, eg, *glucometer*), to quantitative jargon (words for which clinical judgment is required to accurately interpret, eg, *excessive* wheezing), to lay jargon (words for which two meanings exist, one with clinical meaning and the other with lay meaning, eg, your weight is *stable*).

Clinicians are often unaware of the mismatch between their process of giving information and patients' process of recalling, understanding, and acting on the information.[47–49] Patients with limited literacy often lack skills needed to write a list of questions for the visit or to take notes during a visit or on a phone call with their provider. Providers may fail to detect knowledge or comprehension deficits because patients with limited health literacy may be less likely to challenge or ask questions of the provider[50,51] and disclose poor understanding and they may handle the interaction by being passive or appearing uninterested.[52,53] Finally, clinicians tend to misjudge the information needs of patients[54] and underuse interactive teaching strategies that may be especially useful for patients with limited health literacy.[32]

Barriers in Home-Based Monitoring and Clinical Support

Chronic disease care involves an ongoing process of patient assessments, adjustments to treatment plans, and reassessments to measure change in patient health status. Without timely and reliable information about patients' health status, symptoms, and self-care,

TABLE 11-1

Results from an Ongoing Study of Physicians' Use of Jargon Among Diabetic Patients with Limited Health Literacy*

Example 1: Lay Jargon		Example 2: Technical Jargon		Example 3: Quantitative Jargon	
Weight is Stable		**Dialysis**		**Wide Range**	
MD: "Your weight is stable since I saw you a couple of months ago."		MD: "Do you know what the number one cause for people in this country being on dialysis is? Diabetes"		MD: "How have your sugars been running?…That's a wide range!"	
Would you please tell me in your own words what weight is stable means?	In your own words, what do you think the doctor was trying to tell the patient?	Would you please tell me in your own words what dialysis means?	In your own words, what do you think the doctor was trying to tell the patient?	Would you please tell me in your own words what wide range means?	In your own words, what do you think the doctor was trying to tell the patient?
"I don't know."	"Saying uh…I didn't weigh as much as I did the last time."	"Check something every day."	"Sugar is too high."	"I don't know."	"That means it's high."
"I can't explain."	"Very good."	"What? Is that about your toes?"	"I can't say it"	"I don't know."	"OK my blood test, my blood pressure is OK. That's not high, it's low."
"That my body's stable weight—stable means the body's losing or gaining."	"He says that the weight has to gain."	"It means that your diabetes is going worse that you have to exercise to make diabetes."	"Means that more people are getting diabetes."	"Wide range could mean something is wrong with the body. It could mean blood, heart, liver, kidneys."	"That the sugar is getting out of control—it would be too high."

Adapted from: Babel babble: physicians' use of jargon with diabetes patients. Castro et al. Journal of General Internal Medicine. 2004;19 (suppl):124–125.

* Patients were asked to define jargon terms and were then presented with excerpts from audiotaped clinic visits and asked to provide their interpretations of jargon-containing phrases.

the necessary health education, treatments, or behavioral adjustments may come late or not at all, compromising patients' health and increasing the likelihood of poor outcomes.

To effectively manage their disease, patients must remember any self-care instructions they have received from their provider, be able to correctly interpret symptoms or results of self-monitoring, adjust treatment regimens as needed, and know when and how to contact the provider should the need arise. A number of studies demonstrate that patients remember and understand as little as half of what they are told by their physicians[53,55–58] and that, the more information they are provided, the less they are able to recall.[59] Patients with limited health literacy are likely to understand and remember at even lower rates. In addition, they may be less equipped to overcome gaps when they are at home due to knowledge deficits[27,43] and difficulties reading or interpreting instructions.[27,58] Cross-sectional studies involving patients with diabetes suggest that traditional self-management education may not eliminate health literacy–related disparities in chronic disease outcomes.[27,29,43]

Unfortunately, a minority of clinical practices provides any form of care management that involves outreach and support in the patient's home.[60] In addition, home-based disease-specific education, monitoring, and clinical support increasingly rely on patients and providers interacting via Web-based or e-health interfaces.[61] These interfaces may present overwhelming barriers to patients with limited health literacy because of difficulty accessing Web sites,[62] reading from these sites,[63,64] and navigating through them.[61,65,66] Simply transforming text versions of disease-specific education to more visually oriented media (ie, CD-ROM), while increasing satisfaction, does not appear to increase knowledge among patients with limited health literacy. Focus groups of patients with limited health literacy have identified "health system navigation," such as knowing whom, for what, and when to call for assistance with a problem, as a particularly daunting aspect of chronic disease management.[51, 67]

Community and Environmental Barriers

Data from the National Adult Literacy Survey[68] demonstrate regional variation in literacy rates that parallels neighborhood patterns of socioeconomic status, immigrant status, age, and race and ethnicity. Studies in health care settings[7,8] indicate that patients with limited health literacy comprise a large sector of patients in public hospitals and community clinics that predominantly serve socioeconomically disadvantaged populations and in private health systems that serve the elderly or those with low incomes, such as Medicare and Medicaid managed care organizations.[69] Much of the variation in literacy in the

United States likely reflects disparities in access to and quality of education, a problem of greatest significance for older disadvantaged populations, as well as for immigrants who have had only limited schooling. It is important to point out, however, that among individuals with limited literacy skills, the majority are Caucasian and poor.[68]

Little work has been done to explore how community factors can either assist or hamper disease management efforts for patients with limited health literacy. Communities that have high rates of limited health literacy may be less able to assert political power and advocate for the health and health care needs of their community.[1] Residents of medically underserved areas experience greater difficulties accessing a regular source of health care, a problem that has been shown to be associated with preventable hospitalizations for chronic conditions.[70] Other environmental attributes of communities, such as the availability of goods and services that promote health, access to adult basic education, the quality of the air and recreational physical space, and occupational risks associated with neighborhood employment, may each interact with limited health literacy to lead to worse health. In addition, recent studies demonstrate racial and ethnic differences in level of trust in the health care system that may influence how these communities interact with the health care system.[37] Finally, the focus of health promotion messages and activities that take place at the community level may not be aligned with the needs of patients with limited health literacy.[1]

SHAPING THE CHRONIC CARE MODEL FOR PATIENTS WITH LIMITED HEALTH LITERACY

One underlying assumption of the Chronic Care Model is that the reorganization of health care will lead to more productive interactions between informed, involved patients and prepared, proactive practice teams that will, in turn, lead to better outcomes (Figure 11-1). In order for this assumption to hold true for populations with limited health literacy, communication across the levels described earlier (Figure 11-2) must be successful.

Previous research indicates that patients want practical, concise information focused on identification of the problem, what specifically the patient needs to do, why it is in their best interest, and what outcomes they can expect.[48,71,72] Communication strategies commonly employed by health professionals are often only marginally effective for those with limited health literacy. At present, clinicians do not have the means to determine how patients learn best, nor the tools to more effectively engage patients who do not appear to be maximally benefiting from clinical interactions.

FIGURE 11-2

Improving Chronic Disease Care: A Framework Based on Health Literacy and Related Research

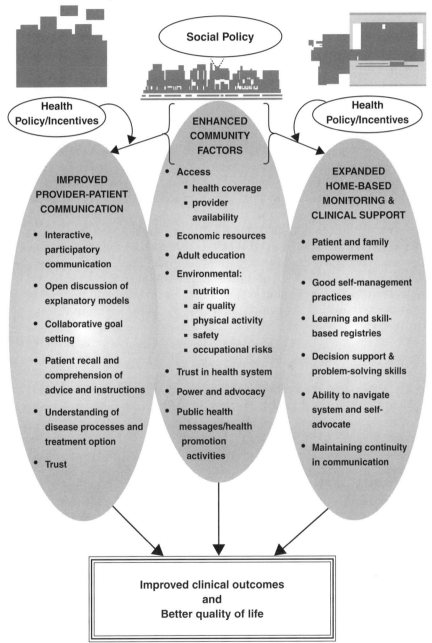

Some principles derived from the field of adult education may be relevant to chronic disease communication.[73–75] Patients should be actively involved in developing health education messages, materials, and programs.[76–78] This involvement helps ensure that the education is relevant, understandable, culturally sensitive, and empowering. Moreover, adult learning theory indicates provider-patient education should involve exploration and problem-based learning.[79] Patient education should be designed to engage patients in ways relevant to their lives and their conditions and that enhance problem-solving skills.[80] Such educational focus may lead to patient-generated goal-setting, an important intermediate objective in successful chronic disease care.[81,82] Group medical visits, an innovation in which groups of patients who share a common condition regularly meet with a health provider, have the potential to operate via these principles. Results of a small trial with diabetes patients suggest that, when designed with the collaboration of an expert in adult education, such visits can dramatically improve outcomes.[83,84]

As chronic disease education, monitoring, and clinical support move beyond the office walls to include e-health and other forms of telemedicine, it is critical that patients with limited health literacy not be left behind.[61,63,85] Individuals with limited health literacy must be involved in all stages of intervention design and testing. This participatory development method[86,87] allows for input during the generative phase of an intervention, provides opportunities for feedback during multiple points of pilot testing, and can engender trust and participation during the evaluation phase. As an example, our recent work at San Francisco General Hospital involves development of an automated telephone diabetes management system for patients with limited health literacy. The idea for a telephone-based intervention was generated, in part, by patients. Through the active involvement of adult learners and patients with limited health literacy, we significantly altered numerous aspects of the program. Patients wanted confirmation that we were actively listening and caring about their well-being. They preferred narratives instead of instruction, recommended we reduce the speed at which messages are delivered, and suggested that we limit the amount of technical language. We are currently evaluating the impact of this system on diabetes-related outcomes.

As health care systems design disease registries and implement registry-driven care, attention should be paid to developing and including the following: measures of patients' learning preferences and abilities so that a heterogeneous set of providers can communicate consistently; checklists of critical self-management skills that have been mastered so as to stratify efforts based on self-management skills, not just distal clinical outcomes; and lists of resources available in patients' communities to support their self-care. Evidence from a small randomized trial suggests that these types of disease management strategies can reduce health literacy–related disparities in diabetes care[30] and that tailoring communication to those with limited health literacy can affect outcomes in prevention efforts,[76,86] chronic anticoagulation,[31] and diabetes care.[32,33]

If all patients with chronic diseases are to benefit from emerging technologies, particularly interventions that involve the Internet, research must explore how to best design such programs for patients with limited literacy.[61] Such research will also require professional collaboration between disciplines such as computer science, health communication, education, economics, marketing, sociology, and library and information science. In addition, given the expansion and evolution of direct-to-consumer marketing, we must pay particular attention to the effects of this strategy on those with limited health literacy and foster the development of a critical consciousness.

If we are to redesign the health care delivery system and better support patients in their self-management, we must recognize the needs that patients with limited health literacy have expressed with regard to system navigation. We must better understand the elements of successful system navigation and apply this understanding to enhance patients' navigational and self-advocacy skills and better equip patients to get what they need from a complex system. This can be done by partnering with patients with limited health literacy to identify those aspects of the system that represent bottlenecks and to design solutions that lower such barriers. The fragmentation resulting from discontinuity in health care negatively impacts communication and self-care[88] and likely affects those with limited health literacy to a great extent. Emerging issues in the delivery of health care, such as legislated policies related to privacy, may create unintended, additional burdens for patients with limited health literacy and their providers by potentially depriving them of the assistance of friends and family in safely and effectively carrying out care plans.

A crucial component of reducing the burden of limited health literacy lies with health care providers. A solution commonly proposed to improve care for patients with limited health literacy has been to measure patients' health literacy levels and then provide this information to the treating clinicians. Preliminary results of a trial exploring the impact of health literacy screening of patients with feedback of results to physicians found that feedback led to higher rates of recommended physician communication strategies, but lower physician confidence and satisfaction.[89] This work suggests that future efforts should focus less on identifying patients with limited health literacy and more on clinician skill-building regarding patient assessment and engagement. Training of all health professionals that focuses on communication strategies to enhance clinician self-awareness,[90] mutual learning, partnership-building, collaborative goal-setting, and behavior change for chronic disease patients is essential.[9,91] Such training should be expanded to include all members of the multidisciplinary health team, including lay health educators, both as learners and teachers. Training efforts must be informed by new health communication research that involves patients with limited health literacy, a segment often underrepresented in clinical research.

Community efforts should focus on developing relationships that foster trust, providing resources to measure and meet community needs, creating stronger links between the delivery system and community resources, and ultimately preparing community members to effectively advocate for the needs of their community.[92] Adult basic education should be promoted and curricula should be expanded to include issues of health and health care. Public health and health promotion messages should take into account the health literacy skills of the population to whom the message is being targeted, involve the population from the beginning, and make use of appropriate channels to convey these messages.[93]

MEASURING PROGRESS

To promote progress in chronic care delivery for patients with limited health literacy, quality-of-care measures must be designed to capture health literacy–related performance. If incentives are aligned to improve quality, the development of quality measures can, in turn, lead to the creation of standards of care and improve practice. The main challenge is to establish new incentives that will create such a case,[94] rather than demonstrate that there is a "business case" for improving health care quality for those with limited health literacy.

There are several ways to measure the extent to which health systems are meeting the needs of patients with limited health literacy. An indirect approach, advocated by policymakers and clinicians involved in initiatives to reduce racial and ethnic disparities in quality of care,[37,95] is to use existing measures of quality, such as Medicaid Health Plan Employer Data and Information Set (HEDIS) indicators (which currently do not include any health literacy–specific indicators) and to stratify a system's performance by race/ethnicity or, in this case, health literacy level. Such an approach makes it possible to compare performance in process or outcome measures among those with inadequate literacy vs those with adequate literacy. A health system could be considered to show improvement if overall performance improved and if the extent of health literacy–related variation in performance narrowed over time. The main challenge to this strategy is the complexity involved in measuring health literacy (see Chapter 10).

Current instruments assess literacy in the context of health care, require in-person administration, and can take between 3 and 7 minutes to administer.[6,96] Education level may not be a useful proxy for health literacy, because there is only a modest correlation between education and health literacy. Also, there are interactions between education and other demographic characteristics (eg, ethnicity, age, or primary language) of health literacy.[97] Nonetheless, a recent study suggests that, among native English speakers, an eight-item medical pronunciation test may adequately measure health literacy.[98] A strategy that reduces health literacy–related disparities by measuring health literacy–related quality can succeed only if more rapid and reliable measures of health literacy are developed and validated.

A second approach is to develop novel measures of quality that may be less disease-specific yet have particular relevance to patients with limited health literacy across chronic conditions. One such measure has been developed by the National Center for Quality Assurance (NCQA) for managed care organizations and involves measuring the readability of a specific form, the patient appeal of denial services form.[99] While arguably of importance, the approach of assessing quality by measuring document readability is obviously very narrow in scope and does not capture a more comprehensive view of the patient experience. Other possibilities include measuring patients' reports of their experiences of communication with health care providers[33]; the rates of discordance between patients' and providers' reports of medication regimens[31]; the extent to which home monitoring and support for chronic disease is available[12, 100]; the range of learning options and media available to patient; the ease with which one can navigate a health system; or the degree to which a health system has a family and community orientation.[101] In order for significant progress to be made, research to develop appropriate quality indicators for health literacy–related performance must be performed.

CONCLUSION

Limited health literacy is a dilemma with roots that extend into the core of our society and its legacy of unequal opportunity and the promise of emerging technology. The consequences of limited health literacy, however, appear to be heavily influenced by the extent to which health care providers are unaware of the problem and are poorly trained to respond to it. The consequences are also influenced by the extent to which the current design of the health care system places care management demands on patients without providing them with the preparation and support to succeed in these efforts. Modern chronic disease care requires patients to play an active role in their care and requires clinicians and the health systems in which they work to partner with patients to promote successful outcomes. Meeting these goals is often most challenging for those patients who have the greatest needs. These patients often have the least ability to comprehend and independently act on chronic disease information and are disadvantaged in navigating and functioning in our current health care system.

When considered as a barrier to successful health communication as well as a marker for problems with navigation and self-advocacy, it becomes clear that the concerns related to limited health literacy are inescapably linked to the challenges of chronic disease management. In order to ensure that the Chronic Care Model and increasingly sophisticated chronic disease management programs benefit patients with limited health literacy, programs must be designed and implemented with the involvement of patients with limited health literacy. In addition, programs must be expanded to reach all those with limited health literacy. By promoting meaningful, collaborative communication between patients and the providers and systems that serve them, such a reorganization is likely to benefit all patients.

REFERENCES

1. Nutbeam D. Health literacy as a public health goal: a challenge for contemporary health education and communication strategies into the 21st century. *Health Promot Int*. 2000;15:259–267.

2. US Department of Health and Human Services. Health Communication (Chapter 11). *Healthy People 2010*. 2nd ed. *Understanding and Improving Health* and *Objectives for Improving Health*. 2 vols. Washington, DC: US Government Printing Office, November 2000.

3. Ad Hoc Committee on Health Literacy for the Council on Scientific Affairs, American Medical Association. Health literacy: report of the Council on Scientific Affairs. *JAMA*. 1999;281:552–557.

4. Davis TC, Crouch MA, Long SW, et al. Rapid assessment of literacy levels of adult primary care patients. *Fam Med*. 1991;23:433–435.

5. Parker RM, Baker DW, Williams MV, Nurss JR. The test of functional health literacy in adults: a new instrument for measuring patients' literacy skills. *J Gen Intern Med*. 1995;10:537–541.

6. Davis TC, Michielutte R, Askov EN, Williams MV, Weiss BD. Practical assessment of adult literacy in health care. *Health Educ Behav*. 1998;25:613–624.

7. Williams MV, Parker RM, Baker DW, et al. Inadequate functional health literacy among patients at two public hospitals. *JAMA*. 1995; 274: 1677–1682.

8. Gazmararian JA, Baker DW, Williams MV, et al. Health literacy among Medicare enrollees in a managed care organization. *JAMA*. 1999;281: 545–551.

9. Wagner EH. *The Chronic Care Model*. Improving Chronic Illness Care; 2003. Available at www.improvingchroniccare.org/change/model/components.html. Accessed March 12, 2003.

10. *Chronic Care in America: A 21st Century Challenge*. Princeton, NJ: The Institute for Health & Aging, University of California, San Francisco and The Robert Wood Johnson Foundation; 1996.

11. Von Korff M, Gruman J, Schaefer J, Curry SJ, Wagner EH. Collaborative management of chronic illness. *Ann Intern Med*. 1997;127:1097–1102.

12. Norris SL, Nichols PJ, Caspersen CJ, et al. The effectiveness of disease and case management for people with diabetes: a systematic review. *Am J Prev Med*. 2002;22:15–38.

13. Wagner EH. Population-based management of diabetes care. *Patient Educ Couns*. 1995;26:225–230.

14. The Diabetes Control and Complications Trial Research Group. The effect of intensive treatment of diabetes on the development and progression of long-term complications in insulin-dependent diabetes mellitus. *N Engl J Med*. 1993;329:977–986.

15. The Diabetes Control and Complications Trial Research Group. Lifetime benefits and costs of intensive therapy as practiced in the diabetes control and complications trial. *JAMA*. 1996;276:1409–1415.

16. UK Prospective Diabetes Study (UKPDS) Group. Intensive blood-glucose control with sulphonylureas or insulin compared with conventional treatment and risk of complications in patients with type 2 diabetes (UKPDS 33). *Lancet*. 1998;352:837–853.

17. Bodenheimer T. Disease management—promises and pitfalls. *N Engl J Med*. 1999;340:1202–1205.

18. McCulloch DK, Price MJD, Hindmarsh M, Wagner EH. Improvement in diabetes care using an integrated population-based approach in a primary care setting. *Disease Manag*. 2000;3:75–82.

19. Piette JD. Satisfaction with care among patients with diabetes in two public health care systems. *Med Care*. 1999;37:538–546.

20. Economic consequences of diabetes mellitus in the US in 1997. American Diabetes Association. *Diabetes Care*. 1998;21:296–309.

21. National Diabetes Fact Sheet. Atlanta, Ga: Centers for Disease Control and Prevention; 2000.

22. Vinicor F, Burton B, Foster B, Eastman R. Healthy people 2010: diabetes. *Diabetes Care*. 2000;23:853–855.

23. Fiscella K, Franks P, Gold MR, Clancy CM. Inequality in quality: addressing socioeconomic, racial, and ethnic disparities in health care. *JAMA*. 2000;283:2579–2584.

24. Wagner EH. Chronic disease management: what will it take to improve care for chronic illness? *Eff Clin Pract*. 1998;1:2–4. Available at www.acponline.org/journals/ecp/augsep98/cdmfg1.htm

25. Lorig KR, Sobel DS, Stewart AL, et al. Evidence suggesting that a chronic disease self-management program can improve health status while reducing hospitalization: a randomized trial. *Med Care*. 1999;37:5–14.

26. Piette JD. Interactive voice response systems in the diagnosis and management of chronic disease. *Am J Manag Care*. 2000;6:817–827.

27. Williams MV, Baker DW, Honig EG, Lee TM, Nowlan A. Inadequate literacy is a barrier to asthma knowledge and self-care. *Chest*. 1998;114:1008–1015.

28. Kalichman SC, Rompa D. Functional health literacy is associated with health status and health-related knowledge in people living with HIV-AIDS. *J Acquir Immune Defic Syndr*. 2000;25:337–344.

29. Schillinger D, Grumbach K, Piette J, et al. Association of health literacy with diabetes outcomes. *JAMA*. 2002;288:475–482.

30. Rothman R, Pignone M, Malone R, Bryant B, Crigler B. A primary care-based, pharmacist-led, disease management program improves outcomes for patients with diabetes: a randomized controlled trial. *J Gen Intern Med*. 2003;18:155.

31. Schillinger D, Machtinger E, Win K, et al. Are pictures worth a thousand words? Communication regarding medications in a public hospital anticoagulation clinic. *J Gen Intern Med*. 2003;18:187.

32. Schillinger D, Piette J, Grumbach K, et al. Closing the loop: physician communication with diabetic patients who have low health literacy. *Arch Intern Med*. 2003;163:83–90.

33. Schillinger D, Bindman A, Stewart A, Wang F, Piette J. Health literacy and the quality of physician-patient interpersonal communication. *Patient Educ Couns*. 2004;3:315–323.

34. Cleland JG, Van Ginneken JK. Maternal education and child survival in developing countries: the search for pathways of influence. *Soc Sci Med*. 1988;27:1357–1368.

35. Grosse RN, Auffrey C. Literacy and health status in developing countries. *Annu Rev Public Health*. 1989;10:281–297.

36. *Crossing the Quality Chasm: A New Health System for the 21st Century*. Washington, DC: National Academy Press, Institute of Medicine Committee on Quality of Health Care in America; 2001.

37. Smedley BD, Stith AY, Nelson AR. *Unequal Treatment: Confronting Racial and Ethnic Disparities in Health Care*. A report of the Institute of Medicine. Washington, DC: National Academy Press; 2002.

38. Newman AP, Beverstock C. *Adult Literacy: Contexts and Challenges*. Bloomington, Ind: International Reading Association; ERIC Clearinghouse on Reading and Communication Skills, Indiana University; 1990.

39. Weiss BD, Hart G, McGee DL, D'Estelle S. Health status of illiterate adults: relation between literacy and health status among persons with low literacy skills. *J Am Board Fam Pract*. 1992;5:257–264.

40. Baker DW, Parker RM, Williams MV, Clark WS, Nurss J. The relationship of patient reading ability to self-reported health and use of health services. *Am J Public Health*. 1997;87:1027–1030.

41. Baker DW, Parker RM, Williams MV, Clark WS. Health literacy and the risk of hospital admission. *J Gen Intern Med*. 1998;13:791–798.

42. *Diverse Communities, Common Concerns: Assessing Health Care Quality for Minority Americans*. New York, NY: The Commonwealth Fund; 2002.

43. Williams MV, Baker DW, Parker RM, Nurss JR. Relationship of functional health literacy to patients' knowledge of their chronic disease: a study of patients with hypertension and diabetes. *Arch Intern Med*. 1998;158:166–172.

44. Williams MV, Parker RM, Baker DW, Coates W, Nurss J. The impact of inadequate functional health literacy on patients' understanding of diagnosis, prescribed medications, and compliance. *Acad Emerg Med*. 1995;2:386.

45. Win K, Machtinger E, Wang F, Chan LL, Rodriguez ME, Schillinger D. Understanding of warfarin therapy and stroke among ethnically diverse anticoagulation patients at a public hospital. *J Gen Intern Med*. 2003;18:278.

46. Kalichman SC, Ramachandran B, Catz S. Adherence to combination antiretroviral therapies in HIV patients of low health literacy. *J Gen Intern Med*. 1999;14:267–273.

47. Doak CC, Doak LG, Friedell GH, Meade CD. Improving comprehension for cancer patients with low literacy skills: strategies for clinicians. *CA Cancer J Clin*. 1998;48:151–162.

48. Davis TC, Williams MV, Marin E, Parker RM, Glass J. Health literacy and cancer communication. *CA Cancer J Clin*. 2002;52:134–149.

49. Williams MV, Davis T, Parker RM, Weiss BD. The role of health literacy in patient-physician communication. *Fam Med*. 2002;34:383–389.

50. Street RL, Jr. Information-giving in medical consultations: the influence of patients' communicative styles and personal characteristics. *Soc Sci Med*. 1991;32:541–548.

51. Baker DW, Parker RM, Williams MV, et al. The health care experience of patients with low literacy. *Arch Fam Med*. 1996;5:329–334.

52. Cooper LA, Roter DL. Patient-provider communication: the effect of race and ethnicity on process and outcomes in health care. In: Smedley BD, Stith AY, Nelson AR, eds. *Unequal Treatment: Confronting Racial and Ethnic Disparities in Health Care*. A report of the Institute of Medicine. Washington, DC: National Academy Press; 2002:336–354.

53. Roter DL. The outpatient medical encounter and elderly patients. *Clin Geriatr Med*. 2000;16:95–107.

54. Cegala DJ. A study of doctors' and patients' communication during a primary care consultation: implications for communication training. *J Health Commun*. 1997;2:169–194.

55. Cole SA, Bird J. *The Medical Interview: The Three-Function Approach*. 2nd ed. St. Louis, Mo: Mosby; 2000.

56. Bertakis KD. The communication of information from physician to patient: a method for increasing patient retention and satisfaction. *J Fam Pract*. 1977;5:217–222.

57. Rost K, Roter D. Predictors of recall of medication regimens and recommendations for lifestyle change in elderly patients. *Gerontologist*. 1987;27:510–515.

58. Crane JA. Patient comprehension of doctor-patient communication on discharge from the emergency department. *J Emerg Med*. 1997; 15:1–7.

59. Chow KM. Information recall by patients. *J R Soc Med*. 2003;96:370.

60. Casalino L, Gillies RR, Shortell SM, et al. External incentives, information technology, and organized processes to improve health care quality for patients with chronic diseases. *JAMA*. 2003;289:434–441.

61. *A Research Dialogue: Online Behavior Change and Disease Management*. The National Cancer Institute and the Robert Wood Johnson Foundation; 2001. Available at www.rwjf.org/publications/publicationsPdfs/ onlineBehaviorChange.pdf. Accessed April 2003.

62. *Seeking Health Care Information: Most Consumers Still on the Sidelines*. Washington, DC: Center for Studying Health System Change; 2003.

63. Kusec S, Brborovic O, Schillinger D. Diabetes websites accredited by the Health On the Net Foundation code of conduct: Readable or not? In: Baud R, Fieschi M, Le Beux P, Ruch P, eds. *The New Navigators: from Professionals to Patients*. Amsterdam, The Netherlands: IOS Press; 2003:95.

64. Berland GK, Elliott MN, Morales LS, et al. Health information on the Internet: accessibility, quality, and readability in English and Spanish. *JAMA*. 2001;285:2612–2621.

65. Zarcadoolas C, Blanco M, Boyer JF, Pleasant A. Unweaving the Web: an exploratory study of low-literate adults' navigation skills on the World Wide Web. *J Health Commun*. 2002;7:309–324.

66. Annual Report 2001. Princeton, NJ: The Robert Wood Johnson Foundation; 2002.

67. Davis TC, Rudd R. personal communication; 2003.

68. Kirsch IS. Educational Testing Service, National Center for Education Statistics. *Adult Literacy in America: A First Look at the Results of the*

National Adult Literacy Survey. Washington, DC: Office of Educational Research and Improvement, US Department of Education: Supt. of Docs. US G.P.O. distributor; 1993.

69. *California HealthCare Foundation: Home.* California HealthCare Foundation; 2003. Available at www.chcf.org. Accessed July 2003.

70. Bindman AB, Grumbach K, Osmond D, et al. Preventable hospitalizations and access to health care. *JAMA.* 1995;274:305–311.

71. Davis TC, Fredrickson DD, Arnold CL, et al. Childhood vaccine risk/benefit communication in private practice office settings: a national survey. *Pediatrics.* 2001;107:E17.

72. Davis TC, Fredrickson DD, Bocchini C, et al. Improving vaccine risk/benefit communication with an immunization education package: a pilot study. *Ambul Pediatr.* 2002;2:193–200.

73. Brookfield S. *Understanding and Facilitating Adult Learning.* San Francisco, Calif: Jossey-Bass; 1986.

74. Roter DL, Stashefsky-Margalit R, Rudd R. Current perspectives on patient education in the US. *Patient Educ Couns.* 2001;44:79–86.

75. Wallerstein N, Bernstein E. Introduction to community empowerment, participatory education, and health. *Health Educ Q.* 1994;21:141–148.

76. Davis TC, Berkel HJ, Arnold CL, Nandy I, Jackson RH, Murphy PW. Intervention to increase mammography utilization in a public hospital. *J Gen Intern Med.* 1998;13:230–233.

77. Davis TC, Fredrickson DD, Arnold C, Murphy PW, Herbst M, Bocchini JA. A polio immunization pamphlet with increased appeal and simplified language does not improve comprehension to an acceptable level. *Patient Educ Couns.* 1998;33:25–37.

78. Rudd RE, Comings JP. Learner developed materials: an empowering product. *Health Educ Q.* 1994;21:313–327.

79. Cooper HC, Booth K, Gill G. Patients' perspectives on diabetes health care education. *Health Educ Res.* 2003;18:191–206.

80. *Equipped for the Future: Tools & Standards For Building & Assessing Quality Adult Literacy Programs.* New York, NY: Council for Advancement of Adult Literacy; 2003.

81. Anderson RM, Funnell MM, Butler PM, Arnold MS, Fitzgerald JT, Feste CC. Patient empowerment: results of a randomized controlled trial. *Diabetes Care.* 1995;18:943–949.

82. Anderson RM. Patient empowerment and the traditional medical model. A case of irreconcilable differences? *Diabetes Care.* 1995; 18:412–415.

83. Trento M, Passera P, Bajardi M, et al. Lifestyle intervention by group care prevents deterioration of type II diabetes: a 4-year randomized controlled clinical trial. *Diabetologia.* 2002;45:1231–1239.

84. Trento M, Passera P, Tomalino M, et al. Group visits improve metabolic control in type 2 diabetes: a 2-year follow-up. *Diabetes Care*. 2001; 24:995–1000.

85. Murray E, Lo B, Pollack L, et al. The impact of health information on the Internet on the physician-patient relationship: patient perceptions. *Arch Intern Med*. 2003;163:1727–1734.

86. Jacobson TA, Thomas DM, Morton FJ, Offutt G, Shevlin J, Ray S. Use of a low-literacy patient education tool to enhance pneumococcal vaccination rates: a randomized controlled trial. *JAMA*. 1999; 282:646–650.

87. Houts PS, Witmer JT, Egeth HE, Loscalzo MJ, Zabora JR. Using pictographs to enhance recall of spoken medical instructions. *Patient Educ Couns*. 1998;35:83–88.

88. Piette J, Schillinger D, Potter M, Heisler M. Dimensions of patient-provider communication and diabetes self-care in an ethnically diverse patient population. *J Gen Intern Med*. 2003;18:624–633.

89. Schillinger D, Piette J, Daher C, Liu H, Bindman AB. Should we be screening for functional health literacy problems among patients with diabetes? *J Gen Intern Med*. 2001;16(s1):172.

90. Frankel RM, Stein T. Getting the most out of the clinical encounter: the four habits model. *J Med Pract Manage*. 2001;16:184–191.

91. Youmans S, Schillinger D. Functional health literacy and medication management: the pharmacist's role. *Ann Pharmacother*. 2003; 37:1726–1729.

92. *Communication for Social Change: An Integrated Model for Measuring the Process and Its Outcomes*. New York, NY: The Rockefeller Foundation and Johns Hopkins University Center for Communication Programs; 2002.

93. Bird JA, McPhee SJ, Ha NT, Le B, Davis T, Jenkins CN. Opening pathways to cancer screening for Vietnamese-American women: lay health workers hold a key. *Prev Med*. 1998;27:821–829.

94. Steinberg EP. Improving the quality of care: can we practice what we preach? *N Engl J Med*. 2003;348:2681–2683.

95. Sehgal AR. Impact of quality improvement efforts on race and sex disparities in hemodialysis. *JAMA*. 2003;289:996–1000.

96. Baker DW, Williams MV, Parker RM, Gazmararian JA, Nurss J. Development of a brief test to measure functional health literacy. *Patient Educ Couns*. 1999;38:33–42.

97. Beers BB, McDonald VJ, Quistberg DA, Ravenell KL, Asch DL, Shea JA. Disparities in health literacy between African American and non-African American primary care patients. *J Gen Intern Med*. 2003;18:169.

98. Bass PF, Wilson JF, Griffith CH. A shortened instrument for literacy screening. *J Gen Intern Med*. 2003;18:1036–1038.

99. *NCQA: Measuring the Quality of America's Health Care*. National Committee for Quality Assurance; 2003. Available at www.ncqa.org/. Accessed July 2003.

100. Norris SL, Nichols PJ, Caspersen CJ, et al. Increasing diabetes self-management education in community settings: a systematic review. *Am J Prev Med*. 2002;22:39–66.

101. Starfield B. *Primary Care: Balancing Health Needs, Services, and Technology*. Rev. ed. New York, NY: Oxford University Press; 1998.

chapter 12

Health Literacy and Health Outcomes: Overview of the Literature

Darren A. DeWalt, MD, MPH, and Michael Pignone, MD, MPH

Note: This chapter is based, in part, on Evidence Report/Technology Assessment Number 87, *Literacy and Health Outcomes* (2004). (*See detailed footnote below.) The opinions expressed in this chapter are those of the authors and do not represent the official position of AHRQ or the US Department of Health and Human Services.

O ver the past 10 to 20 years, an increasing body of research has examined the relationship between low health literacy and adverse health outcomes. Early research demonstrated an alarming discrepancy between the readability of medical information and the reading ability of the population for which it was intended. More recently, several studies have begun to directly examine the association between literacy and health outcomes.

The Measurement of Health Literacy

To examine the association between health literacy and health outcomes, a method to measure health literacy is needed. In epidemiologic terms, health literacy is considered the exposure variable, which leads to the outcome of interest. Health literacy has been defined as a constellation of skills, including the ability to perform basic reading and numerical tasks required to function in the health care environment.[1]

---

* Berkman ND, DeWalt DA, Pignone MP, Sheridan SL, Lohr KN, Lux L, Sutton SF, Swinson T, Bonito AJ. Literacy and Health Outcomes. Evidence Report/Technology Assessment No. 87 (Prepared by RTI International–University of North Carolina Evidence-based Practice Center under contract No. 290-02-0016). AHRQ Publication No. 04-E007-2. Rockville, MD: Agency for Healthcare Research and Quality. January 2004.

It has also been defined as: "the cognitive and social skills which determine the motivation and ability of individuals to gain access to, understand and use information in ways which promote and maintain good health."[2] However, published studies of health literacy have used the patient's ability to read as their main measure, which, as described in Chapter 10, may simply be a surrogate measure.

The three predominant instruments used in this research are the Rapid Estimate of Adult Literacy in Medicine (REALM),[3] Wide Range Achievement Test-Revised 3 (WRAT-R3), and the Test of Functional Health Literacy in Adults (TOFHLA).[4] The tests are described briefly below and in greater detail in Chapter 10. The REALM and WRAT-R3 are both word recognition and pronunciation tests in which subjects are asked to read aloud a list of words of increasing difficulty. The REALM uses medical terms but is highly correlated with the WRAT-R3 ($r = 0.88$), which does not use medical terms. The TOFHLA uses two other methods to measure a person's facility with health information. In the first method, subjects are given prompts and asked to respond to questions (eg, subjects are given a prescription bottle and asked when they would next take the medication). The second method used by the TOFHLA is a modified Cloze procedure in which subjects read health materials with every fifth to seventh word removed and are asked to select the best choice to fill in each "blank." The TOFHLA requires some knowledge of context and word meaning, while such knowledge is not required for the REALM or WRAT-R3. However, the TOFHLA is highly correlated with these word recognition instruments ($r = 0.74$–0.84), suggesting that they measure similar underlying constructs that are akin to one another. No studies have examined whether health-specific literacy evaluations (like REALM and TOFHLA) are more specifically correlated with health outcomes than other measures, such as the WRAT-R3. Because instruments used to measure health literacy appear to measure basic reading skill, we use the term *literacy* throughout this chapter.

Health Outcomes to Consider

After defining literacy, one must consider what is meant by a health outcome. For this chapter, we define health outcomes very broadly because the body of literature is relatively small. This choice also gives us the opportunity to look at intermediate outcomes, or consequences, of a disease process that may lead to health outcomes that people can feel. For instance, in diabetes, glycated hemoglobin (Hb A_{1C}) is measured as an intermediate outcome. It indicates how well an individual's blood sugar is controlled. We know from other research that a person's hemoglobin A_{1C} is related to whether or not he or she develops eye or kidney disease that would be considered the true outcome of the diabetes. However, it would take years to follow people until they develop these conditions. Methodologically, it is much easier to measure a biochemical test to get an idea of the risk of outcomes. This approach is best applied when the intermediate outcome clearly predicts or leads to the final outcome.

The most commonly measured intermediate outcome in literacy research is knowledge or comprehension of health information. Patients require at least some knowledge about their disease or treatment to participate in care and to achieve an optimal outcome. We reasonably assume that literacy level can affect the ability to acquire or use that knowledge. For this reason, many researchers have used knowledge as a proxy for future adverse outcomes. However, the relationship between knowledge and adverse outcomes is often poorly understood or described. Yet, because of the theoretical importance of knowledge and comprehension in the path from low literacy to poor health, we have included studies that only measure knowledge. Readers should recognize that the relationship between the measured knowledge and an actual health outcome is generally not clear.

Measuring the health outcome is not always straightforward in low-literacy populations. When measuring a biochemical or biometric outcome, the result holds the same value for low- and high-literacy populations. However, when self-report questionnaires are used, measurement bias may become a problem. Patients with low literacy may have difficulty completing a written questionnaire, and many investigators will read questions aloud to overcome this barrier. A more subtle problem may exist in the ability to respond to complicated questions, even when the questions are presented verbally. For example, some people with low literacy skills have difficulty completing questionnaires with Likert-type response scales. The effects of these measurement issues are not known, and research is needed to help us understand the best way to measure important outcomes like quality of life and symptoms.

Analyzing the Relationship Between Literacy and Health Outcomes

Etiologic research focuses on understanding the relationship between exposures and outcomes of interest. In this chapter, we explore whether low literacy (the exposure) leads to worse health outcomes. However, confounders (other variables that are related to both exposure and outcome) may influence (ie, bias) the observed relationship between literacy and health outcomes. For example, low literacy is often associated with lack of health insurance, lower-income level, and age. Each of these variables is also associated with worse health outcomes. Therefore, when a study observes a relationship between literacy and a particular health outcome, it is important to question whether or not that relationship represents a true association or is a result of confounding. To do this, many researchers employ statistical methods to adjust for confounders in calculating an unbiased estimate of the relationship between literacy and outcomes.

Data analysis for literacy-related questions becomes more complicated because greater levels of adjustment may not always lead to a better (unbiased) estimate. This is particularly true if the potential confounder actually mediates (ie, is in the causal pathway between) the effect of literacy on the outcome. Education serves as a good example of this phenomenon. Low literacy may lead to fewer years of school completed (or vice versa), and completing fewer years of school may then be independently associated with worse health outcomes. In this case, the years of school completed may mediate the effect of literacy on the health outcome. Adjusting for education might lead us to underestimate the effect of literacy; in other words, this would be an overadjustment. If literacy truly causes less education, which in turn causes worse health, it might be acceptable to attribute that effect to literacy, and not adjust according to educational status. In reality, because the links from literacy to education to health are not well understood, we cannot make a definitive statement about whether or not to adjust for education. Careful assessment of potential confounders, clear presentation of data by the authors, and careful interpretation of results is the best that can be expected given our current understanding.

In this chapter, we indicate whether or not adjustment was performed and highlight a few examples where the lack of adjustment or the overadjustment may have biased the result. Although this chapter describes all studies that have evaluated the relationship between literacy and health outcomes, we focus in-depth analysis on only a few studies to illustrate the complexity of these issues for the reader. In general, research efforts in this area are laudable and study design has improved over time. The intent of critical analysis is to encourage others to take the next step in health literacy research. We find it difficult to confidently state a "correct" method for analyzing the data from these studies and look forward to future research that will elucidate the connections between literacy and health outcomes.

METHODS

We searched MEDLINE, Cumulative Index to Nursing and Allied Health Literature (CINAHL), Educational Resources Information Center (ERIC), Public Affairs Information Service (PAIS), Industrial and Labor Relations Review (ILRR), PsychInfo, and Ageline from 1980 to 2003. In addition, we accepted articles suggested by experts. In MEDLINE and CINAHL, we used the following "keyword" searches: *literacy*, *numeracy*,

WRAT, Wide Range Achievement, Rapid Estimate of Adult, TOFHLA, Test of Functional Health, reading ability, and *reading skill.* In databases that cover a variety of literacy-related issues, we used only the key term *health literacy.* Articles were included in our review if they measured literacy or reported a health outcome other than dementia or dyslexia. Dementia and dyslexia were excluded because of the ambiguous cause-effect relationship with measured literacy.

OVERVIEW OF THE LITERATURE

Most studies that have measured the relationship between literacy and a health outcome have been conducted in the past 10 years. In our systematic review, we identified 42 observational studies—30 studies were cross-sectional, meaning all the data were collected at one point in time; 10 were cohort studies, meaning patients were followed over time and the exposure and outcome were separated by time; and 2 were case-control studies, meaning subjects were selected purposefully by the presence or absence of an outcome. Theoretical disadvantages of a cross-sectional study design include the inability to measure incident outcomes and the inability to assign cause and effect. However, when cross-sectional studies measure literacy in nonelderly adults, we can often safely assume that the same level of literacy predated the health outcome. This assumption, while obviously not appropriate for children, may also be inappropriate for elderly adults in whom literacy levels may change over time.[5] Additionally, medical illness may more profoundly affect literacy in these groups. In terms of health outcomes, 10 studies had health-specific knowledge or comprehension as the only measured outcome.[6–15] We identified one study that addressed the role of literacy in health care costs[16] and one study that looked at the interaction between literacy and race, ethnicity, or culture in terms of their effect on health outcomes.[17] Most measured health outcomes are addressed in only one study.

In the studies we identified, the number of participants enrolled ranged from 26 to 3,260. The largest and most rigorously conducted study was performed on enrollees in the Prudential Medicare health maintenance organization (HMO), which produced four articles.[18–21] Most studies presented information on the participants' age, ethnicity, and education levels, and about half of the studies included information on participants' income level. Literacy was most often measured with REALM (12 studies), TOFHLA or short TOFHLA (11 studies), or WRAT-R3 (6 studies). Several other literacy instruments were used in only one study each. The range and distribution of participants' literacy levels varied widely among studies. Age groups ranged from school-aged children to elderly adults, and most participants in the studies were Caucasian, African American, or Hispanic/Latino.

Knowledge or Comprehension

Several studies designate knowledge as one of their outcomes or as the only outcome. These studies measure knowledge about smoking,[22] postoperative care,[6,15] mammography,[14] contraception,[13] HIV,[10,12,23,24] cervical cancer screening,[11] emergency department discharge instructions,[7] informed consent,[9] parental understanding of child diagnosis and medication,[8] heart healthy lifestyle,[25] hypertension,[26] diabetes,[26] and asthma.[27] Table 12-1 illustrates the populations and knowledge tested for each study. Three of the HIV knowledge studies measured the same knowledge outcome (although there was significant overlap among the patients in these studies); all other knowledge outcomes have only one study each evaluating them. In general, the included studies found a positive relationship between participants' knowledge and literacy level. Only two studies did not demonstrate a statistically significant higher level of knowledge for the higher-literacy group.[6,8]

Health Behaviors

Several studies examined the relationship between literacy and certain health behaviors.

Breastfeeding

Two studies evaluated a relationship between literacy and breast-feeding.[28,29] Kaufman et al[28] studied 61 mothers in Albuquerque, NM. They reported that those with literacy levels greater or equal to the ninth grade (REALM) were more likely to breastfeed for at least 2 months than mothers with literacy levels at the seventh- to eighth-grade level (54% vs 23%, $P = .018$), but they did not adjust for potential confounders.[28] Fredrickson et al[29] had a much larger study (646 mothers). However, they only reported that "bivariate comparison showed significant associations between reading ability (WRAT) and never breastfeeding, . . . significant at the $P < .05$ level." Again, the magnitude of the association was not reported. These studies suggest that mothers with lower levels of literacy are less likely to breastfeed their babies.

Problem Behavior in Children

One study evaluated the relationship between literacy and adolescent behaviors,[30] and another evaluated the relationship between reading ability and "problem behaviors" in younger children.[31] Of 386 students, those who were more than two grades behind expected reading level (Slosson Oral Reading Test–Revised) were more likely than others to carry a weapon (OR = 1.9; CI, 1.1 = 3.5), carry a gun (OR = 2.6; CI, 1.1 = 6.2), miss school because it was unsafe (OR = 2.3; CI, 1.3 = 4.3), and to be in a physical fight that required medical

TABLE 12-1

Studies that Measure Knowledge or Comprehension as an Outcome

Authors	Population	Result
Arnold et al[22]	Predominantly Medicaid-insured or uninsured pregnant women.	Low literacy predicts lower knowledge about smoking effects.
Conlin and Schumann[15]	Patients recovering from open heart surgery at a teaching hospital.	Lower literacy level is correlated with a lower score on knowledge test.
Davis et al[14]	Low-income women at an ambulatory clinic at LSU Shreveport	Lower literacy is correlated with less knowledge about mammograms.
Gazmararian et al[13]	Female Medicaid managed care enrollees in Memphis, TN.	Lower literacy is associated with less knowledge of the time women are most likely to get pregnant during the menstrual cycle.
Kalichman et al[23]	HIV-infected individuals living in Atlanta, GA.	Those with higher literacy are more likely to understand the meaning of the CD4 count or viral load.
Kalichman and Rompa[24]	HIV-infected individuals living in Atlanta, GA.	Lower literacy was associated with less understanding of the meaning of CD4 counts and viral load; lower literacy was associated with less disease and treatment knowledge based on 14-item questionnaire.
Kalichman et al[12]	HIV-infected individuals living in Atlanta, GA.	Patients who knew their CD4 counts and viral load had higher literacy levels than those who did not.
Lindau et al[11]	Females in women's health clinics at an academic medical center in Chicago; predominantly Medicaid-insured.	Higher literacy was associated with more knowledge about cervical cancer screening.
Miller et al[9]	Participants enrolling in anti-infective clinical trials.	There was a moderate correlation between literacy and comprehension of informed consent.
Miller et al[10]	HIV-infected patients in a public hospital–affiliated clinic.	Literacy was associated with knowledge of antiretroviral medication.

Continued

TABLE 12-1

Studies that Measure Knowledge or Comprehension as an Outcome, cont'd

Authors	Population	Result
Moon et al[8]	Parents of children in urban and suburban pediatric practices in Washington, DC.	Literacy does not correlate with parental knowledge of health maintenance procedures or child health measures.
Spandorfer et al[7]	Impoverished inner-city patients at an emergency department in Philadelphia.	Reading ability was the best predictor of comprehension of discharge instructions.
TenHave et al[25]	Community members coming to a cholesterol screening at a local supermarket.	Higher literacy was associated with more "heart healthy knowledge."
Williams et al[28]	Patients with diabetes or hypertension attending a primary care clinic at a public hospital in Los Angeles or Atlanta.	Higher literacy was associated with more knowledge about hypertension and diabetes.
Williams et al[27]	Adult asthma patients in the emergency depart ment at Grady Memorial Hospital in Atlanta, GA.	Higher literacy was associated with more asthma knowledge.
Wilson and McLemore[6]	Patients hospitalized for knee or hip surgery.	There was no correlation between literacy level and patients' level of knowledge about self-care after receiving written education materials.

treatment (OR = 3.1; CI, 1.6-6.1) after controlling for age, race, and gender.[30] Stanton et al[32] found that reading ability (Burt Word Reading Test) was an independent predictor of problem behavior in their sample of 779 children, even after adjustment for early problem behavior, school age IQ, and family adversity (magnitude unknown). They also demonstrated that, as family adversity increases, reading ability decreases.

Smoking

Three studies examined the relationship between literacy and smoking and found mixed results.[22,29,31] Fredrickson et al[29] selected 646 adults waiting for child-related services in private and public clinics in Wichita, Kansas. They reported "significant associations between low reading ability (WRAT) and smoking . . . significant at the $P < .05$ level," but did not report the magnitude of the association. Arnold et al[22] also evaluated the relationship between literacy (REALM) and smoking practices among 600 pregnant women. They found no difference in rates of smoking according to literacy status.

The study by Hawthorne[31] aimed to identify predictors of early adolescent drug use among 3,019 students in Australia. They categorized students into low, middle, or high levels of literacy (literacy assessment unclear) and examined the relationship between literacy and whether or not a student self-reported ever using tobacco or having used tobacco in the last month. In multivariate analysis, they found a modest relationship (low literacy vs high literacy OR = 1.7; 95% CI, 1.1-2.7) between literacy and ever having used tobacco among boys, but no relationship among girls. However, there was a stronger relationship between literacy and using tobacco in the last month among both boys and girls.

Alcohol Use in Adolescence
Hawthorne[31] used multivariate analysis of a cross-sectional data collection to study the relationship between literacy level in adolescence and alcohol use. Although the odds of having ever used alcohol in adolescence did not differ according to literacy status, the odds of having misused alcohol was higher among boys with lower literacy levels compared to boys with higher literacy levels (OR = 2.6; 95% CI, 1.4-4.8). The relationship was not statistically significant among girls (OR = 2.1; 95% CI, 0.8-5.5).

Proper Use of Asthma Medications
Williams et al[27] studied the relationship between literacy (REALM) and correct metered dose inhaler (MDI) technique, an important skill for patients with asthma, in 469 patients. Those with higher literacy had better MDI technique based on a measurement of the number of steps that were performed correctly (difference in number of correct steps (out of 6) = 1.3 steps, 95% CI, 0.9-1.7), adjusted for education and whether or not the patient had a regular source of care.

Screening and Prevention

Several studies examined the relationship between literacy and use of screening and preventive services.

Sexually Transmitted Disease Screening
One study evaluated the relationship between literacy (REALM) and screening for gonorrhea.[33] For the study, 722 patients were selected from clinical and nonclinical sites in four cities around the country.

Literacy assessments were incomplete for many of the patients, but the authors attempted to control for this shortcoming in their analysis. The bivariate analysis demonstrated that people who read at the ninth-grade level or higher were more likely than people who read below the ninth-grade level to be screened for gonorrhea in the previous year. After controlling for incomplete data and several other covariates, a reading level at or above ninth grade was associated with a 10% increase in the probability of having a gonorrhea test in the past year. This result was found even though subjects with a reading level below ninth grade perceived greater risk for acquiring gonorrhea.

Immunization

One study evaluated the relationship between literacy (short TOFHLA) and adult immunization rates.[21] Participants in the study were enrollees in a Medicare managed care health plan; the authors evaluated the percentage of these patients who had received influenza and pneumococcal immunizations. In multivariate analysis of 2,722 patients, adjusting for age, sex, and study location, patients with inadequate literacy had 1.4 (95% CI, 1.1-1.9) times the odds of not having had an influenza immunization and 1.3 (95% CI, 1.1-1.7) times the odds of not having had a pneumococcal immunization than patients with adequate literacy.

Cancer Screening

Scott et al[21] evaluated cancer screening rates by measuring the percentages of female patients who had never had a Pap smear or had not had a mammogram in the last two years. This study yielded mixed results. Patients with inadequate literacy had slightly greater odds of never having had a Pap smear (adjusted OR = 1.7; 95% CI, 1.0-3.1) and slightly greater odds of not having a mammogram in the last two years (adjusted OR = 1.5; 95% CI, 1.0-2.2) than patients with adequate literacy, adjusted for age, sex, and study location. However, for Pap smears, those participants who had marginal literacy (between inadequate and adequate) had 2.4 times the odds of never having had a Pap smear than participants with adequate literacy. Thus, the odds of not ever having had a Pap smear were higher in patients with marginal literacy than for patients with inadequate literacy.

Adherence

The relationship between literacy and adherence was evaluated in three studies.[34–36] Both Kalichman et al[34] and Golin et al[35] measured medication adherence among patients taking anti-retrovirals for HIV infection. Kalichman et al studied 184 patients in an HIV clinic.

After adjusting for race, income, social support, and education, they found that lower literacy (modified TOFHLA) increased the odds of poor adherence (OR = 3.9; 95% CI, 1.1–13.4), defined as missing any dose during the previous 48 hours and measured by 48-hour recall during the study interview. Golin et al[35] measured adherence over 48 weeks using electronic bottle caps, pill counts, and self-reports in a prospective cohort study among 117 patients in a university HIV clinic. They did not find a relationship between literacy (short TOFHLA) and adherence ($r = -0.01, P = .88$).

Li et al[36] evaluated adherence to breast conservation therapy among 55 low-income women with early-stage breast cancer. Only 36% had full adherence, defined as attendance at all X-ray therapy sessions and follow-up clinical sessions. They found no relationship to reading ability (REALM).

Biochemical and Biometric Health Outcomes

The relationship between literacy and disease status has been examined in several studies designating biochemical or biometric markers as the health outcome.

Diabetes

The relationship between literacy and diabetes outcomes was assessed in three studies.[26,37,38] Ross and colleagues[37] evaluated glycemic control, measured by hemoglobin A_{1C}, in 78 children with type 1 diabetes mellitus and its relationship to the child's literacy and the parent's literacy. Children were ages 5–17 years. At these ages, it is likely that the parent still had an impact in the child's care. They found no correlation between the child's score on the WRAT-R3 and glycemic control ($r = 0.1$, "nonsignificant"). However, the parent's score on the National Adult Reading Test (NART) was weakly correlated with the child's glycemic control ($r = 0.28, P = .01$).[37] This analysis did not control for confounders.

Both Williams et al[26] and Schillinger et al[38] evaluated the relationship between patient literacy and hemoglobin A_{1C} in adults with type 2 diabetes mellitus using a cross-sectional study design. The study by Williams et al. was designed to look at diabetes-related knowledge; HbA_{1C} values were available for only 55 patients (48%). Average HbA_{1C} levels tended to be higher among those with inadequate literacy (TOFHLA) vs adequate literacy. However, in this small study, the difference was not statistically significant (8.3% vs 7.5%; $P = .16$).

The primary aim of the Schillinger et al study was to measure the independent relationship between literacy and glycemic control. Of the 408 patients from a public hospital internal medicine or family practice clinic, patients with lower literacy appeared to have worse glycemic control. Among those with inadequate literacy on the short TOFHLA ($N = 156$), 20% of patients had "tight" glycemic control (HbA$_{1C}$ < 7.2), compared with 33% of those with adequate literacy ($N = 198$) (adjusted OR = 0.57, P = .05). Similarly, those with inadequate literacy were more likely to have poor glycemic control (HbA$_{1C}$ > 9.5, adjusted OR = 2). Schillinger et al also performed multivariate linear regression to examine literacy and hemoglobin A$_{1C}$ as continuous variables. They found that the HbA$_{1C}$ increased by 0.02% for every 1-point decrease on the short TOFHLA. This relationship did not change after adjusting for age, race/ethnicity, sex, education, language, insurance, depressive symptoms, social support, receipt of diabetes education, treatment regimen, and years with diabetes. This thoughtful approach to the analysis supports the notion that the literacy–HbA$_{1C}$ relationship was not mediated by these confounders. However, depressive symptoms, diabetes education, and treatment regimen may be intermediates between literacy and HbA$_{1C}$, and their inclusion in the model could have led to a misestimation of the effect.

Schillinger et al[38] also evaluated the relationship between literacy and important diabetes complications, but data was collected by patient self-report (later confirmed through administrative data). Patients with inadequate literacy were more likely to report retinopathy (adjusted OR = 2.33; 95% CI, 1.2-4.6) and cerebrovascular disease (adjusted OR = 2.71; 95% CI, 1.1-7.0). While other diabetes complications also appeared to be more prevalent among patients with inadequate literacy, these did not individually reach statistical significance (self-reported lower extremity amputation (adjusted OR, 2.48; 95% CI, 0.74, 8.3), nephropathy (adjusted OR = 1.71; 95% CI, 0.75-3.9), ischemic heart disease (adjusted OR = 1.73; 95% CI, 0.83-3.6), perhaps due to the relatively low number of events.

Rothman et al[39] published a research letter to the editor in response to the Schillinger paper. They reported no association between literacy (REALM) and glycemic control among patients enrolled in a diabetes disease management program. Eligibility for enrollment included poor glycemic control (HbA$_{1C}$ ≥ 8%). The lack of association may be partially due to exclusion of patients with HbA$_{1C}$ < 8%, many of whom may have higher literacy levels.

In summary, the studies on glycemic control and literacy have yielded mixed results, but the larger, more inclusive studies seem to suggest a relationship. The relationship may be stronger for achievement of excellent, as opposed to good, glycemic control. The mediators of this relationship are being explored in further research. Schillinger et al[40] have published a subsequent report from the same study in which patients with lower literacy levels reported worse communication with their physician. Another report from this same study suggests that patients whose physicians asked them to "teach-back" important aspects of the diabetes treatment recommendations had better glycemic control, independent of literacy.[41]

Hypertension

The relationship between literacy and hypertension was evaluated in two studies.[26,42] Battersby et al[42] performed a case-control study to compare literacy of 90 patients with a diagnosis of hypertension to 90 age-, race-, and sex-matched controls without hypertension. They did not find a statistically significant difference in unadjusted literacy scores between patients with or without hypertension (Schonell-graded word reading test: cases 78.4; controls 81.3).

Williams et al[26] performed a cross-sectional study of 402 patients in two public hospitals. To participate in the study, patients had to have a diagnosis of hypertension. Thus, this study actually examined the relationship between literacy and level of control of hypertension. It was found that patients with inadequate literacy, measured by the TOFHLA, had higher systolic blood pressures than those with adequate literacy (unadjusted 155 mm Hg vs 147 mm Hg; $P = .04$, $N = 408$). However, when they adjusted for age, the relationship was no longer statistically significant.

These two studies did not identify an independent relationship between literacy and presence or control of hypertension. However, both studies were relatively small and could not completely exclude an important relationship.

Human Immunodeficiency Virus Infection

The relationship between literacy and control of HIV infection has been reported in three cross-sectional studies.[23,24,43] All studies were conducted by the same research group and enrolled patients from an HIV-positive population in Atlanta, Georgia. Each study was conducted independently, but approximately 60% of the subjects were repeat participants. Each study measured literacy using a modified TOFHLA and then dichotomized literacy into high-literacy and low-literacy groups at levels different from the recommended cutoffs for inadequate, marginal, and adequate literacy. The cutoff was set at 85% correct on the three reading comprehension passages. At this cutoff, some patients who would be categorized as adequate on the traditional TOFHLA would fall into the low-literacy group. Additionally, the results were presented differently for each study.

One study of 294 patients[23] found no relationship between literacy and CD4 lymphocyte counts (a measure of immune system function) or number of symptoms. However, the same study found that higher-literacy patients had 2.9 (95% CI, 1.1-8.1) times the odds of having an undetectable viral load than those with lower literacy.[23] In another study of 339 patients, Kalichman and Rompa[24] showed that patients with higher literacy had 6.2 (95% CI, 2.1-18.5) times the odds of having an undetectable viral load than patients with lower literacy. In the same study, Kalichman and Rompa found that lower-literacy patients had 2.3 (95% CI, 1.1-5.1) times the odds of having a CD4 count that was less than 300 compared to higher-literacy patients. The third study found no association between literacy status and undetectable viral load in 294 patients.[43] In each of these studies, the authors reported only crude bivariate analyses and did not adjust for other potential confounders, such as education, income, adherence, or race/ethnicity. From these findings, it is difficult to draw definite conclusions regarding the relationship between HIV infection markers and literacy status.

Measures of Disease Prevalence, Incidence, or Morbidity

The relationship between literacy and disease prevalence, incidence, or morbidity has been examined in several studies.

Depression

Five studies have examined the relationship between literacy and depression and all have yielded mixed results.[19,25,43–45] All studies used previously validated self-report questionnaires to measure depression, and two of the studies evaluated depression in the context of specific chronic diseases—rheumatoid arthritis[44] and HIV infection.[43]

The largest study was a cross-sectional evaluation of patients enrolled in a Medicare managed care plan.[19] In this study, depression was assessed using the well-validated Geriatric Depression Scale (GDS). The authors approached 6,734 patients, of whom 3,171 participated—a response rate of about 47%. This study found an unadjusted OR for being depressed of 2.7 (95% CI, 2.2-3.4) in those patients with inadequate literacy compared to those with adequate literacy as assessed by the short TOFHLA. However, after adjusting for demographic, social support, health behavior, and health status factors, the adjusted OR of 1.2 (95% CI, 0.9-1.7) was no longer statistically significant. From this large sample, the authors conclude that there is no relationship between literacy and depression. Although this study is the largest and most rigorously reported analysis addressing this question, the limited response rate may introduce bias. For example, people with low literacy who are depressed may be more likely to refuse participation. Additionally, there may have been over-adjustment for covariates. For instance, worse health status could be a result of depression rather than a confounder of the relationship between literacy and depression.

TenHave et al[25] evaluated depression scores among 339 subjects recruited for participation in a cardiovascular dietary education program. As part of their study, they evaluated a screening instrument to assess literacy. They measured depression (Beck Depression Inventory [BDI]–Short Form) and literacy (Cardiovascular Dietary Education System [CARDES] scale) in 339 patients and found a statistically significant relationship. Lower scores on the literacy assessment were associated with higher scores on the depression assessment, suggesting more propensity of depression among those with lower literacy (P <.001).

Zaslow et al[45] evaluated depression and literacy (Tests of Applied Literacy Skills) among 351 mothers and the relationship between maternal literacy and childhood depression and antisocial behavior. Risk of depression was increased among mothers who had lower literacy skills (estimated RR, 1.60; 95% CI, 1.21-2.12). No relationship was detected between maternal literacy and childhood depression or antisocial behavior (P >.10).

Kalichman and Rompa[43] compared scores on the Centers for Epidemiologic Studies Depression (CES-D) scale with scores on the TOFHLA in a group of 294 patients infected with HIV. They found that scores for CES-D questions or subscales were higher (representing more depression) for participants with lower literacy. However, the total scores on the depression scale did not differ by literacy status.

Gordon et al[44] used the Hospital Anxiety and Depression (HAD) scale on 123 consecutive patients with rheumatoid arthritis, all of whom had their literacy assessed by the REALM. They found that the percentage of patients with a score of 15 or above on the HAD scale was higher among those who read below the ninth-grade level than for those who read at or above the ninth-grade level on the REALM (61% vs 44%; P = .011).

Of these five studies, three found statistically significant and clinically important associations between lower literacy and higher rates of depression. However, the largest study failed to show this relationship. The discrepancy in results may be related to study design and analysis. For instance, since different literacy assessments were used in each study, the cutoff between high and low literacy differed between studies. Additionally, the populations were all quite different. The study by Gazmararian et al[19] only included patients over age 65 for whom there was not necessarily a coexistent chronic condition. The study by TenHave et al[25] enrolled community-dwelling people aged 40 to 70. Zaslow et al[45] enrolled mothers of young children. Gordon et al[44] enrolled only patients with rheumatoid arthritis, while Kalichman and Rompa[24] enrolled only patients with HIV infection.

Because of the substantial differences in patient populations, it is difficult to reach a general conclusion about the relationship between literacy and depression. Last, differences in adjustment for covariates may have affected results. Gazmararian et al[19] adjusted for age and health status. Prior to adjustment, a relationship between literacy and depression had been identified. TenHave et al[25] adjusted for age but did not adjust for health status. Kalichman and Rompa[24] and Gordon et al[44] reported only bivariate relationships. The relationship between literacy and depression appears to decrease after adjustment for certain variables, especially age. An important relationship between literacy and depression may exist in certain populations, but further studies with careful attention to confounders are needed.

Arthritis and Functional Status
One study of 123 consecutive patients with rheumatoid arthritis evaluated functional status and literacy.[44] Functional status was measured using the Health Assessment Questionnaire (HAQ). There was no difference in HAQ scores according to literacy dichotomized at the ninth-grade level on the REALM ($\geq$ninth 1.9 vs <ninth 2.0; P <.5). The authors did not adjust for potential confounders.

Migraine
One study evaluated the relationship between literacy and migraine headaches in 64 children.[46] Andrasik et al[46] performed a case-control study of children with migraine headaches and control children without migraine headaches. Literacy was measured using the WRAT-R3. This small study found no difference in literacy scores between the cases and controls, but it may have been underpowered to detect a difference.

Prostate Cancer
One study evaluated the relationship between literacy and stage of presentation of prostate cancer in 212 patients.[17] Bennett et al[17] performed the REALM and dichotomized literacy at the sixth-grade level into high and low groups. They found that those with lower literacy were more likely to present with late-stage prostate cancer than those with higher literacy (unadjusted proportions 55% vs 38%; P = .022). After adjustment for race, age, and location of care, the relationship between literacy and stage of presentation was smaller and no longer statistically significant (OR 1.6 = 95% CI, 0.8-3.4). They found a similar relationship for race and late stage of presentation. The bivariate relationship demonstrated that African American patients were more likely than white patients to present with late-stage cancer (unadjusted 49.5% vs 35.9%; P = .045). However, after adjustment for literacy, age, and location of care, the relationship was smaller and no longer statistically significant (OR 1.4; 95% CI, 0.7-2.7). The authors

concluded that literacy mediates some of the relationship between race and stage of presentation for prostate cancer. In support of this hypothesis, the point estimate of the odds ratio changed somewhat (unadjusted OR = 1.74, adjusted; OR = 1.4), but the loss of statistical significance is likely due to the small size of the study (212 patients) and the loss of precision after controlling for several variables.

Global Health Status Measures

Four studies evaluated the relationship between literacy and a global health status measure.[20,47,48] All studies found an association between lower literacy and worse health status. Gazmararian et al[20] reported findings from a cohort of 3,260 patients enrolled in a Medicare managed care health plan. Patients were asked to self-report their health as excellent, good, fair, or poor. They found that patients with lower literacy (short TOFHLA) were more likely to self-report fair or poor health than patients with higher literacy (43% vs 20%; $P < .001$), but they did not adjust for confounders.[20]

Baker et al[49] asked 2,659 patients at two public hospitals to report whether their health was poor or not poor. This study included both English- and Spanish-speaking patients, and literacy was assessed in the preferred language (TOFHLA). After controlling for potential confounders (eg, age, gender, race, and socioeconomic indicators), patients with inadequate literacy had about two times the odds of reporting poor health than patients with adequate literacy.

Weiss et al[47] assessed global health status using the sickness impact profile (SIP) in 193 relatively young participants with a mean age of 28 years. Literacy was dichotomized at the fourth-grade level (Tests of Adult Basic Education [TABE] and Mott Basic Language Skills Program). Lower-literacy patients scored worse than higher-literacy patients on the overall SIP after adjustment for age, sex, ethnicity, marital status, insurance status, occupation, and income (10.4 vs 6.0; $P = .02$). Patients with lower literacy scored worse on both the physical and psychosocial components of the SIP.

Sullivan et al[48] measured general health status among 697 patients with type 2 diabetes using the short form-36 (SF-36). Literacy was assessed using the Questionnaire Literacy Screen (QLS), which was being developed at the time of the study. They found no difference in scores on the SF-36 according to whether or not the subject passed the QLS.

Use of Health Care Resources

Several studies have examined the relationship between literacy and the use of health care resources.

Hospitalization

Two studies evaluated the risk of hospitalization according to literacy status.[18,50] In a study performed at two public hospitals (1,937 patients),[50] the odds of being hospitalized over the course of one year was 1.69 (95% CI, 1.13-2.53) times higher for patients with inadequate literacy (TOFHLA) than for patients with adequate literacy after adjusting for age, sex, race, health status, receiving financial assistance, and health insurance, but not for education. The second study was performed with 3,260 patients enrolled in a Medicare managed care program.[18] After adjusting for age, sex, race/ethnicity, language, income, and educational status, the odds of being hospitalized were 1.29 (95% CI, 1.07-1.55) higher for patients with inadequate literacy (short TOFHLA) than for patients with adequate literacy.

Cost

One published study examined the relationship between health care cost and literacy.[16] Weiss et al. enrolled a cohort of 402 patients that qualified for Medicaid. Literacy was measured using the Instrument for the Diagnosis of Reading (Instrumento Para Diagnosticar Lecturas, or IDL). Health care costs for the previous year were gathered from Medicaid records. Because participants had to be contacted by telephone or respond to a letter in order to be eligible, some people may have been systematically excluded. No relationship was identified between literacy and cost of care ($r^2 = 0.0016; P = .43$). The authors also evaluated several components of medical charges such as inpatient care, outpatient care, emergency care, etc, and no relationship was found between literacy and component costs. A subsequent subgroup analysis of this data focused on 74 patients enrolled because of medical need or medical indigence. In this subgroup, 18 patients reading at or below third grade level had higher mean Medicaid charges than the 56 who read above the third grade level ($10,688 vs $2,891; P = .025).[51] Further research is needed to substantiate this relationship.

Physician Visits

Only two studies have examined the relationship between literacy and number of health care visits. Gorden et al[44] studied 123 patients with rheumatoid arthritis and found that, while patients with lower literacy reported similar levels of functional disability compared to patients with higher literacy, they made three times more outpatient visits over the prior year. This study did not adjust for potential confounders. Baker et al[49] asked 2,659 patients about the number of physician visits in the past 3 months, presence of regular source of care, and whether needed medical care was received during the past 3 months. After adjusting for confounders (age, health status, and economic indicators), they found no relationship between literacy status

(TOFHLA) and self-reported access to physician visits. However, these participants were recruited from emergency rooms and walk-in clinics, and they may represent a population that is already accessing the health care system to some degree.

CONCLUSION

Elucidation of the relationship between literacy and health outcomes remains an emerging area of research. Based on the published literature, literacy is related to knowledge and comprehension, hospitalization, global measures of health, and outcomes of some chronic diseases. However, in many cases, the evidence is mixed and depends on the study design and method of analysis. Although literacy may be related to health outcomes in bivariate associations, when controlling for covariates such as measures of education or socioeconomic status, the relationship becomes weaker and is often statistically nonsignificant. Furthermore, most available data comes from cross-sectional studies that suffer from inability to measure incident outcomes and do not include the element of elapsed time. Although the relationship between literacy and certain health outcomes seems reasonably well proven, the magnitude of that relationship and the specific avenues between literacy and those outcomes need more exploration.

As discussed in Chapter 11, it can be quite difficult to delineate the effect of literacy and other closely tied measures of socioeconomic status and educational level on health outcomes. The measurement of health literacy has focused on measuring an individual's reading ability. Many factors, including quality and length of schooling, parental influences, economic opportunity, learning potential, and social conditions, can lead to differential levels of reading ability. These factors may also influence health outcomes through avenues other than an individual's reading ability. In addition, an individual's ability to read may influence length of schooling, economic opportunity, and social conditions, which, in turn, can influence health. We have found it challenging to map the complex relationships among measured reading ability, other socioeconomic factors, and a health outcome. Opportunity awaits researchers who can delineate these pathways and help us all understand the relationship between literacy and health outcomes.

Although we can measure an individual's literacy, the impact of the literacy level may go far beyond the ability to understand written or even spoken instructions. The literacy level of the patient may insidiously affect patient-physician communication dynamics and inadvertently lead to substandard medical care for patients with low literacy. Studies on patient-physician communication suggest that this may be part of the pathway from low literacy to worse health.[40]

Future research in this area may elucidate the various pathways from low literacy to worse health. Studies of focused interventions to improve health outcomes beyond knowledge will help to identify modifiable factors that mediate the relationship between literacy and health. Observational studies that refine the measurement of intermediates such as self-efficacy, participation in medical decision-making, and trust will help to focus the interventions of the future. Intervention studies should incorporate the knowledge from observational studies into their design and report the results stratified by literacy status.

REFERENCES

1. Ad Hoc Committee on Health Literacy for the Council on Scientific Affairs, American Medical Association. Health literacy: report of the Council on Scientific Affairs. *JAMA*. 1999;281:552–557.
2. Nutbeam D. Health promotion glossary. *Health Promot Int*. 1998;13:349–364.
3. Davis TC, Long SW, Jackson RH, et al. Rapid estimate of adult literacy in medicine: a shortened screening instrument. *Fam Med*. 1993;25: 391–395.
4. Parker RM, Baker DW, Williams MV, Nurss JR. The test of functional health literacy in adults: a new instrument for measuring patients' literacy skills. *J Gen Intern Med*. 1995;10:537–541.
5. Baker DW, Gazmararian JA, Sudano J, Patterson M. The association between age and health literacy among elderly persons. *J Gerontol B Psychol Sci Soc Sci*. 2000;55:S368–S374.
6. Wilson FL, McLemore R. Patient literacy levels: a consideration when designing patient education programs. *Rehabil Nurs*. 1997;22:311–317.
7. Spandorfer JM, Karras DJ, Hughes LA, Caputo C. Comprehension of discharge instructions by patients in an urban emergency department. *Ann Emerg Med*. 1995;25:71–74.
8. Moon RY, Cheng TL, Patel KM, Baumhaft K, Scheidt PC. Parental literacy level and understanding of medical information. *Pediatr*. 1998;102:e25.
9. Miller CK, O'Donnell DC, Searight HR, Barbarash RA. The Deaconess Informed Consent Comprehension Test: an assessment tool for clinical research subjects. *Pharmacother*. 1996;16:872–878.
10. Miller LG, Liu H, Hays RD, et al. Knowledge of antiretroviral regimen dosing and adherence: a longitudinal study. *Clin Infect Dis*. 2003; 36:514–518.
11. Lindau ST, Tomori C, Lyons T, Langseth L, Bennett CL, Garcia P. The association of health literacy with cervical cancer prevention knowledge

and health behaviors in a multiethnic cohort of women. *Am J Obstet Gynecol*. 2002;186(5):938–943.

12. Kalichman SC, Rompa D, Cage M. Reliability and validity of self-reported CD4 lymphocyte count and viral load test results in people living with HIV/AIDS. *Int J STD AIDS*. 2000;11:579–585.

13. Gazmararian JA, Parker RM, Baker DW. Reading skills and family planning knowledge and practices in a low-income managed-care population. *Obstet Gynecol*. 1999;93(2):239–244.

14. Davis TC, Arnold C, Berkel HJ, Nandy I, Jackson RH, Glass J. Knowledge and attitude on screening mammography among low-literate, low-income women. *Cancer*. 1996;78:1912–1920.

15. Conlin KK, Schumann L. Literacy in the health care system: a study on open heart surgery patients. *J Am Acad Nurse Pract*. 2002;14:38–42.

16. Weiss BD, Blanchard JS, McGee DL, et al. Illiteracy among Medicaid recipients and its relationship to health care costs. *J Health Care Poor Underserved*. 1994;5:99–111.

17. Bennett CL, Ferreira MR, Davis TC, et al. Relation between literacy, race, and stage of presentation among low-income patients with prostate cancer. *J Clin Oncol*. 1998;16(9):3101–3104.

18. Baker DW, Gazmararian JA, Williams MV, et al. Functional health literacy and the risk of hospital admission among Medicare managed care enrollees. *Am J Public Health*. 2002;92:1278–1283.

19. Gazmararian J, Baker D, Parker R, Blazer DG. A multivariate analysis of factors associated with depression: evaluating the role of health literacy as a potential contributor. *Arch Intern Med*. 2000;160:3307–3314.

20. Gazmararian JA, Baker DW, Williams MV, et al. Health literacy among Medicare enrollees in a managed care organization. *JAMA*. 1999;281(6):545–551.

21. Scott TL, Gazmararian JA, Williams MV, Baker DW. Health literacy and preventive health care use among Medicare enrollees in a managed care organization. *Med Care*. 2002;40:395–404.

22. Arnold CL, Davis TC, Berkel HJ, Jackson RH, Nandy I, London S. Smoking status, reading level, and knowledge of tobacco effects among low-income pregnant women. *Prev Med*. 2001;32:313–320.

23. Kalichman SC, Benotsch E, Suarez T, Catz S, Miller J, Rompa D. Health literacy and health-related knowledge among persons living with HIV/AIDS. *Am J Prev Med*. 2000;18:325–331.

24. Kalichman SC, Rompa D. Functional health literacy is associated with health status and health-related knowledge in people living with HIV-AIDS. *J Acquir Immune Defic Syndr Hum Retrovirol*. 2000;25:337–344.

25. TenHave TR, Van Horn B, Kumanyika S, Askov E, Matthews Y, Adams-Campbell LL. Literacy assessment in a cardiovascular nutrition education setting. *Patient Educ Couns.* 1997;31:139–150.

26. Williams MV, Baker DW, Parker RM, Nurss JR. Relationship of functional health literacy to patients' knowledge of their chronic disease: a study of patients with hypertension and diabetes. *Arch Intern Med.* 1998;158:166–172.

27. Williams MV, Baker DW, Honig EG, Lee TM, Nowlan A. Inadequate literacy is a barrier to asthma knowledge and self-care. *Chest.* 1998;114:1008–1015.

28. Kaufman H, Skipper B, Small L, Terry T, McGrew M. Effect of literacy on breast-feeding outcomes. *South Med J.* 2001;94:293–296.

29. Fredrickson DD, Washington RL, Pham N, Jackson T, Wiltshire J, Jecha LD. Reading grade levels and health behaviors of parents at child clinics. *Kansas Med.* 1995;96:127–129.

30. Davis TC, Byrd RS, Arnold CL, Auinger P, Bocchini JAJ. Low literacy and violence among adolescents in a summer sports program. *J Adolesc Health.* 1999;24:403–411.

31. Hawthorne G. Preteenage drug use in Australia: the key predictors and school-based drug education. *J Adolesc Health.* 1997;20:384–395.

32. Stanton WR, Feehan M, McGee R, Silva PA. The relative value of reading ability and IQ as predictors of teacher-reported behavior problems. *J Learn Disabil.* 1990;23:514–517.

33. Fortenberry JD, McFarlane MM, Hennessy M, et al. Relation of health literacy to gonorrhoea related care. *Sex Trans Infect.* 2001; 77:206–211.

34. Kalichman SC, Ramachandran B, Catz S. Adherence to combination antiretroviral therapies in HIV patients of low health literacy. *J Gen Intern Med.* 1999;14:267–273.

35. Golin CE, Liu H, Hays RD, et al. A prospective study of predictors of adherence to combination antiretroviral medication. *J Gen Intern Med.* 2002;17:756–765.

36. Li BD, Brown WA, Ampil FL, Burton GV, Yu H, McDonald JC. Patient compliance is critical for equivalent clinical outcomes for breast cancer treated by breast-conservation therapy. *Ann Surg.* 2000; 231:883–889.

37. Ross LA, Frier BM, Kelnar CJ, Deary IJ. Child and parental mental ability and glycaemic control in children with type 1 diabetes. *Diabetic Med.* 2001;18:364–369.

38. Schillinger D, Grumbach K, Piette J, et al. Association of health literacy with diabetes outcomes. *JAMA.* 2002;288:475–482.

39. Rothman R, Malone R, Bryant B, Dewalt D, Pignone M. Health literacy and diabetic control. *JAMA.* 2002;288:2687–2688.

40. Schillinger D, Bindman A, Stewart A, Wang F, Piette J. Health literacy and the quality of physician-patient interpersonal communication. *Patient Educ Couns.* 2004;3:315–323.

41. Schillinger D, Piette J, Grumbach K, et al. Closing the loop: physician communication with diabetic patients who have low health literacy. *Arch Intern Med*. 2003;163:83–90.

42. Battersby C, Hartley K, Fletcher AE, Markowe HJL, Brown RG, Styles W. Cognitive function in hypertension: a community based study. *J Hum Hypertens*. 1993;7:117–123.

43. Kalichman SC, Rompa D. Emotional reactions to health status changes and emotional well-being among HIV-positive persons with limited reading literacy. *J Clin Psychol Med Setting*. 2000;7:203–211.

44. Gordon MM, Hampson R, Capell HA, Madhok R. Illiteracy in rheumatoid arthritis patients as determined by the Rapid Estimate of Adult Literacy in Medicine (REALM) score. *Rheumatol*. 2002;41:750–754.

45. Zaslow MJ, Hair EC, Dion MR, Ahluwalia SK, Sargent J. Maternal depressive symptoms and low literacy as potential barriers to employment in a sample of families receiving welfare: are there two-generational implications? *Women & Health*. 2001;32:211–251.

46. Andrasik F, Kabela E, Quinn S, Attanasio V, Blanchard EB, Rosenblum EL. Psychological functioning of children who have recurrent migraine. *Pain*. 1988;34:43–52.

47. Weiss BD, Hart G, McGee DL, D'Estelle S. Health status of illiterate adults: relation between literacy and health status among persons with low literacy skills. *J Am Board Fam Pract*. 1992;5:257–264.

48. Sullivan LM, Dukes KA, Harris L, Dittus RS, Greenfield S, Kaplan SH. A comparison of various methods of collecting self-reported health outcomes data among low-income and minority patients. *Med Care*. 1995;33:AS183–AS194.

49. Baker DW, Parker RM, Williams MV, Clark WS, Nurss J. The relationship of patient reading ability to self-reported health and use of health services. *Am J Public Health*. 1997;87:1027–1030.

50. Baker DW, Parker RM, Williams MV, Clark WS. Health literacy and the risk of hospital admission. *J Gen Intern Med*. 1998;13:791–798.

51. Weiss BD, Palmer R. Relationship between health care costs and very low literacy skills in a medically needy and indigent Medicaid population. *J Am Board Fam Pract*. 2004;17:44–47.

Appendix A: Glossary

Adult Basic Learning Examination (ABLE): A test designed to measure the educational achievement of adults who have not completed 12 years of schooling and to evaluate efforts to raise the educational level of these adults. The ABLE contains six subtests (vocabulary, reading comprehension, spelling, language, number operations, and quantitative problem solving) for each of three levels corresponding to skills commonly taught in grades 1 to 4, 5 to 8, and 9 to 12.

Adult Education and Literacy (AEL) Survey: Literacy survey of participants in federally sponsored adult education programs, undertaken by the US Department of Education. The AEL survey uses measures of literacy from the Adult Literacy and Lifeskills (ALL) Survey and will report results on the same scales as the National Assessment of Adult Literacy (NAAL) allowing direct comparisons between survey populations. Analysis of the AEL survey is anticipated to be completed in 2005.

Adult Literacy and Lifeskills (ALL) Survey: International assessment of adult literacy skills undertaken by the Organisation for Economic Co-operation and Development (OECD). The ALL survey is modeled after the International Adult Literacy Survey (IALS) but includes a new test of problem-solving ability as well as a broader measure of math skills. Analysis of the ALL survey is anticipated to be completed in 2005.

Agency for Healthcare Research and Quality (AHRQ): A US Department of Health and Human Services agency whose mission includes both translating research findings into better patient care and providing policymakers and other health care leaders with information needed to make critical health care decisions.

Beck Depression Inventory (BDI): A 21-item survey used to assess the intensity of depression in individuals aged 13 to 80 years. A seven-item short form ("Fast Screen") is also available.

Brochureware: A slang term used to describe Web sites that consist only of information placed on a Web page with no interactive or user-centric features.

Burt Word Reading Test: A reading recognition test for children consisting of 110 words in differing font sizes graded in order of difficulty.

Centers for Epidemiologic Studies-Depression (CES-D) scale: A series of 20 questions used to screen for depressive symptoms in general populations and in psychiatric populations.

Chall, Jeanne (1921-1999): Founder and director for more than 20 years of the Harvard Reading Laboratory, and leading expert in reading research and instruction. Chall produced the

229

definitive study of reading instruction in her book, *Learning to Read: The Great Debate* (1967), and was among the first to describe learning to read as a developmental process. Chall's Stages of Reading Development include *learning to read*, the stage at which individuals learn to map printed language to oral language; *fluency*, in which individuals become fluent and automatic decoders of language; and *reading to learn the new*, in which individuals use their reading skills to learn new information, ideas, attitudes, and values.

Chronic Care Model: A model developed by Ed Wagner, MD, MPH, that summarizes the basic elements for improving chronic illness care in health systems at multiple levels. The elements of self-management support, decision support, delivery system design, and clinical information systems exist under the levels of the community and the health system. These elements feed into the productive interactions between the prepared, proactive practice team and the informed, activated patient to produce improved functional and clinical outcomes.

Chronic condition: A medical condition that has been present 3 months or longer.

Cloze-type procedure: Procedure in which a subject is asked to supply words that have been systematically deleted from a text. This procedure requires that the subject understand the context of the text to supply the missing words.

Commonwealth Fund 2001 Health Care Quality Survey: A survey conducted to collect information on the health care experiences of a cross section of adults living in the United States representing people from a diverse range of racial/ethnic backgrounds. From April 30 to November 5, 2001, Princeton Survey Research Associates conducted 25-minute telephone interviews in English, Spanish, Cantonese, Mandarin, Korean, and Vietnamese with a random national sample of 6,722 adults aged 18 years and older living in the continental United States. Key findings from the survey fell into one of four broad categories: (1) interactions with the health care system, (2) cultural competence and health care, (3) quality, medical errors, preventive care, and chronic disease management, and (4) access to health care.

Computer literacy: The ability to understand the concepts, terminology, and operations that relate to general computer use, and the knowledge needed to function independently with a computer.

Confounder: An extraneous variable whose effects on a given outcome cannot be distinguished from the effects of one or more independent variables being examined.

Contextualized language: Language in which shared physical context and background knowledge are utilized. For example, a contextualized description of allergy symptoms might be: "You know how your nose gets all stuffy and you feel pressure behind it? That's how I feel right now."

Decontextualized language: Language in which meaning is conveyed via linguistic cues that are independent of the immediate communicative context and shared experience. For example, a decontextualized description of chest pain might be: "I feel like an elephant is sitting on my chest," as opposed to the contextualized description: "My chest hurts here; I feel bad."

Digital divide: The gap that exists between those who have access to technology and related services (eg, telephones, computers, or the Internet) and those who do not have access to them.

Document literacy: The ability to locate selected information on a short form or graphical display of information (eg, job application, transportation schedule, or map), apply selected information presented in documents, and use writing to complete documents and survey forms that require filling in information.

Ecological model: A model that characterizes the complex factors surrounding an issue that, through various interactions, can influence the issue's outcome.

Flesch-Kincaid formula: Formula for determining the readability of text based on the average number of syllables per word and the average numbers of words per sentence. The score is expressed as a grade-school reading level. The formula has been validated in adults up to a 16th-grade readability level, although Microsoft Word's application of the formula truncates the upper readability level at Grade 12.

Freire, Paulo (1921–1997): Brazilian educator best known for his approach to teaching low-literate and illiterate people. Significant aspects of Freire's work include his emphasis on dialogue

(ie, informal education is dialogical, or conversational, and should involve people working with each other rather than one person acting on others); praxis (ie, dialogue should be informed and linked to certain values, and its process should enhance community and build social capital); conscientization (ie, education should develop consciousness, so that those who are educated have a voice in their community); and experience (ie, education should be situated in the lived experiences of participants). Books by Freire include *Pedagogy of the Oppressed* (1972), *Pedagogy of the City* (1993), *Education for Critical Consciousness* (1993), *Pedagogy of Hope: Reliving Pedagogy of the Oppressed* (1995), and *Pedagogy of the Heart* (1997).

Fry Readability Formula: Formula for determining the readability of text based on the number of sentences and syllables in three 100-word passages selected from the text. The score can be expressed as either a school-based reading level (Grades 1 through 12 or college level) or an age-based reading level (ages 6 through 19 years).

Geriatric Depression Scale (GDS): A basic screening measure for depression in older adults. In addition to the original 30-question version, a 15-question version is also available.

Health Assessment Questionnaire (HAQ): An assessment of five generic patient-centered health dimensions (avoiding disability, staying free of pain and discomfort, avoiding adverse treatment effects, keeping dollar costs of treatment low, and postponing) used to measure health-related quality of life.

Health communication: The art and technique of informing, influencing, and motivating individual, institutional, and public audiences about important health issues. The scope of health communication includes disease prevention, health promotion, health care policy, and the business of health care as well as the enhancement of the quality of life and the health of individuals within the community.

Health Insurance Portability and Accountability Act (HIPAA): An act passed into law by the US Congress on August 21, 1996, to improve portability and continuity of health insurance coverage in the group and individual markets; to combat waste, fraud, and abuse in health insurance and health care delivery; to promote the use of medical savings accounts; to improve access to long-term care services and coverage; to simplify the administration of health insurance; and for other purposes. The first HIPAA rules, issued in 2003, also include the first-ever federal privacy standards to protect patients' medical records and other health information provided to health plans, doctors, hospitals, and other health care providers.

Health literacy: (1) The degree to which individuals have the capacity to obtain, process, and understand basic health information and services needed to make appropriate health decisions. (2) A constellation of skills, including the ability to perform basic reading and numerical tasks required

to function in the health care environment. Literacy skills alone may be necessary, but not sufficient, for health literacy. (3) An individual's ability to read health-related materials, as measured by the Rapid Estimate of Adult Literacy in Medicine (REALM), Test of Functional Health Literacy in Adults (TOFHLA), and other screening tools.

Health Plan Employer Data and Information Set (HEDIS): A set of standardized performance measures developed by the National Committee for Quality Assurance (NCQA) that ensures consumers have the information they need to compare the performance of managed care plans.

Health promotion: Any planned combination of educational, political, regulatory, and organizational supports for actions and conditions of living conducive to the health of individuals, groups, or communities.

Healthy People 2010 (HP 2010): As coordinated by the US Department of Health and Human Services, HP 2010 is a statement of national health objectives designed to identify the most significant preventable threats to health and to establish national goals to reduce these threats. The two overarching goals of HP 2010 are (1) to help individuals of all ages increase life expectancy and improve their quality of life and (2) to eliminate health disparities among different segments of the population.

Hospital Anxiety and Depression Scale (HADS): A questionnaire consisting of seven items to assess patients' anxiety and depression while in inpatient care.

Hyperlink: A highlighted image or portion of text on a Web page that is linked to another Web page. Clicking on this image, the hyperlink, takes the user to the linked Web page.

Informed consent: A communication process by which a subject agrees to a procedure based on a fair understanding of the risks, benefits, and alternatives to the proposed procedure. Consent is sometimes, but not always, elicited and granted through use of a formal written consent document signed by the subject.

Instrument for Diagnosis of Reading: A comprehensive Spanish-reading assessment instrument that tests comprehension of written text. This test is also known as the Instrumento Para Diagnosticar Lecturas (IDL).

International Adult Literacy Survey (IALS): International assessment of adult literacy skills modeled after the National Adult Literacy Survey (NALS). Twenty countries participated in the IALS between 1994 and 1999.

Internet: A global communication system that connects computers through a unique address space based on the Internet Protocol (IP) or its subsequent extensions or follow-ons.

Likert scale: A scale in which the respondent indicates a level of agreement or disagreement with a particular statement pertaining to the topic under study.

Literacy: (1) The ability to read, write, and speak in English and to compute and solve problems at levels of proficiency necessary to function on the job and in society, to achieve one's goals, and to develop one's knowledge and potential. (2) A term often used interchangeably with "health literacy," as health literacy is frequently measured in terms of literacy skills in the health care setting.

Literacy Assessment for Diabetes (LAD): A 60-word reading recognition test modeled after the Rapid Estimate of Adult Literacy in Medicine (REALM). The LAD's word list is comprised of words commonly encountered in diabetes education.

Meaning skills: Skills for understanding the meanings of given words. Strong meaning skills include both knowing the meanings of numerous words ("breadth of vocabulary knowledge") and knowing the multiple meanings and nuances assumed by these words in different contexts ("depth of vocabulary knowledge").

Media literacy: The ability to develop an informal and critical understanding of the nature of mass media, the techniques used by them, and the impact of these techniques.

Medical Achievement Reading Test (MART): A 42-word reading recognition test modeled after the Wide Range Achievement Test-Revised 3 (WRAT-R3). The MART was designed to assess medical literacy in a nonthreatening manner. Its print resembles a prescription label.

National Adult Literacy Survey (NALS): Survey undertaken by the US government in 1992 to determine the range of literacy skills in the US adult population and how many US adults have skills sufficient to function effectively as workers, parents, and citizens. Twenty-six thousand Americans aged 16 years and older participated in NALS by undergoing tests of prose literacy, document literacy, and quantitative literacy skills.

National Adult Reading Test (NART): A reading recognition test consisting of 50 words that do not follow the usual rules of pronunciation (eg, ache and thyme). The NART is commonly used to estimate a subject's premorbid level of intellectual ability.

National Assessment of Adult Literacy (NAAL): Survey of adult literacy skills undertaken by the US Department of Education in 2003. NAAL follows the same format and includes many of the same items as the National Adult Literacy Survey (NALS), but expands the number of background questions related to health and includes additional health-related tasks as part of the item pool. Analysis of NAAL is expected to be completed in 2005.

National Institutes of Health (NIH): A US Department of Health and Human Services agency that is one of the world's foremost medical research centers, and the federal focal point for medical research in the United States. The goal of NIH research is to acquire new knowledge to help prevent, detect, diagnose, and treat disease and disability, from the rarest genetic disorder to the common cold.

Participatory decision-making (PDM): A process that considers the input of both the patient and physician to be equally important in determining patient care. PDM is distinguished by three elements: (1) Information exchange, in which the patient and physician share information regarding the patient's symptoms and options for treatment, respectively, (2) deliberation, or the process of expressing and discussing treatment preferences, and (3) deciding on the treatment to implement, with the patient and physician reaching an agreement.

Paternalism: The practice (by an individual, agency, or government) of deciding what is in the best interests of other people rather than letting them choose for themselves.

Patient communication: Information for individuals with medical conditions to help them maximize recovery, maintain therapeutic regimens, and understand alternative approaches. It includes educational resources, provider-patient communication, and, increasingly, peer-to-peer communication.

Peabody Individual Achievement Test-Revised (PIAT-R): A test including components on mathematics, reading recognition, reading comprehension, spelling, and general information. For reading assessment, subjects are first administered the reading recognition test; if the subject scores below the first-grade reading level, the reading comprehension subtest is not administered. In the reading comprehension subtest, the subject reads a sentence and identifies which of four illustrations best matches the sentences.

Print skills: Skills for decoding the written symbols of language (eg, letters of the alphabet) into the sounds of real words. They require knowledge of letter-sound correspondences (phonics), recognition of spelling patterns at the syllable level, and automatic and fluent word recognition.

Prose literacy: The ability to locate requested information within written text documents (eg, editorials, news stories, poems, or fiction), to integrate disparate information presented in the texts, and to write new information based on the texts.

Quantitative literacy: The ability to locate numbers within graphs, charts, prose texts; and documents; to integrate quantitative information from texts; and to perform appropriate arithmetic operations on text-based quantitative data.

Radio button: A computerized form that presents users with a list of selections. A selection can be made by clicking on the appropriate button.

Rapid Estimate of Adult Literacy in Medicine (REALM): A health word recognition test designed specifically to screen for low literacy in health care settings. The REALM consists of three lists of 22 words, including common medical terms and lay terms for body parts and illnesses. The REALM was first developed in 1991 and revised in 1993, and a short version was created in 2002.

Reading comprehension test: A literacy test that assesses an individual's ability to read and understand text written at different levels of difficulty. Examples of reading comprehension tests include the reading

comprehension subtest of the Peabody Individual Achievement Test-Revised (PIAT-R) and the Cloze portion of the Test of Functional Health Literacy in Adults (TOFHLA).

Reading recognition test: A literacy test that assesses an individual's ability to pronounce a list of words. Examples of reading recognition tests include the Wide Range Achievement Test-Revised 3 (WRAT-R3) and Slosson Oral Reading Test-Revised (SORT-R). The Rapid Estimate of Adult Literacy in Medicine (REALM) is a word recognition test that was developed specifically for use in the health care setting.

REALM: See Rapid Estimate of Adult Literacy in Medicine (REALM).

Search box: A box into which Web users type a search term they wish to find on an individual Web site or across the Internet.

Sickness impact profile (SIP): A behavior-based instrument developed to measure the impact of disease on health status. The SIP consists of 136 items grouped into 12 dimensions (sleep and rest, emotional behavior, body care and movement, home management, mobility, social interaction, ambulation, alertness behavior, communication, work, recreation and pastimes, and eating).

Slossan Oral Reading Test–Revised (SORT-R): A reading recognition test widely used in educational settings, composed of 10 lists of 20 core words for each grade level from kindergarten to high school. The test was designed for individuals aged 5 years and older, and was restandardized in 2000.

SMOG Readability Formula: "Simple Measure of Gobbledegook" formula for determining the readability of text based on the number of polysyllabic words (three or more syllables) in three 10-sentence passages selected from the text. The score is expressed as a school-based reading level.

Tailoring: Creating messages and materials to reach *one specific person* based on characteristics unique to that person, related to the outcome of interest, and derived from an assessment of that individual.

Targeting: Creating messages and materials intended to reach a *specific segment of a population*, usually based on one or more demographic or other characteristics shared by its members.

Test of Functional Health Literacy in Adults (TOFHLA): A test that is commonly used for health literacy research in medical and community settings. The TOFHLA consists of a reading comprehension and numeracy section, both composed of materials that subjects might encounter in health care settings. The reading comprehension section uses a modified Cloze-type procedure, while the numeracy section assesses subjects' ability to accurately interpret instructions on a prescription bottle and blood glucose results, and to understand appointment slips. TOFHLA is available in both English and Spanish in the standard version, short version (short

TOFHLA), and very short version (very short TOFHLA).

Tests of Adult Basic Education (TABE) Forms 7 & 8: A set of tests designed to measure achievement of basic skills commonly found in adult basic education curricula and taught in instructional programs. The TABE's seven sections assess reading vocabulary, reading comprehension, mathematics computation, mathematics concepts and applications, language mechanics, language expression, and spelling. A Spanish version, the TABE Español, is appropriate for adults who speak various Spanish dialects.

TOFHLA: See Test of Functional Health Literacy in Adults (TOFHLA).

Two-way communication ability: The ability to exchange information by speaking and listening.

US Department of Health and Human Services (HHS): The US government's principal agency for protecting the health of all Americans and providing essential human services, especially for those who are least able to help themselves. HHS includes more than 300 programs, covering a spectrum of activities from health and social sciences research to disease prevention.

Web: See **World Wide Web**.

Wide Range Achievement Test-R3 (WRAT-R3): A nationally standardized achievement test that assesses reading, spelling, and arithmetic. The test was divided and restandardized in 1993 to develop two equivalent forms

(Tan and Blue) and has been normalized on individuals aged 5 to 75 years.

World Wide Web: An Internet retrieval system in which pages of information (Web pages) reside in various computers around the world and are identified by a Uniform Resource Locator (URL).

Appendix B: Information for Ordering Literacy Tests

Reading Recognition Tests

LAD
Charlotte Nath, EdD
Robert C. Byrd Health
Sciences Center
Department of Family Medicine
PO Box 9152
Morgantown, WV 26505-9152 or
www.hsc.wvu.edu/som/fammed/lad

MART
E. Christine Hansen, PhD, Director
US Scientific Initiatives and Cus-
tomer Support Health Economics
and Outcomes Research
AstraZeneca
919 363-8338
fax: 919 363-7579

REALM
Prevention & Education Project—
LSUHSC, Terry C. Davis, PhD
PO Box 33932, Box 598
Shreveport, LA 71130-3932
318 675-4585
or tdavis1@lsuhsc.edu

SORT-R
Slosson Educational
Publications, Inc.
PO Box 280
538 Buffalo Road
East Aurora, NY 14052-0280
888 756-7766
fax: 800 655-3840

WRAT-R3
Wide Range, Inc.
PO Box 3410
Wilmington, DE 19804-0250
800 221-9728.

Reading Comprehension Tests

Instrument for Diagnosis of Reading (Instrumento Para Diagnosticar Lecturas)
Available from Kendall-Hunt
Publications
4050 Westmark Dr.
PO Box 1840
Dubuque, IA 52004-1840.

TOFHLA, short TOFHLA, and very short TOFHLA (English and Spanish)
Peppercorn Books and Press
PO Box 693
Snow Camp, NC 27349
877 574-1634

PIAT-R
American Guidance Service, Inc.
PO Box 99
Circle Pines, MN 55014
800 328-2560

Adult Education Tests

ABLE
Psychological Corporation Order
Service Center
PO Box 839954
San Antonio, TX 78283
800 211-8378

TABE
CTB/McGraw-Hill
20 Ryan Ranch Road
Monterey, CA 93940
800 538-9547; 408 393-0700
fax: 800 282-0266

Index